The Algorithmic Soc

MW00834239

We live in an algorithmic society. Algorithms have become the main mediator through which power is enacted in our society. This book brings together three academic fields – Public Administration, Criminal Justice and Urban Governance – into a single conceptual framework, and offers a broad cultural-political analysis, addressing critical and ethical issues of algorithms.

Governments are increasingly turning towards algorithms to predict criminality, deliver public services, allocate resources, and calculate recidivism rates. Mind-boggling amounts of data regarding our daily actions are analysed to make decisions that manage, control, and nudge our behaviour in everyday life. The contributions in this book offer a broad analysis of the mechanisms and social implications of algorithmic governance. Reporting from the cutting edge of scientific research, the result is illuminating and useful for understanding the relations between algorithms and power. Topics covered include:

- Algorithmic governmentality
- Transparency and accountability
- Fairness in criminal justice and predictive policing
- Principles of good digital administration
- Artificial Intelligence (AI) in the smart city

This book is essential reading for students and scholars of Sociology, Criminology, Public Administration, Political Sciences, and Cultural Theory interested in the integration of algorithms into the governance of society.

Marc Schuilenburg is Professor at the Department of Criminal Law and Criminology, VU University Amsterdam.

Rik Peeters is Research Professor of public administration at the Centre for Research and Teaching in Economics (CIDE), Mexico City.

Routledge Studies in Crime, Security and Justice

Contemporary social scientific scholarship is being transformed by the challenges associated with the changing nature of, and responses to, questions of crime, security and justice across the globe. Traditional disciplinary boundaries in the social sciences are being disturbed, and at times broken down, by the emerging scholarly analysis of both the increasing merging of issues of 'crime' and 'security' and the unsettling of traditional notions of justice, rights and due process in an international political and cultural climate seemingly saturated by, and obsessed with, fear, insecurity and risk. This series showcases contemporary research studies, edited collections and works of original intellectual synthesis that contribute to this new body of scholarship both within the field of study of criminology and beyond to its connections with debates in the social sciences more broadly.

Edited by
Adam Edwards, Cardiff University
Gordon Hughes, Cardiff University
Reece Walters, Queensland University of Technology

For more information about this series, please visit: https://www.routledge.com/Routledge-Studies-in-Crime-Security-and-Justice/book-series/RSCSJ

The Algorithmic Society

Technology, Power, and Knowledge

Edited by Marc Schuilenburg and Rik Peeters

Routledge
Taylor & Francis Group

LONDON AND NEW YORK

First published 2021
by Routledge
2 Park Square, Milton Park, Abingdon, Oxon OX14 4RN

and by Routledge
52 Vanderbilt Avenue, New York, NY 10017

Routledge is an imprint of the Taylor & Francis Group, an informa
business

British Library Cataloguing-in-Publication Data
A catalogue record for this book is available from the British
Library

Library of Congress Cataloging-in-Publication Data
A catalog record has been requested for this book

ISBN: 978-0-367-20431-0 (hbk)
ISBN: 978-0-429-26140-4 (ebk)

Typeset in Bembo
by SPi Global, India

Contents

Contributors

Fernando Ávila is a Vanier CGS Scholar and a PhD candidate at the Centre for Criminology and Sociolegal Studies at the University of Toronto, Canada. His research focuses on punishment, human rights and criminal justice systems.

Cary Coglianese is the Edward B. Shils Professor of Law and Professor of Political Science at the University of Pennsylvania, where he directs the Penn Program on Regulation. He specializes in the study of regulation and regulatory processes, with a particular emphasis on alternative regulatory strategies and technologies. His recent books include *Achieving Regulatory Excellence* (Brookings Institution Press, 2017) and *Regulatory Breakdown: The Crisis of Confidence of U.S. Regulation* (University of Pennsylvania Press, 2012). He served as a founding editor of Regulation & Governance and is the founder of *The Regulatory Review.*

Stephan Grimmelikhuijsen is an Associate Professor at the Utrecht University School of Governance at Utrecht University. His work centres on issues concerning digital government, transparency, citizen-state interactions, behavioural public administration and citizen trust in government.

Kelly Hannah-Moffat is Professor in Criminology and Sociolegal Studies and Sociology at the University of Toronto. She is the author of 'Algorithmic risk governance: Big data analytics, race and information activism in criminal justice debates' (*Theoretical Criminology*, 2019). Her interdisciplinary research focuses on human rights, criminal records disclosures, big data, AI and risk algorithms, punishment and diverse populations, solitary confinement and institutional risk management practices.

Keith Hayward is Professor of Criminology at the Faculty of Law, University of Copenhagen, Denmark. He is the author, editor, or co-editor of 12 books, and has written widely in areas such as of criminological theory, cultural criminology, space and crime, and terrorism and extremism.

Paul Henman is Professor of Digital Sociology and Social Policy at the University of Queensland, Australia. For over 20 years he has been studying the nexus of digital technologies, government policy and public administration. His recent work has deployed new digital methods for examining digital government.

Recent publications include *Performing the State* (Routledge, 2018) and *Governing Electronically* (Palgrave, 2010). He is a Chief Investigator of the ARC Centre of Excellence for Automated Decision Making and Society.

Paula Maurutto is an Associate Professor in the Department of Sociology and cross-appointed faculty at the Centre of Criminology and Sociolegal Studies at the University of Toronto, Canada. Her research focuses on the areas of risk theory, surveillance, and the intersection between urban security and social welfare. Her current research explores digital security and safe cities across North America.

Michael McGuire is Senior Lecturer in Criminology at the University of Surrey. His work focusses upon the study of technology, crime, social control and more recently, the culture and politics of the smart city. His publications *The Laughing Policebot: Automation and the End of Policing* (Policing and Society, 2020) and *Platform Criminality* (Routledge, 2021) develop new themes in these areas.

Albert Meijer is Professor of Public Management at the Utrecht University School of Governance in the Netherlands. His research focuses on new forms of public management and governance in an information age. Professor Meijer is co-editor in chief of the journal Information Polity and co-chair of the permanent study group on e-government of the European Group for Public Administration.

Brunilda Pali is a Senior Researcher at the Leuven Institute of Criminology KU Leuven. She is co-editor of *Critical Restorative Justice* (Hart, 2017) and *Restoring Justice and Security in Intercultural Europe* (Routledge, 2018). Her areas of interest are gender, critical social theory, social justice, restorative justice, and arts. Her website is: www.restorotopias.com.

Rik Peeters is a Research Professor at the Centre for Research and Teaching in Economics (CIDE) in Mexico City. He analyses the interactions between state and citizens through studies of bureaucracy, digital government and administrative burdens. In various publications (with others) on 'the digital cage' and 'low-trust bureaucracy' he develops an understanding of the social costs of dysfunctional bureaucracies.

Marc Schuilenburg is Assistant Professor at the Department of Criminal Law and Criminology, VU University Amsterdam. His work focuses on politics and crime control, governance of security, social order, theoretical criminology and French philosophy. His recent books include *The Securitization of Society: Crime, Risk, and Social Order* (NYU-Press, 2015) and *Hysteria: Crime, Media, and Politics* (Routledge, 2021). His website is: www.marcschuilenburg.nl.

Rosamunde van Brakel is a Research Professor at the Law, Science, Technology and Society Research Group coordinating the VUB Research Chair in Surveillance Studies and a Postdoctoral Researcher at the imec-SMIT research group at the Vrije Universiteit Brussel (VUB) working on a research project on privacy and smart cities. She has done research on the social and ethical consequences of surveillance technologies such as child risk profiling, CCTV and predictive policing since 2006. Currently, she is doing research on the (history of) governance of surveillance and crime control in Belgium.

Marlies van Eck is Assistant Professor of Law and Digital Technology at eLaw Institute, Leiden University. Her expertise is Legal Protection of Citizens in the Digital Government. She participated in the free online National AI course for all Dutch citizens and advises the government as consultant at Hooghiemstra & Partners.

Gwen van Eijk is Assistant Professor of Criminology at the School of Law at Erasmus University Rotterdam. Her research focuses on the ways in which social inequality is produced and reproduced through policy and practice, in particular in criminal justice and urban development. Her recent publications explore socioeconomic bias in algorithmic risk assessment. Her website is www.gwenvaneijk.nl.

Arjan Widlak is academic director of the Kafka Brigade Foundation (Kafkabrigade), an independent not-for-profit research organization that aims to understand what bureaucratic dysfunction is, what its causes are and how to create the conditions for change. His academic publications as well as his action research focuses on the digital transformation of government, standardization and administrative justice from a citizen's perspective. More information can be found on www.kafkabrigade.nl or www.kafkabrigade.org.

Chapter 1

The algorithmic society
An introduction

Rik Peeters and Marc Schuilenburg

How will they shape you?

Algorithms are everywhere, from simply suggesting online search results or friends 'you may know' on social media, to more critical matters like helping doctors determine your cancer risk, to decide whether you can have a mortgage, or to predict crimes such as gang violence and burglary. Because it is so hard to spot, you might not have even noticed how much of our life is influenced by algorithms. The content we consume on Facebook, the music we listen to on Spotify, the movies we watch on Netflix – it relies on predictive modelling by algorithms. With each click, the algorithms learn to personalise their 'feed' and the marketing for our best experience. Although many of these examples are driven by commercial interests, they are also used in the public sector, such as in health care, education, criminal justice and tax administration. Public organisations increasingly use new forms of data analysis in order to improve public services. We find algorithms used by judges to decide whether a criminal defendant is likely to reoffend or not. We see algorithms used by municipalities to identify optimal routes for waste collection. We encounter algorithms used by teachers for assigning students to schools. Algorithms are here to stay and – the story goes – to help us. The idea is that algorithms are a solution to the mayor challenges of our time, such as security, public services, health care, and environmental protection.

We are living in the midst of a significant transformation of our lives, and while it is an incredible time and place to be in, we must be wary of the effects that come along with it. Mind-boggling amounts of data are generated regarding our daily actions with algorithms processing and acting upon these data to make decisions that manage, control, and nudge our behaviour in everyday life. The use of algorithms not only expands the possibilities of current control and surveillance, but also introduces a new paradigm characterised by an increased rationality of governance, a shift in the functioning of power, and closure of decision-making procedures. We can refer to this by using the term 'algorithmic governance' – the replacement of human, legible and accountable judgements with 'black-box' algorithms – or, as sociologist Aneesh Aneesh dubbed it, 'algocracy' (2006, 2009; Engin & Treleaven, 2019). The term 'algorithmic governance' signifies three distinctive, but related elements with a direct bearing on our behaviour. While automation in decision-making is not particularly new, the impact of algorithms is increasingly becoming *systemic* in terms of (1) automation; (2) architecture; and (3) anticipatory applications.

Full *automation* means that human agency can be almost completely designed out of decision-making processes – even though the extent to which this happens varies in practice. Algorithms collect information (input), process it (throughput), apply it (output) and learn to improve output (feedback) (Zarsky, 2013; Citron & Pasquale, 2014; Danaher et al., 2017). Artificial intelligence, databases, websites, and automated procedures are replacing human agency from actual decision-making (Henman, 2010; Peeters & Widlak, 2018; Van der Voort et al., 2019). Moreover, decision-making becomes a matter of classification rather than judgement of individual cases (Peeters & Schuilenburg, 2018). As a consequence, new actors or experts are now entering the game (usually not trained in social sciences). The discretionary space shifts to the IT professionals that design algorithms, to the data analysts that identify behavioural patterns, and in a certain way also to the algorithms themselves that recognise new patterns and adjust their decision-making procedures accordingly through machine learning (Hannah-Moffat, 2019).

Moreover, algorithms are not merely embedded in existing organisational practices or procedures, but instead form the core of an information *architecture* that determines to a large extent how commercial organisations and public services operate. The widespread use of algorithms fits into a historical development of the digitalisation of organisational operations. In the 1980s, information technology was used primarily to convert organisational documentation into standardised and printable formats. A next step was the digitalisation of files and information into databases, which then could be used to digitalise decision-making procedures and organisational analytics. Pre-filled tax returns are a classic example of this development. Organisational practices changed accordingly. Computer screens replaced paper and system-level information technology replaced individual decision-making based on formal-legal procedures (Bovens & Zouridis, 2002; Landsbergen, 2004). The most recent development is the use of information technology to share data among networks of organisations. Automated decisions by one organisation can now be based on information coming from another organisation, which not only implies the harmonisation of technology (Olson & Subodh, 2010) but can also include the harmonisation of definitions, classifications, and legal frameworks (Widlak & Peeters, 2018). Algorithms – which form the core of digital data sharing and decision-making procedures – should, therefore, be understood as part of a broader information architecture (cf. Yeung, 2011, 2018). Supra-organisational information systems function as an infrastructure that allows for the free flow of information but also guides and constrains its use (Bowker & Star, 2000; Cordella, 2010).

Finally, the application range of algorithm-based organisational practices has expanded considerably in recent years. Most importantly, algorithms are no longer merely used to automate existing internal procedures but, instead, play a key role in new forms of governing society. In the examples given above, algorithms are used to predict, nudge or constrain human behaviour (Danaher et al., 2017). They do so through scores, rankings, profiles and patterns. In 'surveillance capitalism' (Zuboff, 2019), analysis and prediction of client behaviour is a powerful business model that underpins the digital world and is applied in e-commerce, by credit card companies and by social media platforms such as Facebook and Google (Mayer-Schoenberger & Cukier, 2013). The 'proliferation of scoring and ranking citizens' (Harcourt, 2015: 205) also extends to the public domain, where algorithmic risk assessments are used for making no-fly lists, for probation decisions (Smith, Bennett Moses & Chan, 2017: 260), for determining police surveillance resource allocation (Bennett Moses & Chan, 2018), or for algorithmically producing the 'other' as an anomaly in big data analysis (Aradau & Blanke, 2017). Here, algorithmic *anticipation* highlights behavioural patterns and profiles by reducing humans and their behaviour to a set of variables – such as age, gender, educational level, consumer behaviour, criminal record, and income. Individuals have become 'dividuals' (Deleuze, 1990), persons who are defined by the data sets that profile and predict their conduct. As a consequence, the paradigm of the autonomous and sovereign subject no longer serves as a heuristic point of departure. (In)dividuals are entities with many roles, represented in different data banks (Koopman, 2019).

Understanding algorithms

Algorithmic governance is central to the functioning of public and private organisations. For instance, police forces use them to predict where, when and by whom crimes are more likely to be committed (Perry et al., 2013; Asquer, 2014; Van Brakel, 2016; Smith & O'Malley, 2017; Williams, Burnap & Sloan, 2017; Bennett Moses & Chan, 2018). In criminal justice, algorithms are used to predict future dangerousness of defendants and convicts (Sjöstedt & Grann, 2002; Kleiman, Ostrom & Cheeman, 2007; Berk, 2012; Berk & Bleich, 2013; Hamilton, 2015; Goel, Rao & Shroff, 2016; Douglas et al., 2017). Marketeers use algorithms to analyse consumer audiences from online search queries, credit card purchase data, and behavioural data (Sadin, 2009; Mager, 2012; Reigeluth, 2014; Harcourt, 2015; Zuboff, 2019). Government agencies are turning towards algorithms to, among other things, identify welfare fraud, deliver public services, allocate regulatory oversight resources, and assess risks in child protection (Coglianese & Lehr, 2017; Van Eck, 2018; Yeung, 2018; Engin & Treleaven, 2019; Henman, 2019).

The very word 'algorithm', however, is an ancient one. It is often cited as originated from the 9th century Persian mathematician Al-Khwarizmi, who was influenced by the Indian procedures in mathematics and wrote a book on the art of Hindu reckoning. At face value, an algorithm is nothing more than a set of precise steps to accomplish a designated task that will lead to some desirable outcome. For an algorithm to be considered valid it must have three characteristics: (1) it should be finite; (2) it should have well-defined instructions; and (3) it should be effective. Cooking recipes are algorithms of a sort, since they are a list of instructions to be completed in consecutive order. Yet algorithms are far from trivial. When people say they are worried about the influence of algorithms in their day-to-day lives, they are talking about the application of advanced statistical methods and techniques by private and public organisations to automate decision-making on individual people's access to rights and services and to pick out patterns and correlations out of enormous data sets in order to make predictions about their behaviour.

Decisions and predictions

It is crucial to understand that a conceptual and analytical distinction must be made between algorithmic decisions and algorithmic predictions, which may or may not exist side by side in organisational contexts. Algorithmic decisions are the digitalised versions of traditional bureaucratic decision-making. They are forms of classification and categorisation most commonly used to automate routinised non-complex administrative decision-making to determine a citizen's or client's status as eligible for rights, services or obligations (Bovens & Zouridis, 2002). Algorithmic prediction, however, is a form of statistical analysis used to identify individuals from a broader group based on specific characteristics or behavioural patterns. Rather than an extension of traditional decision-making, algorithmic prediction is a more recent addition to the tools of government. In itself, algorithmic prediction does not entail an administrative decision, even though this could also be designed into the algorithm. Instead, predictive algorithms are often used to inform human decision-makers about ways to single out people or other targets for tailor-made attention and treatment through risk analysis or behavioural interventions. Canadian criminologist Kelly Hannah-Moffat (2019) speaks of 'psychology informed risk technologies'.

The statistical model underlying algorithmic prediction can be pre-programmed by humans, but may also be 'outsourced' to the algorithm itself through machine learning and artificial intelligence. Although these two terms are often used interchangeably, they are not quite the same thing. Machine learning is a current application of artificial intelligence based around the idea that by giving machines access to data they learn for themselves, without explicit programming, to make accurate predictions. Based on training models, these algorithms, which are not fully pre-designed but adaptive, 'learn' new ways of classification or prediction by analysing large data sets (Binns, 2018). As the name suggests, artificial intelligence carries out tasks in a way that people would consider 'smart'. It is any technology that enables a system to demonstrate human-like intelligence. Artificial intelligence differs from machine learning in that it cannot exist without machine learning – although machine learning can exist without artificial intelligence. Taken together, algorithms, machine learning and artificial intelligence form the new digital infrastructure of our society.

Algorithms and rationalisation

Algorithms can only exist in a stable environment of standardised codes and classifications. They work according to pre-designed 'recipes'. Or, in the case of machine learning, they become autopoietic or self-reproducing (cf. Luhmann, 1990). Data flows silently through the various steps of a recipe unhindered by human interference (Introna & Wood, 2004) – besides the design of the objective function of the algorithm and its data input. Algorithms produce outcomes that do not 'argue'. They do not present an argument or a reasoning, they do not reveal sources or assumptions, but instead merely construct specific forms of knowledge around things like taste, lifestyle, health and so on, which, in turn, reproduce power. This black box may be opened to make the algorithmic design transparent, but any interference in the functioning of the algorithm is impossible. We consider, therefore, algorithms to be 'instruments of rationalisation' (Peeters & Schuilenburg, 2018) or a 'rationalizing force' (Pasquale, 2015: 15).

By seeing algorithms as similar to bureaucratic or administrative mechanisms rather than to intelligent systems (Caplan & Boyd, 2018: 2), we can better understand the effects they have on the governance of our behaviour in everyday life. Algorithms classify, categorise and process data in organisations in the way forms, procedures and rules do in classic bureaucratic organisations – albeit with a greater speed and a greater amount of data than any human is capable of processing. They are, just like all information technology, characterised by 'simplification' and 'closure' (Kallinikos, 2005). *Simplification* is the process of breaking down a task or problem into a set of operations that needs to be performed sequentially. *Closure*, the necessary complement to simplification, entails 'the isolation and black boxing of the sequential operations, ensuring their execution is protected from external interference' (Cordella & Tempini, 2015: 281). The use of algorithms makes decision-making processes more machine-like. They standardise and formalise tasks in a similar way as the rules and procedures of the classic bureaucracy aimed to do (Gajduschek, 2003).

In two important aspects, however, the analogy between algorithms and bureaucracy falls short. First, algorithms do not leave a paper trail. They are not only less tangible than forms, files and documents, but also less transparent – in both the procedures they follow and in the decisions they make to reach their conclusions. The procedures are designed by IT professionals or adapt themselves through machine learning. The outcomes are produced by a closed system of digital operations. Neither citizens nor the people working with algorithms on a daily basis have insight in or influence on these proceedings. This brings us to a second difference between algorithms and bureaucracies: the exclusion of human agency. As automation becomes more complete, there are ever fewer points of access for people to understand, influence or question the functioning of the system (Eubanks, 2018). Algorithms cannot be held accountable for their actions the way human decision-makers can be. In many cases, decision-makers cannot fully explain how algorithms produce their results. Even if algorithmic outcomes need to be followed up by human decision-making, an organisation that depends on algorithms for its core administrative mechanisms can become a 'digital cage' (Peeters & Widlak, 2018), in which very few people (not even the developers of algorithms) understand how the system works nor the means to influence it.

Algorithmic power

Over the past decade, the power of algorithms has made itself felt in many spheres of society. This suggests that we need to think in terms of algorithms as one of the forms through which power is enacted in our society. Yet, at the same time, an algorithm's power lies not just in the computer code, but also in the way that it becomes part of 'a code of normalization' (Foucault, 2014: 38). This means that algorithms do not simply have power in the classical sense, as in the sovereign manner of power exertion. Rather, they constitute technologies of government as they provide 'actionable insights' (Ekbia et al., 2015) for techniques that seek to nudge, manipulate or manage behaviour at both the collective and individual level. This means that they do not obstruct, but − instead − provide a 'script' for action (cf. Akrich & Latour, 1992). Or, in the words of Michel Foucault, algorithms 'structure the possible field of action of others' (1982: 221).

To understand this, we should look beyond explanations of algorithms that focus solely on their technological qualities. This means that we should not be preoccupied with the technological question: 'What is an algorithm?' − a question that risks essentialism and functionalism. Instead, we must ask questions involving the functioning of algorithms. How do they work? In which domains? What are their effects on our behaviour? How do governments use them to govern society? By posing these questions one obtains more insight in the specific ways algorithms are deployed in our society. Roughly speaking, we can identify three types of applications: (1) status determination, (2) risk assessment, and (3) population management.

Status determination: algorithms are used to automatically determine someone's status or eligibility for the provision of services or the imposition of duties. Automated tax returns and student grant allocation are two typical examples (Bovens & Zouridis, 2002). This is the most basic type of algorithmic application, which has, in some ways, more to do with classic government − determining rights and obligations − than with contemporary governance. However, in the context of full automation and information architecture, algorithmic status determination can affect the governance of an entire system of public and private organisations. Nowadays, someone's status may be determined by one organisation (for instance, a person's residence status), but this information is used by a potentially infinite number of organisations to determine eligibility for all kinds of services (Peeters & Widlak, 2018).

Risk assessment: algorithms are used to generate automated estimations of probability and risk for the allocation of resources and for the personalised treatment of individuals. Algorithms are used to make operational decisions about the focus of regulatory efforts, of policing, and of fraud detection (Smith & O'Malley, 2017; Yeung, 2018; Engin & Treleaven, 2019), as well as to make decisions regarding the treatment of risky individuals, such as juvenile delinquents (Asquer, 2014; Goel, Rao & Shroff, 2016; Aradau & Blanke, 2017). Risk assessments have enabled actuarial, pre-emptive and preventative forms of governance which try to make 'the future secure and certain' (Schuilenburg, 2015: 67–68).

Population management: algorithms are used to generate behavioural insights on specific target populations for the purpose of actively influencing their future behaviour. In the private sector, customer information is not only used to predict behaviour but also to actively anticipate through personalised offers (Mayer-Schoenberger & Cukier, 2013). The most prominent form of population management in the public sector are 'smart cities', where behavioural insights are used to manage the flow of people in the public domain (Vanolo, 2014; Sadowski & Pasquale, 2015; Morozov & Bria 2018). The smart city implies a way of managing public space by deploying techniques to profile and actively modify the behaviour of the people in order to stimulate an efficient, safe and consumption-focused use of space (McGuire, 2018; Schuilenburg & Peeters, 2018; Pali & Schuilenburg, 2019).

For a better understanding of algorithmic power, it is necessary to analyse how algorithmic tools reshape power relations between state, private companies, and citizens. Critical theory often frames the politics of data in a trajectory from disciplinary to control societies. In an extension of Deleuze's writings (1990; 2003), numerous authors have tried to conceptualize the power of data. Whether one defines this in terms of 'infopower' (Koopman), 'expository power' (Harcourt), 'datapower' (Chamayou) or 'psycho-power' (Stiegler), it is clear that the embedded nature of algorithms and their potential role in social processes needs to be addressed. This means that we need to think not just about the impact and consequences of algorithms, but also about the powerful ways in which algorithms oscillate in social ordering processes populated by images, legends, stories, symbols, fictions and so on, that are shared by large groups of people, if not the whole society (Ferrell, Hayward & Young, 2015). By exploring the social imaginary of the algorithm, we are, according to David Beer (2017), likely to find broader rationalities, knowledge-making and norms – both in terms of how the algorithm is used to promote certain visions of calculative objectivity and also in relation to the wider governmentalities that this concept can help to open up.

The dark side of algorithmic governance

Every day, we rely on algorithms to make our lives better. The idea is that algorithms are capable of being fairer and more efficient than humans ever could be. Decision-making becomes more reliable, easier, more time-efficient and less costly. However, there are some concerns to be aware of. The ongoing discussion regarding the use of algorithms focuses on the following elements: (1) the eradication of the human factor in decision-making; (2) the focus on efficiency in automated decision-making; and (3) the comprehensiveness of computational analyses (Harcourt, 2007; Christin, Rosenblat & Boyd, 2015; Domingos, 2015; Goel, Rao & Shroff, 2016; Smith, Bennett Moses & Chan, 2017).

First, proponents claim that by eliminating the wicked problem of the human factor, and all the ways it can negatively impact the lives of millions of people, algorithms will make decision-making less prone to bias or sentiments (Sandvig, 2015; Zarsky, 2016). However, critics point out that algorithms often behave in ways that reflect patterns and prejudices that are deeply embedded in society. How do we know we can trust an algorithm's decision? Although algorithms lack the conscious intention to be racist, they can reproduce biases or propagate specific values that reflect the biases of system designers or of input data (Nissenbaum, 2001). For instance, there is a growing concern that 'dirty data' in police practices, created from flawed, racially biased, and unlawful practices, cause discriminatory results, leading to over-policing of high-poverty and non-white urban areas (Richardson, Schultz & Crawford, 2019). This also holds true for algorithmic decision-making based on machine learning. Biased data that reflects unjust socioeconomic inequalities based on education, employment, income or other attributes may lead algorithms to 'learn' to find new proxies for them (Van Eijk, 2017; Binns, 2018). Models might give a higher risk score to individuals or groups that have been historically more prone to, for instance, defaulting on their loans or being convicted of a crime.

Second, algorithms are able to process a bigger volume of data at a higher velocity than human decision-makers are able to (Laney, 2001). The use of algorithms for risk assessment can also improve efficiency since resources can be allocated more specifically to high-risk areas of control or regulation (Harcourt, 2007). However, critics point out that efficiency comes at a price. First of all, opacity and a lack of transparency are, to a large extent, inherent to algorithms (Grimmelikhuijsen & Meijer, 2014). The reasoning behind the outputs of knowledge-based systems (i.e. systems using predetermined input data and processing procedures) can, in principle, be explained – contrary to machine learning algorithms, which are intrinsically opaque (Danaher, 2016). However, the screen-level bureaucrats who use automatically generated decisions on a daily basis often have no such insight in how algorithms work and produce their results (Peeters & Widlak, 2018). Furthermore, many algorithms are protected by proprietary laws, which further complicate accountability (Pasquale, 2015). In many cases, algorithms have the legal protection of trade secrets and are as closely guarded as the formula for Coca-Cola. Another objection against the efficiency of algorithms are legal concerns regarding privacy and data protection (Polonetsky & Tene, 2013) as well as their compatibility with administrative justice and principles of good governance (Van Eck, 2018). Finally, several authors argue that efficiency for the organisation does not necessarily translate into efficiency or fairness for citizens subjected to automated decisions (Peeters, 2019). Eliminating discretionary space for human decision-making, for instance, complicates the proportional and reasonable treatment of complicated individual cases. In principle, all pathological tendencies of classic bureaucracies also apply to automated decision-making (Peeters & Widlak, 2018).

Third, algorithms are not only able to produce outcomes faster than humans; they are also able to find new patterns and process a number of variables that far exceeds human capacities (Kitchin, 2014). This potential is especially put to use in predictive algorithms (Smith & O'Malley, 2017), which project representations of reality into the future to, for instance, identify crime patterns and suspicious individuals based on data ranging from criminal statistics to the mining of social media (Williams, Burnap & Sloan, 2017). However, comprehensiveness is not the same as accuracy. Critics point out various epistemic concerns. Full prediction is unattainable, since 'universal and perfect surveillance' (Smith, Bennett Moses & Chan, 2017: 267) would be needed to assemble a truly complete data set. Moreover, a theoretical model would always need to be designed into an algorithm to identify the relevant data (ibid.: 268) and prevent them from being lost 'in a fog of possible correlations' (Crawford, 2014). Furthermore, even correct predictions generated by algorithms are based on correlations rather than causal explanations (Mckinlay, 2017), which can complicate the adequate identification of objects of intervention. Besides epistemic complications, critics also warn about the normative implications of comprehensive algorithmic governance. Algorithms are often used for purposes of control, which leads to concerns about privacy and totalitarian tendencies (Yeung, 2011; Dixon & Gellman, 2014; Edwards, 2016; Bayamlioğlu et al., 2018). Technocratic classifications and codes are by their very nature contested, since they highlight specific elements of a complex reality while ignoring others (Bowker & Star, 2000). The design and use of algorithms, therefore, always implies ethical choices.

Beyond the critique

This book aims to understand the mechanisms and social implications of algorithmic governance. How are algorithmic tools reshaping power relations between state, private companies and citizens? The primary objective is to develop an in-depth analysis of the use of algorithms in our society and the logics, values and assumptions inscribed within it. How can we conceptualise algorithmic governance? What are the dynamics and preconditions that are at its core? We have structured the book around three domains – public administration, criminal justice and smart cities – in order to obtain a deeper understanding of the role of algorithms in our society. Specifically, we aim to make two contributions to the existing research on algorithms.

First, this book brings together three currently dispersed academic discourses: public administration, criminal justice and urban governance. What are the social and organisational consequences of algorithms in the core mechanisms of public authorities, such as decision-making, regulation and service delivery? How do algorithmic applications transform practices of policing and justice? How can we understand the 'smart mentality' of our new cityscapes? Where most studies focus on sectoral applications, the ambition here is to analyse the systemic nature of algorithmic governance and how this translates into new modes of governing society and managing behaviour. While the importance of algorithms has been picked up in various academic debates, this book brings them together into a single conceptual framework. This allows for a full understanding of the importance of algorithms in the governing of society.

Second, this book goes beyond a pragmatic description and offers a constructive critique of algorithmic governance. In many cases, the use of algorithms tends to be self-authorising, running the risk of lacking democratic, moral and juridical legitimacy. However, as algorithmic structures proliferate, it is vital that they are designed and applied in a way that is consistent with the values of social justice, inclusion and solidarity. Our assumption is that algorithms are 'here to stay' and the relevant question, therefore, is how to deal with them. How can we ensure that algorithmic governance is fair and reasonable, just and unbiased? What solutions can be formulated to mitigate the negative effects or implications of algorithmic governance? In short, what could be an ethical and legal framework for the use of algorithms? Each chapter in this book combines critical analysis with a perspective on how we can try to make algorithmic governance compatible with democratic, legal and social values.

Outline of the book

In the first part of the book, the outlines of algorithmic governance are explored in the core mechanisms of public organisations, such as decision-making, regulation, service delivery, and rule enforcement. The contributions in this section conceptualise various aspects of algorithmic governance and explore the way this transforms the governance of society and the internal dynamics of government. Following our editorial introduction, Paul Henman analyses the algorithmic governmentality in the second chapter of this book and argues for instituting greater legal protections and valorising collective modes of being in order to challenge machinic judgement in government. In Chapter 3, Cary Coglianese offers an overview of the main critiques against the use of algorithms in governmental regulation and argues for human capacity building as a means to mitigate them. In Chapter 4, Albert Meijer and Stephan Grimmelikhuijsen raise the question how the use of algorithms may undermine citizens' trust in government and formulate a set of assessment questions to guide public organisations in the implementation of responsible and accountable algorithmic applications. This theme is further developed in the fifth chapter by Arjan Widlak, Marlies van Eck and Rik Peeters in the form of principles of good digital administration to ensure fairness, accountability and proportionality in automated decision-making.

Key aspects of algorithmic justice, such as predictive policing and predictive criminal justice, are conceptualised and analysed in the second part of the book. Predictive policing and predictive justice raise questions about the relation between algorithmic security and values of justice, dignity and solidarity. In the sixth chapter, Fernando Ávila, Kelly Hannah-Moffat and Paula Maurutto argue that it is problematic to assume that the use of machine learning algorithms and big data will lead to more accurate and fairer decisions in criminal justice. The lack of precision and consistency in conceptualisations of fairness and the decontextualised nature of data analysis raise concerns regarding the obfuscation of social values and the discriminatory effects of risk assessment. In Chapter 7, Rosamunde van Brakel proposes to rethink predictive policing in a more empowering, inclusive and democratic way inspired by approaches of democratic technology, digital democracies and positive criminology. Gwen van Eijk discusses the ethical concerns of algorithmic justice in risk-based rehabilitation practices in Chapter 8. She argues that the problem is not in the first place a technological problem, but a problem of human-algorithm interaction, specifically human interpretation of algorithmic prediction and the rationalisation of algorithms.

In the third part of the book, contributions analyse the changing ways our behaviour is governed in public spaces. The focus is on smart cities, the nexus of algorithms and urban governance. In Chapter 9, Marc Schuilenburg and Brunilda Pali look beyond the techno-utopian vision of smart cities and seek to repoliticise the debate by analysing the neoliberal ethos of market-led and technocratic solutions to city governance and development. In Chapter 10, Michael McGuire analyses the way smart cities sponsor an artificial, hygienically controlled urban space. Traditional anxieties about urban spaces are designed out of the smart city and replaced by a personalised, but ultimately unsubstantial and highly controlled experience of security, wellbeing and connectivity. In Chapter 11, Keith Hayward develops an understanding of what it means to live in an urban space that is ultimately defined and enforced by a computational system. He outlines five putative 'smart city futures' and identifies emerging cultures of resistance to the threat of transitioning from a socio-technical imaginary to a technologically-determined reality.

The concluding chapter, by the editors of this book, draws together the various strands of the arguments of the individual chapters and the guiding theme of the book. The chapter offers five observations on the link between the process of algorithmisation and the governance of society. In an attempt to generalise the most important findings of the chapters, we define the algorithmic society as 'a set of practices and discourses, implicating hybrid connections between governmental and private parties, that is underpinned by a repertoire of relatively new data-driven technologies, which adds new layers to the governance of society through own modes of knowledge, and particular ways of forming new subjects'. We conclude the chapter with directions for new research and further theorising.

References

Akrich, M. and B. Latour. 1992. A summary of a convenient vocabulary for the semiotics of human and nonhuman assemblies. In *Shaping technology/building society: Studies in sociotechnical change*, edited by W. Bijker and J. Law, 259–264. Cambridge, MA: The MIT Press.

Aneesh, A. 2006. *Virtual migration: The programming of globalization*. Durham, NC: Duke University Press.

Aneesh, A. 2009. Global labor: Algocratic modes of organization. *Sociological Theory*, 27 (4): 347–370.

Aradau, C. and T. Blanke. 2017. Governing others: Anomaly and the algorithmic subject of security. *European Journal of International Security*, 3 (1): 1–21.

Asquer, A. 2014. Big data and innovation in the delivery of public services: The case of predictive policing in Kent. In *Handbook of research on democratic strategies and citizen-centered E-Government services*, edited by C. Dolićanin, E. Kajan, D. Randjelović and B. Stojanović, 20–37. Hershey, PA: IGI Global.

Bayamlioğlu, E., I. Baraliuc, L. Janssens and M. Hildebrandt, eds. 2018. *Being profiled: Cogitase ergo sum − 10 years of 'profiling the European citizen'*. Amsterdam: Amsterdam University Press.

Beer, D. 2017. The social power of algorithms. *Information, Communication & Society*, 20 (1): 1–13.

Bennett Moses, L. and J. Chan. 2018. Algorithmic prediction in policing: Assumptions, evaluation, and accountability. *Policing and Society*, 28 (7): 806–822.

Berk, R.A. 2012. *Criminal justice forecasts of risk: A machine learning approach*. New York: Springer.

Berk, R.A. and J. Bleich. 2013. Statistical procedures for forecasting criminal behavior. *Criminology & Public Policy*, 12 (3): 513–544.

Binns, R. 2018. Algorithmic accountability and public reason. *Philosophy & Technology*, 31 (4): 543–556.

Bovens, M. and S. Zouridis. 2002. From street-level to system-level bureaucracies: How information and communication technology is transforming administrative discretion and constitutional control. *Public Administration Review*, 62 (2): 174–184.

Bowker, G.C. and S.L. Star. 2000. *Sorting things out*. Cambridge, MA: The MIT Press.

Caplan, R. and D. Boyd. 2018. Isomorphism through algorithms: Institutional dependencies in the case of Facebook. *Big Data & Society*, doi: 10.1177/2053951718757253, accessed 08-06-2020.

Christin, A., A. Rosenblat and D. Boyd. 2015. Courts and predictive algorithms. *Data & Civil Rights: A New Era of Policing and Justice*. http://www.datacivilrights.org/pubs/2015-1027/WDN-Courts_and_Predictive_Algorithms.pdf; accessed 21-05-2020.

Citron, D. and F. Pasquale. 2014. The scored society: Due process for automated predictions. *Washington Law Review*, 89 (1): 1–33.

Coglianese, C. and D. Lehr. 2017. Regulating by robot: Administrative decision making in the machine-learning era. *The Georgetown Law Journal*, 105: 1147–1223.

Cordella, A. 2010. Information infrastructure: an actor-network perspective. *International Journal of Actor-Network Theory and Technological Innovation*, 2 (1): 27–53.

Cordella, A. and N. Tempini. 2015. E-government and organizational change: Reappraising the role of ICT and bureaucracy in public service delivery. *Government Information Quarterly*, 32 (3): 279–286.

Crawford, K. 2014. The anxieties of big data. *The New Inquiry*, May 30, 2014.

Danaher, J. 2016. The threat of algocracy: reality, resistance and accommodation. *Philosophy & Technology*, 29 (3): 245–268.

Danaher, J., M.J. Hogan, C. Noone, R. Kennedy, A. Behan, A. De Paor, H. Felzmann, et al. 2017. Algorithmic governance: Developing a research agenda through the power of collective intelligence. *Big Data & Society*, doi: 10.1177/2053951717726554; accessed 28-04-2020.

Deleuze, G. 1990. *Pourparlers 1972–1990*. Paris: Minuit.

Deleuze, G. 2003. *Deux régimes de fous: Textes et entretiens, 1975–1995*. Paris: Minuit.

Dixon, P. and R. Gellman. 2014. The scoring of America: How secret consumer scores threaten your privacy and your future. *World Privacy Forum*, April 2, 2014.

Domingos, P. 2015. *The master algorithm: How the quest for ultimate machine learning will remake our world*. New York: Basic Books.

Douglas, T., J. Pugh, I. Singh, J. Savulescu and S. Fazel. 2017. Risk assessment tools in criminal justice and forensic psychiatry: The need for better data. *European Psychiatry*, 42: 134–137.

Edwards, A. 2016. Big data, predictive machines and security: the minority report. In *The Routledge handbook of technology, crime and justice*, edited by M. McGuire and T. Holt, 451–460, London: Routledge.

Ekbia, H., M. Mattiolo, I. Kouper, G. Arave, A. Ghazinejad, R. Suri, A. Tsou, S. Weingart and C.R. Sugimot. 2015. Big data, bigger dilemmas: A critical review. *Advances in Information Science*, 68 (8): 1523–1545.

Engin, Z. and P. Treleaven. 2019. Algorithmic government: Automating public services and supporting civil servants in using data science technologies. *The Computer Journal*, 62 (3): 448–460.

Eubanks, V. 2018. *Automating inequality: How high-tech tools profile, police and punish the poor*. New York: St. Martin's Press.

Ferrell, J., K. Hayward and J. Young 2015. *Cultural criminology: An invitation*. Newbury Park: Sage.

Foucault, M. 1982. The subject and power: afterword. In *Michel Foucault: Beyond structuralism and hermeneutics*, edited by H.L. Dreyfus and P. Rabinow, 208–226. Sussex: Harvester Press.

Foucault, M. 2014. *On the government of the living: Lectures at the collège de France 1979–1980*. Basingstoke: Palgrave Macmillan.

Gajduschek, G. 2003. Bureaucracy: Is it efficient? Is it not? Is that the question? Uncertainty reduction: An ignored element of bureaucratic rationality. *Administration & Society*, 34 (6): 700–723.

Goel, S., J.M. Rao and R. Shroff. 2016. Personalized risk assessments in the criminal justice system. *American Economic Review: Papers & Proceedings*, 106 (5): 119–123.

Grimmelikhuijsen, S.G. and A.J. Meijer. 2014. Effects of transparency on the perceived trustworthiness of a government organization: Evidence from an online experiment. *Journal of Public Administration Research and Theory*, 24 (1): 137–157.

Hamilton, M. 2015. Adventures in risk: Predicting violent and sexual recidivism in sentencing law. *Arizona State Law Journal*, 47 (1): 1–62.

Hannah-Moffat, K. 2019. Algorithmic risk governance: Big data analytics, race and information activism in criminal justice debates. *Theoretical Criminology*, 23 (4): 453–470.

Harcourt, B.E. 2007. *Against prediction: Profiling, policing, and punishing in an actuarial age.* Chicago, IL: Chicago University Press.

Harcourt, B.E. 2015. *Exposed: Desire and disobedience in the digital age.* Cambridge: Harvard University Press.

Henman, P. 2010. *Governing electronically: E-government and the reconfiguration of public administration, policy, and power.* Basingstoke: Palgrave Macmillan.

Henman, P. 2019. Of algorithms, apps and advice: digital social policy and service delivery. *Journal of Asian Public Policy*, 12 (1): 71–89.

Introna, L. and D. Wood. 2004. Picturing algorithmic surveillance: The politics of facial recognition systems. *Surveillance & Society*, 2 (2/3): 177–198.

Kallinikos, J. 2005. The order of technology: Complexity and control in a connected world. *Information and Organization*, 15: 185–202.

Kitchin, R. 2014. *The data revolution: Big data, open data, data infrastructures and their consequences.* London: Sage.

Kleiman, M., B.J. Ostrom and F.L. Cheeman. 2007. Using risk assessment to inform decisions for nonviolent offenders in Virginia. *Crime & Delinquency*, 53 (1): 1–27.

Koopman, C. 2019. *How we became our data: A genealogy of the informational person*, Chicago, IL: The University of Chicago Press.

Landsbergen, D. 2004. Screen level bureaucracy: Databases as public records. *Government Information Quarterly*, 21 (1): 24–50.

Laney, D. 2001. 3D management: Controlling data volume, velocity and variety. https://blogs. gartner.com/doug-laney/files/2012/01/ad949-3D-Data-Management-Controlling-Data-Volume-Velocity-and-Variety.pdf; accessed 28-04-2020.

Luhmann, N. 1990. *Essays in self-reference.* New York: Columbia University Press.

Mager, A. 2012. Algorithmic ideology. *Information, Communication & Society*, 15(5): 769–787.

Mayer-Schoenberger, V. and K. Cukier. 2013. *Big data: A revolution that will transform how we life, work, and think.* London: John Murray Publishers.

Mckinlay, S.T. 2017. Evidence, explanation and predictive data modelling. *Philosophy & Technology*, 30 (4): 461–473.

McGuire, M. 2018. Beyond flatland: When smart cities make stupid citizens. *City, Territory and Architecture*, 5 (22): 1–11.

Morozov, E. and F. Bria 2018. *Rethinking the smart city: Democratizing urban technology.* New York: Rosa Luxembourg Stiftung.

Nissenbaum, H. 2001. How computer systems embody values. *Computer*, 34 (3): 118–120.

Olson, D. and K. Subodh. 2010. Enterprise information systems: Contemporary trends and issues. *World Scientific*, 2: 13–16.

Pali, B. and M. Schuilenburg. 2019. Fear and fantasy in the smart city. *Critical Criminology: An International Journal*, doi:10.1007/s10612-019-09447-7; accessed 28-04-2020.

Pasquale, F. 2015. *The black box society: The secret algorithms that control money and information.* Boston: Harvard University Press.

Peeters, R. 2019. The political economy of administrative burdens: A theoretical framework for analyzing the organizational origins of administrative burdens. *Administration & Society*, doi: https://doi.org/10.1177/0095399719854367; accessed 28-04-2020.

Peeters, R. and M. Schuilenburg. 2018. Machine justice: Governing security through the bureaucracy of algorithms. *Information Polity*, 23 (3): 267–280.

Peeters, R. and A. Widlak. 2018. The digital cage: Administrative exclusion through information architecture – The case of the Dutch civil registry's master data management. *Government Information Quarterly*, 35 (2): 175–183.

Perry, W.L., B. McInnis, C.C. Price, S.C. Smith and J.S. Hollywood. 2013. *Predictive policing: The role of crime forecasting in law enforcement operations.* Santa Monica: RAND Corporation.

Polonetsky, J. and O. Tene. 2013. Privacy and big data: Making ends meet. *Stanford Law Review*, 66: 25–33.

Reigeluth, T. 2014. Why data is not enough: Digital traces as control of self and self-control. *Surveillance & Society*, 12 (2): 243–254.

Richardson, R., J. Schultz and K. Crawford 2019. Dirty data, bad predictions: How civil rights violations impact police data, predictive policing systems, and justice. *New York University Law Review Online*, 94 (192): 192–233.

Sadin, E. 2009. *Surveillance global.* Paris: Flammarion-Climats.

Sadowski, J. and F. Pasquale 2015. The spectrum of control: A social theory of the smart city. http://firstmonday.org/ojs/index.php/fm/article/view/5903/4660; accessed 28-08-2020.

Sandvig, C. 2015. Seeing the sort: The aesthetic and industrial defense of 'the algorithm'. *Journal of the New Media Caucus*, 10 (3): 1–21.

Schuilenburg, M. 2015. *The securitization of society: Crime, risk, and social order.* New York: New York University Press.

Schuilenburg, M. and R. Peeters, 2018. Smart cities and the architecture of security: Pastoral power and the scripted design of public space. *City, Territory and Architecture*, 5 (13): 1–9.

Sjöstedt, G. and M. Grann. 2002. Risk assessment: What is being predicted by actuarial prediction instruments?. *International Journal of Forensic Mental Health*, 1 (2): 179–183.

Smith, G.J.D., L. Bennett Moses and J. Chan. 2017. The challenges of doing criminology in the big data era: Towards a digital and data-driven approach. *The British Journal of Criminology*, 57 (2): 259–274.

Smith, G.J.D. and P. O'Malley. 2017. Driving politics: Data-driven governance and resistance. *The British Journal of Criminology*, 57 (2): 275–298.

Van Brakel, R. 2016. Pre-emptive big data surveillance and its (dis)empowering consequences: The case of predictive policing. In *Exploring the boundaries of big data*, edited by B. van der Sloot et al., 117–141. Amsterdam: Amsterdam University Press.

Van der Voort, H.G., A.J. Klievink, M. Arnaboldi & A.J. Meijer. 2019. Rationality and politics of algorithms: Will the promise of big data survive the dynamics of public decision making?. *Government Information Quarterly*, 36 (1): 27–38.

Van Eck, M. 2018. *Geautomatiseerde ketenbesluiten & rechtsbescherming: Een onderzoek naar de praktijk van geautomatiseerde ketenbesluiten over een financieel belang in relatie tot rechtsbescherming (dissertation).* Tilburg: Tilburg University.

Van Eijk, G. 2017. Socioeconomic marginality in sentencing: The built-in bias in risk assessment tools and the reproduction of social inequality. *Punishment & Society*, 19 (4): 463–481.

Vanolo, A. 2014. Smartmentality: The smart city as disciplinary strategy. *Urban Studies*, 51 (5): 883–898.

Widlak, A. and R. Peeters. 2018. *De digitale kooi: (On)behoorlijk bestuur door informatiearchitectuur – of: hoe we de burger weer centraal zetten in een digitaliserende overheid*. Den Haag: Boom Bestuurskunde.

Williams, M.L., P. Burnap and L. Sloan. 2017. Crime sensing with big data: The affordances and limitations of using open-source communications to estimate crime patterns. *The British Journal of Criminology*, 57 (2): 320–340.

Yeung, K. 2011. Can we employ design-based regulation while avoiding *brave new world?*. *Law, Innovation and Technology*, 3 (1): 1–29.

Yeung, K. 2018. Algorithmic regulation: A critical interrogation. *Regulation & Governance*, 12 (4): 505–523.

Zarsky, T. 2013. Transparent prediction. *University of Illinois Law Review*, 4: 1503–1570.

Zarsky, T. 2016. The trouble with algorithmic decisions: An analytic road map to examine efficiency and fairness in automated and opaque decision making. *Science, Technology and Human Values*, 41 (1): 118–132.

Zuboff, S. 2019. *The age of surveillance capitalism: The fight for a human future at the new frontier of power*. New York: Public Affairs.

Part I

Algorithmic governance

Chapter 2

Governing by algorithms and algorithmic governmentality
Towards machinic judgement

Paul Henman

Introduction

Governing has become algorithmic; and algorithms govern. Consider this current, or near future, scenario of a shopping trip and dinner with friends.

On my drive to the shopping mall, I drive past cameras used to assess my speed, to determine if I am using my phone while driving, to confirm my car registration is paid, and to check if I stop at red lights (Hoang Ngan Le et al., 2016). The cameras also help local authorities automate traffic control (Hu & Ni, 2017). As I enter the precinct car park my registration plates are scanned to assess my parking fee when I exit. My phone app directs me to available car parks. As soon as I enter the shopping precinct the Wi-Fi pings my mobile to detect my presence and connects this with my previous visits, walking paths, and purchase patterns (Oosterlinck et al., 2017).

My movements are also monitored by facial matching and gait detecting CCTV to assess whether or not my past or current conduct would compel my ejection (Lomell, 2004). My presence and activity is used to push advertisements and discount vouchers to my phone and social media accounts (Anacleto et al., 2011). While I browse I listen to music that has been curated for me based on my past activity, my personal characteristics and that of my social media 'friends' (Bu et al., 2010). Feeling peckish, I obtain a snack from a vending machine that uses facial recognition to automatically deduct the cost from my bank account. I see a 'Mr Jihad' T-shirt in the 'Mr Men' genre and laugh, posting a picture on my social media accounts. My post leads to anonymous others calling me a 'terrorist' and to 'go back where I came from'. These responses disturb me, so I then delete the post. Unbeknownst to me, the post also feeds a government algorithm fractionally increasing my assessed security risk level (Trottier, 2016) and also triggers an advertisement on my social media to donate to an organisation supporting civil disobedience.

After online group chats with my friends we meet for dinner. As we talk we discover that one of my friends had her bags checked at each store, but none of the others did, and then she did not receive the same discount from her Voucher-app as the rest of us. We all seem to have read different news stories in the last day from our curated news feeds (Powers, 2017a). After dinner, we proceed to a bar for a relaxing drink, but to enter our drivers' licenses were scanned, which are then stored for reporting to government (Palmer, Warren & Miller, 2013). Our social media posts of us drinking are invisibly evaluated to assess if any of us have a drinking problem, potentially prompting a public health message and offer to refer to support services (Hossain et al., 2016).

During this time all my activity on my phone – which apps and websites I use – is recorded by the shopping precinct (Ren et al., 2017) and the shopping precinct links my presence with information about my purchases which they then use for determining rents for shops and making strategic decisions about the types of shops and services to install in their precinct. My purchases are also recorded by the payment systems via my watch or phone which are then used by my bank for ongoing assessment of my financial credit risk and to identify suspicious transactions, and for on selling to marketing firms. Government algorithms also monitor my social media activity and provide real time risk assessments for a range of social problems (such as alcoholism, terrorism, social disobedience) and potentially prompting social, health or criminal justice interventions. I go about my whole day without feeling any coercion; I feel free to act as I please as a consumer-citizen.

As the above scenario illustrates, algorithms have become extensive and intensive in all aspects of governing us by states, corporations and civil societies (Steiner, 2012). In undertaking my actions I may not feel I am controlled, but my agency, my possible choices, and my possible fields of action are shaped by others in order to maximise profit extraction, to abide by laws and regulations, and to comply with perceived social norms. Algorithms thus govern, and are thus an operation of power. Mostly such algorithmic power is capillary-like, winding tendrils through, nudging and co-constituting everyday activities, though they also may give rise to more coercive forms of power, such as blocking access, exclusion and prompting policing, security and criminal justice interventions (Davis & Chouinard, 2016).

The notion that algorithms govern us is not controversial. A large body of literature has documented and charted these dynamics and developments (Steiner, 2012; Eubanks, 2018; Noble, 2018; Rosenblat, 2018; Benjamin, 2019). The diverse forms of algorithmic governing perhaps suggest that algorithms are simply neutral tools developed and deployed by those who seek to govern and control us for specified purposes. In this viewpoint, algorithms enact modes of governing dictated by those who govern; social democrats use algorithms to enhance social democracy; libertarians use algorithms to enhance liberty, dictators use algorithms to dictate.

There is, however, value in moving beyond such a conceptualisation of governing by algorithm; not simply treating these governmental tools as intentionally encoded by governors to govern. It is important to consider the possibility that despite the great heterogeneity of algorithms and their authors' objectives, algorithmic governing has a shared *modus operandi*, a common mode of governing, similar epistemological ways of seeing the world and enacting on it. In the language of Michel Foucault, is there a distinct 'algorithmic governmentality', and, if there is, what is its particular forms of knowledge and modes of subjectification? This chapter argues that there is a distinct algorithmic governmentality, denoted by digitised knowledge and anticipatory government. To be sure, algorithmic governmentality does not displace, but overlays and entangles with other governmentalities.

The argument develops as follows. The next section provides an outline of the concept of governmentality as articulated by Foucault and as mobilised in subsequent 'governmentality studies'. That section gives attention to how governmentality can accommodate a discussion of algorithms as non-human devices and actors and highlights how previous studies have argued that algorithms have been variously used to enact neoliberal, authoritarian, and other governmentalities. This is then followed by an extended section explicating a distinct algorithmic governmentality, by exploring two themes: (a) algorithms as constituting a particular digitised form of knowledge as a result of their governing of programmers and coders; and (b) algorithms constituting an anticipatory mode of governing. The chapter then discusses the implications of this understanding of algorithmic governmentality, the operation of power in algorithmic societies, and possible counter-conducts to algorithmic governmentality.

Understanding governmentality and governing algorithms

Michel Foucault coined the neologism 'governmentality' in his lectures and writings of the late 1970s and early 1980s (Foucault, 1981, 1982, 1991, 2007, 2008), and instigated a new area of research titled 'governmentality studies'.[1] Building on his previous works in understanding power and their transformations, Foucault argued that 'government' is a particular form of power that arose from the middle ages. Central to Foucault's approach is his utilisation of the older meaning of 'government', one that is not equated with state organisations or apparatuses, but to practices of governing, by which he means to 'structure the possible field of action of others' (Foucault, 1982) or the 'calculated direction of conduct' (Dean, 2010: 18). Governing in this sense is an activity not only of sovereigns and state apparatuses, but also of employers, teachers, parents, selves and so on. In his 1 February 1978 lecture, Foucault explains that 'governmentality' is

> [T]he type of power that we can call 'government' and [involves] the development of a series of specific governmental apparatuses (*appareils*) on the one hand, [and, on the other] to the development of a series of knowledges (*savoirs*).
> (2007: 108–109)

Governmentality provides an important juxtaposition to the long-standing focus on political ideologies and political philosophies relating to the conceptualisation and justification of power. For Foucault, governmentality is also very much concerned with the administering practices of everyday life, which, as the above quote demonstrates, involves both practices, techniques, mechanisms and apparatuses of governing, as well as forms of knowledge and knowing about the subjects of government. Sociologists Peter Miller and Nikolas Rose (2008) re-articulate governmentality as composing both 'political rationalities' and 'technologies of government'. In short, Foucault's historical account of governmentality is one of the emergence of rational and calculated knowledges and techniques as a modern mode of power, which Foucault succinctly frames as 'the conduct of conduct'.

Foucault's intellectual intervention sought to highlight *how* we are governed, and create a different scholarly focus to political philosophy. Even so, governmentality analyses have often been applied to examine particular neoliberal forms of governing (and indeed Foucault spoke a lot about the rise of neoliberal govern-mentality (2007, 2008), as well as the articulation of classical liberal, social demo-cratic and authoritarian governmentalities). Authors have also characterised more localised governmentalities, including risk, international and colonial governmen-talities (Scott, 2005; Dean, 2010).

How might the concept of governmentality relate to algorithms? Much govern-mentality research has typically focused on humans as governing agents and gov-erned subjects, and when 'technologies of government' are considered they are typically positioned as neutral processes and tools being deployed by humans to govern other humans. Yet, as German social theorist Thomas Lemke (2015b) argues, Foucault's writings provide considerable space for a recognition of the role of government of and by things: 'to govern means to govern things' (Foucault, 2007: 97). Lemke concludes:

> [T]he conceptual proposal of a 'government of things' is not restricted to humans and relations between humans. It refers to a more comprehensive reality that includes material environments and the specific constellations and technical networks between humans and non-humans.
>
> (2015b: 17)

Taking such an approach means that things are not only subject to government, but also govern. Governing is a socio-technical activity; it melds humans and things in governing practices and subjects of government. Moreover, Lemke's articulation draws attention to the relational aspects of humans and non-humans, echoing Actor-Network Theory's perspective[2] that all actors are networks and all networks are actors, rather than individual things. Things have agential characteristics. Accordingly, things may not just enact governmentalities, but may actively consti-tute them; the 'technologies of government' can reconfigure and give rise to new 'political rationalities' (Henman, 2010: ch. 1).

How then are we to apprehend algorithms within a governmentality analytic? As the opening scenario vividly attests, algorithms are now part of the very fabric of governing. Several authors have used the governmentality analytic to examine algo-rithmic forms of governing. It is hardly surprising that studies have examined the way in which algorithms operate within and to reinforce contemporary neoliberal governmentality. For example, Christian Borch (2017) examines how algorithmic high-frequency trading constitutes traders in particular neoliberal ways. Nuno Rodrigues (2016) reviews how algorithms in smart cities reinforce neoliberalism. Timothy Graham (2018; Graham & Henman, 2019) demonstrates how algorithms within websites constitute 'hyper-choice' and provide mechanisms for users to navi-gate and tame such choice, thereby heightening the 'freedom' to choose within a marketised ontology as the *sin qua non* of neoliberalism (Rose, 1999). Meanwhile, Lucas Introna (2016) charts the ways in which the TurnItIn algorithm constitutes neoliberal calculative subjectivities of responsibility and notions of plagiarism.

While this body of work highlights how algorithms are, to various extents, handmaidens to wider governmental agendas, the question arises as to whether there is also a discernible algorithmic governmentality operating through and by them. In other words, following Colin Gordon (1991), do algorithms constitute a particular way or system of thinking about the practice of government, a way in which to make governing practicable? Or, following Mitchell Dean's (Dean, 2010: 33) characterisation, do algorithms provide a characteristic way of thinking and seeing, with modes of truth, and particular ways of forming subjects, selves and actors? The following section answers in the affirmative, and articulates the mechanisms and dynamics of algorithmic governmentality.

Algorithmic governmentality

In examining and describing algorithmic governmentality, this section consists of two parts. The first part takes as its point of departure the ways in which the essential makeup of digital computers, including their computer programming languages, governs the way in which computer programmers construct algorithms. If digital algorithms enact an algorithmic governmentality then the ground truth of the materiality of digital computers, coding and data structures, forms the basis of its shape and substance. The need to focus on the formation of algorithms at the operational level of digital computers is a conceptual proposition, while the understanding of the programming of digital computers is based on empirical studies and personal experience.[3] The ways in which the structure of computer code and data, when mobilised within algorithms, then configures governmental knowledge (*savoir*) in a particular, digitised form.

The second part argues that, despite the huge variety of computer algorithms, a discernible and growing dimension of algorithmic governmentality is anticipatory; it creates knowledges and subjects in the present based on their calculated likely futures. One's future becomes one's present. In other words, algorithms constitute a particular, predictive way of thinking about the practice of government, a practical way of governing the future in the present, and the present in the future. The basis of this argument is grounded in empirical studies and informed by other scholars who have examined the question of the existence of an algorithmic governmentality. In particular, Antoinette Rouvroy (2013; Rouvroy & Berns, 2013; Rouvroy & Stiegler, 2016) articulates algorithmic governmentality as an operation of governing individuals based on statistical probabilities of future realities and mathematically constructed truths.

Algorithmic governmentality as programmes of programmers and digitised knowledge

Algorithmic governmentality is grounded in the ways in which computer languages structure the activities of programmers (or coders). In order to encode an algorithm in computers, coders must abide by very strict rules of syntax and data structures. Coding also requires a certain mentality, a way of thinking about processes and actions that is both functionalist and reductionist. Stepwise decomposition, a practice inculcated into programmers, is the process by which a desired algorithm is progressively broken down into increasingly smaller sub-programs, each coded as sub-routines, procedures and data structures, in order to create the overall desired computer action (Beecher, 2017: ch. 3). Abstraction is the complementary aspect of computer programming, whereby procedures and data structures are required to be conceptualised abstractly, rather than specifically. For example, instead of creating code for a wide range of separate activities, the separate activities are grouped and commonalities identified to create more generic procedures. Abstraction is also applied to the program's input, operation and output data. Generic, rather than specific, data structures are pertinent (Beecher, 2017: ch. 4). Computer codes thus constitute an algorithmic governmentality, a way of thinking about the structure of worldly processes and knowledge, as functional outcomes of complex combinations of and basic operations on 0s and 1s. It is one that apprehends the world as largely quantitative, discrete, logical, functionalist, and deterministic (Weizenbaum, 1984; Henman, 1995). This world of code governs programmers and creators of code. Such an algorithmic governmentality thereby creates the possibility of certain digitised forms of knowledge and ways of being, those that are quantifiable, and calculable,[4] and elides those that are more qualitative and organic. It hollows out meaning and reinforces abstracted superficiality.

While the governmental structures of code force themselves on coders, what might this algorithmic governmentality mean for the wider population? When digital algorithms are executed they enact a specific digitised abstract epistemology and ontology defined within the code (Vámos, 2010; Powers, 2017b), which in turn becomes the governmental knowledges (*savoirs*) that construct governable subjects and subjectivities. While categorisation of the world, of people and things, is undoubtedly socially constructed (Bowker & Star, 2000), today's digitised categories that algorithms collect, calculate and circulate, are typically discrete, clearly formed, non-negotiable, abstract and compulsory. They sharply contrast to less rigid and organic classifications more prevalent in previous generations.[5] Consider, for example, Simon Clay's (2018) observation of the obligatory categorisation of self, using pre-fixed, encoded 'tribes' on gay dating app Grindr. These algorithmic categorisations construct particular subjectivities of personalities, body shapes, sexual positions and fetishes. While algorithms shapes conduct, it is the particularity of discrete 'tribes' grounded in an algorithmic governmentality that shapes conduct in particular ways. One becomes classified; the classification become one's self; and one seeks out others by classification. Dating and sex operates by algorithmic categorisation, and digitised categories become the prism by which gay identity is constructed.[6]

Digitised knowledge thus mobilises a wider dynamic of obligatory quantification and categorisation, which David Boyle captures in *Tickbox* (2020), a dynamic that inculcates rigid, unreflecting mindsets and algorithmic decisions. Boyle tells the story of Anthony Bryan, a long-term British resident who is flagged as 'illegal' when applying for a passport, despite being a lawful resident. His mis-categorisation is algorithmically determined because the proper boxes are not ticked in the computer system due to its lack of flexibility in terms of the paperwork required to satisfy its operation. Such mis-categorisation leads to him being imprisoned at length, bankrupt, and deprived of seeing his mother and dying son.

Political scientist Virginia Eubanks (2018) gives a similar account of how the creation of distinct, authoritative and compulsory categories codify, simplify and misrepresent complex realities resulting in human miseries. She reports the case whereby Medicaid systems in the USA encode a category 'failure to cooperate' that captures a wide range of circumstances. She cites the case of six-year-old Sophie Stipes, whose mother was not advised to sign a particular document, that in turn led to Sophie being categorised as 'failure to cooperate'. This resulted in automated cessation of Medicaid coverage thereby denying Sophie access to costly life-saving medical treatment (2018: 39–45).

The above examples illustrate how the specific nature of computer data structures creates digitised forms of knowledge that overlays and displaces the messier realities of lived lives. In doing so we become defined and governed by our digital data (Koopman, 2019). Tarleton Gillespie (2014) uses the phrase 'the production of calculated publics' to capture this dynamic of computer-coded categories enchanted by algorithms to shape the way in which the world is constructed and perceived. Moreover, such digitised knowledge becomes the basis by which we are governed, and, indeed, by algorithms themselves that deny Medicaid, raise welfare debts (Carney, 2019) and terminate employment (Diallo, 2018).

With the rise of machine learning (somewhat euphemistically called Artificial Intelligence), algorithmically produced digitised knowledge is being further severed from human experience. Categories and actions are being algorithmically generated according to a 'logic' the algorithm determines, not encoded by human programmers. Machine learning involves setting up numerous internal variables and connections between those, and providing the algorithm with a learning input dataset (such as income, gender, photos, tweets, x-ray images) and a learning output dataset (e.g. x-rays with/out cancer, individuals who have committed a crime, book purchases, children who have been removed from their families). The algorithm repeatedly modifies its internal variables and weightings between them to best transform input to output data. In doing so, the algorithm creates its own 'categories' and digitised knowledge to achieve the best associations between input and output data.[7]

It is important to note that digitised knowledge and algorithmic governing diverges from the wider neoliberal governmentalities in which they operate. Algorithms create subjects and subjectivities that do not reflect policy principles or legal states, but override policy or law, resulting in abuse of power. Based on algorithmically created 'truths', these cases illustrate that such operations of power diverge from the intent of human governors. People are algorithmically reallocated. Algorithmic government is not a simple enactment of human intent. Algorithmic governmentality enacts an irrational rationality, an alternative program of government, but draws in and deploys human-enacted powers to control, discipline, surveil and 'empower'. At the heart of these operations are new digitised power/knowledges, new truth regimes constructed by the impeccable logic of algorithms, a logic that has become abstractised and riven from human realities. It creates what John Danaher (2016) describes as 'algocracy', organisational governance by algorithms.

Algorithmic governmentality enacts anticipatory judgement

Algorithms do not simply classify and categorise (as the previous section has established). They also make more complex judgements and determinations. These judgements range from sorting individuals into groups, assessing eligibility, calculating risk, and real-time monitoring and regulating. Anticipatory algorithmic governmentality goes beyond traditional application of procedures and rules to facts, to instead compute future realities based on probabilistic logics.[8] Data mining (Zarsky, 2011) and machine learning are the most recent algorithmic forms of this.

Anticipatory algorithmic governmentality is evident in the use of generic search and recommender systems. Using your input search terms, your past search history, geo-location, and so on, Google's algorithms return results based on prior webpage rankings and learning from previous search outcomes. Your search is related to those of others and probabilities of successful suggested webpages are calculated (Feuz, Fuller & Stalder, 2011). Netflix's recommender algorithm uses your past watching habits and compares those with others to recommend new movies and TV series based on calculated probabilities that you will also watch them (Gomez-Uribe & Hunt, 2015). Social media feeds are curated for you to deliver content you are most likely to consume (Rader & Gray, 2015).

Anticipatory algorithmic judgement is precipitously being deployed by states, often in coercive governing of the most marginalised. Child protection and welfare services have been relatively early adopters of anticipatory algorithms to classify the riskiness of children to abuse/neglect. Philip Gillingham (2006, 2019) has been studying the introduction and evolution of risk-based assessments in Australia, New Zealand and the UK, from forms to computerised screen flows to more automated systems. Gillingham observes how such risk-based decision support systems construct digitised knowledge about the future realities of a child based on administrative data. In doing so, they simultaneously challenge and displace the more nuanced and in-depth professional knowledge of child welfare workers' judgement and their capacity for discretion (Høybye-Mortensen, 2013). These are high-stakes outcomes as the tool effectively becomes the basis for deciding whether to remove a child from their parents, or not, with the profound consequences for children in cases of false-negatives or false-positives (Dare & Gambrill, 2016).

Criminal justice has also adopted anticipatory algorithms to supplement or supplant professional human judgement. Most obvious is the rise of predictive policing (Harcourt, 2008; Perry, 2013; Bennett Moses & Chan, 2018). Based on digitised knowledge from algorithms, algorithms deploy data analytics, modelling, and machine learning in order to predict crime, criminals, criminal spaces and criminal identities. For many years, risk assessment tools, such as COMPAS (Northpointe, 2015), Public Safety Assessment (www.psapretrial.org) and LSI-R (Andrews & Bonta, 2000), have been deployed in bail and parole processes. The systems calculate risk of future breach of bail or parole orders, or recidivism by comparing an individual's profile with profiles associated with increased risk (Peeters & Schuilenburg,

2018). While these tools govern specific offenders, new predictive policing tools extent beyond this to make judgements of people, populations and places. Similar to the child protection systems, these algorithms create 'risky' subjects whose (alleged) future criminal acts are (probabilistically) constituted. Use of such tools has been criticised for reproducing, rather than reducing, racial discrimination through the creation of algorithmic models based on historical data reflecting structural racism. Such systems also fundamentally challenge legal principles of due process and assessing the merits of each case individually (Huq, 2018; Washington, 2018; Hannah-Moffat, 2019).

In summary, algorithmic governmentality in criminal justice creates new forms of anticipatory knowledge – new governable subjects ('future criminals') – and new anticipatory governmental techniques, a preventative gaze (Peeters, 2013), based on curtailing predicted futures, rather than the traditional approach of investigating existent crimes and punishing those that have committed the offence. In doing so, they reproduce crime and criminality, and reinforce spirals of disadvantage and exclusion based on the digitised categories of one's case compared. How might this algorithmic governmentality, of comparative categorisation and calculated prediction be understood? How does it relate to forms of power and modes of subjectification? Here, Antoinette Rouvroy and Thomas Berns' characterisation is insightful:

> [W]e thus use the term algorithmic governmentality to refer very broadly to a certain type of (a)normative or (a)political rationality founded on the automated collection, aggregation and analysis of big data so as to model, anticipate and pre-emptively affect possible behaviours. (…) Algorithmic governmentality produces no subjectification, it circumvents and avoids reflexive human subjects, feeding on infra-individual data which are meaningless on their own, to build supra-individual models of behaviours or profiles without ever involving the individual, and without ever asking them to themselves describe what they are or what they could become.
>
> (Rouvroy & Berns, 2013: X)

Drawing this out, Rouvroy and Berns concisely encapsulate the key contours of algorithmic governmentality. First, its origin is in big data made up of digitised characteristics of individuals and their activities. Second, in drawing such data into an algorithm, they are detached from specific individuals, their subjectivities and lived experiences, to instead construct digital personas with calculated characteristics and future behaviours. Third, these digital personas 'produce no subjectification', but construct governable digital subjects that are re-connected to an individual subject. Fourth, the individuals are governed on the basis of the proxy digital and future individuals. At the heart of algorithmic governmentality is a new regime of truth, not about live humans – as biopower or pastoral power would be – but on digitally concocted subjects. Such algorithmic regimes of truth form the basis for machinic judgement to govern human subjects.

Towards judgement machines and their judgement

Algorithms have always been key to making judgements and decisions. What are the social consequences of algorithmic governmentality? There are two key social dynamics that arise from this growing machinic judgement of algorithmic governmentality. The first relates to the nature of individuals and individuality, and the second relates to social structure and individuals' experience of it.

Understanding the nature of selves within society is a long-standing focus of social science. Algorithmic governmentality constitutes individuals in quite different ways to that of neoliberal governmentality (Rose, 1999; Bauman, 2001; Beck & Beck-Gernsheim, 2002), whereby individuals become authors and entrepreneurs of their own life stories, take on risks that were previously socially shared, and define themselves via their choices. In contrast, individuality arising from algorithmic governmentality is a socio-technological process that constructs digital personas via a set of digitised characteristics and classifications that are attached to a person (Henman, 2007) or what Gilles Deleuze calls 'dividuals' (1992). The computerised classifications arising from complex algorithmic calculations denote a dividual as a 'unique' combination of almost unlimited combinations of social categories (such as income, sex/gender, purchasing history, social network). Yet, dividuals are governed in place of real-life persons, an equivalence is assumed, but the governing of dividuals has real effects on real persons; they can be denied entry, given benefits, provided services and charged fines.

The second social inter-related dynamic arising from algorithmic governmentality is a reconfiguration of society and people's experience of the social (Henman, 2010: 228–238). Just as the digitised knowledge of algorithmic governmentality is used to constitute and govern dividuals, digitised knowledge is also the way in which society is constituted and governed. Algorithmic governmentality fragments and splinters society according to digitised knowledge. At one level, algorithmic governmentality re-produces and heightens traditional forms of social discrimination (by gender/sex, race/ethnicity, religion, etc.) and magnifies disadvantage. For example, Safiya Umoja Noble documented Google's race-loaded autosearch (Noble, 2018), Amazon's employment algorithms discriminated by gender (Dastin, 2018), predictive policing further criminalises race and space (Harcourt, 2008), and Microsoft's ill-fated Twitter AI, Tay, spewed vile (Neff & Nagy, 2016).

Moreover, algorithmic governmentality creates ever finer forms of social differentiation; it simultaneously anticipates and excludes. In undertaking to 'model, anticipate and pre-emptively affect possible behaviours' (Rouvroy & Berns, 2013), algorithmic governmentality excludes through machinic judgement using the digitised classifications of dividuals. By feeding different news content, ads, music and television programs to different dividuals (Spohr, 2017), by providing differential prices based on personal characteristics (White House, 2015), by differentiating services to different citizens and consumers (Henman, 2004; Tsiptsis & Chorianopoulos, 2011), by hiring on the basis of machinic judgments (Dastin, 2018), or by differentiated surveillance (Lyon, 2003), people are excluded from a somewhat shared world of news, prices, universal service offerings and work.

Universal public services are progressively 'individualised', resulting in separate citizens treated separately, not knowing what to expect or their rights. There is no level playing field, no universal suffrage.

To be sure, people have always been excluded, for example by price points in markets and workplaces due to lack of skills. But previously one had a better chance of apprehending the overall world – they could see what TV shows were on, could find out the prices of goods and services, to share in news consumption. The world of machinic judgement is far more differentiated. The worlds we each view, engage in and experience become increasingly disconnected from others; differentiated subpopulations develop separate 'taken for granted' knowledge and experiences. Consequently, people have little understanding of others' worlds and how they are governed vis-à-vis to others. There is no shared public. Society is fragmented, where we live in our own digital bubbles constituted by algorithmic governmentality (Henman, 2010: 228–237).

What might be critical and practical responses to algorithmic governmentality? What might be modes of counter-conduct to algorithmic governmentality? One approach is to embrace, yet enhance, algorithmic governmentality so that dividuals accord most closely to individuals. Digital categories can be remade. Just as queer politics has destabilised the male/female dichotomy, resulting in new digitised categories (e.g. non-binary, other), new digitised classifications and data ontologies can be developed to better reflect the complex diversity of human. Instead of using 'failure to cooperate', a more nuanced classificatory system can be devised. Just as digitised music and videos have become acceptable recordings of the analogue world, we could come to have acceptable data structures of people. In enhancing algorithmic governmentality we can also move to ensure that algorithms become more transparent, explainable and accountable, and data about us can be viewed and corrected if erroneous (Mittelstadt et al., 2016; Fjeld et al., 2020).

Such enhancement of algorithmic governmentality may more accurate model ourselves, to better govern us, but there remain two crucial social problems arising from enhancing algorithmic governmentality. First, anticipatory algorithmic governmentality governs dividuals based on calculated realities and futures, not actual realities. This mode of governing undermines basic legal principles and due process (Henman, 2005; Slobogin, 2008; Perry, 2014). Counter-conduct therefore can seek to curtail or override algorithmic governmentality by using long-standing legal principles and social mores about 'fairness'. In addition, a 'no detriment' principle can be instituted such that governmental decisions based on a person's calculated future cannot disadvantage (only advantage) them.

The second problem of enhancing algorithmic governmentality relates to differentiation of dividuals, of creating differential worlds. There are valid and appropriate reasons for treating people differently, such as for health care based on diagnosed need or individualised teaching based on learning profiles. However, there are also strong reasons to eschew dividual differentiation to embrace universality, such as universal health care, education and anti-discrimination. Revaluing equality, universalism, and shared collectivities can counter the differentiation of machinic judgement.

A further form of counter-conduct is to refuse to be categorised. Just as queer theory challenges the categories of gender and sexuality, and liquid modernity (Bauman, 2000) destabilises concretised social norms and expectations, we collectively can refuse to be classified, coded and labelled (Lanier, 2010). We can disrupt algorithms' capacity to operate. And we can refuse to have our futures defined by algorithms saying what we are to be and to become. As Doc Brown in the classic movie *Back to the Future* says: 'Your future hasn't been written yet. No one's has. Your future is whatever you make it. So make it a good one.'

Conclusion

Algorithms govern us. Yet they are not simply tools for enacting political agendas and governmentalities. This chapter argues that, despite the infinite variety in digital computer algorithms, there are shared ways in which algorithms govern, that they enact their own 'algorithmic governmentality' that overlays and entwines with other governmentalities. The basic makeup of digital computers, of code and abstract data types, structures the fields of possibility. In doing so, algorithmic governmentality renders the world as calculable, knowledge becomes digitised. It is also anticipatory, constructed future subjects and scenarios to be governed in the present. The recent growth of machine learning has exacerbated these tendencies. Algorithmic governmentality is machinic judgement. Algorithmic governmentality in turn creates new selves; dividuals, constituted by digitised knowledge, inhabiting an increasing differentiated society of multiple universes reinforcing old and new disadvantages and discriminations. Challenging algorithmic governmentality requires engagement with algorithms, digitised categories and a renewal of our shared humanity.

Notes

1 For text book introductions to 'governmentality' see Dean (2010), Walters (2012) and Lemke (2015a).
2 For an understanding of Actor–Network Theory see: (Callon, 1987; Latour, 1988, 2005; Law, 1992).
3 The author was initially trained as computer scientist in the late 1980s.
4 Alan Turing famously constructed a hypothetical 'universal Turing machine' as a thought experiment to define what is calculable and incalculable (Turing, 1936). The concept – of fixed data sections and limited operations on that data – underpins what computers theoretically can and cannot do.
5 Totaro and Ninno (2014), in arguing that algorithms are an 'interpretative key of modern rationality', point to the centrality of classification in the operation of algorithms, but also argue for the importance of function, that is, procedures of calculation on categories.
6 The exteriority of the category becomes equated to the interiority of the individual, in a parallel fashion Foucault (1978) observed the late 19th century constructed the interior personage of 'the homosexual' from what previously had been an exterior of a physical activity.
7 For more detailed explanation of machine learning see, for example, Alpaydin (2020).
8 For an understanding on rise of probabilistic thinking and risk governmentality, see, for example, Ewald (1991), Ericson & Haggerty (1997) and O'Malley (2004).

References

Alpaydin, E. 2020. *Introduction to machine learning*. Cambridge, MA: MIT Press.

Anacleto, R., N. Luz, A. Almeida, L. Figueiredo and P. Novais. 2011. *Shopping center tracking and recommendation systems*. Paper presented at the *Soft Computing Models in Industrial and Environmental Applications, 6th International Conference SOCO*, Salamanca.

Andrews, D. A. and J. Bonta. 2000. *The level of service inventory-revised*. Toronto: Multi-Health Systems

Bauman, Z. 2000. *Liquid modernity*. Cambridge: Polity.

Bauman, Z. 2001. *The individualized society*. Cambridge: Polity.

Beck, U. and E. Beck-Gernsheim. 2002. *Individualization*. London: Sage.

Beecher, K. 2017. *Computational thinking*. London: BCS.

Benjamin, R. 2019. *Race after technology*. Cambridge: Polity.

Bennett Moses, L. and J. Chan. 2018. Algorithmic prediction in policing. *Policing and Society*, 28(7), 806–822.

Borch, C. 2017. Algorithmic finance and (limits to) governmentality. *Le foucaldien*, 3 (1): 1–17.

Bowker, G.C. and S.L. Star. 2000. *Sorting things out: Classification and its consequences*. Cambridge, MA: MIT Press.

Boyle, D. 2020. *Tickbox*. London: Little Brown.

Bu, J., S. Tan, C. Chen, C. Wang, H. Wu, L. Zhang and X. He. 2010. *Music recommendation by unified hypergraph*. Paper presented at the *Proceedings of the 18th ACM International Conference on Multimedia*, Firenze.

Callon, M. 1987. Society in the making: The study of technology as a tool for sociological analysis. In *The social construction of technological systems*, edited by W.E. Bijker, T.P. Hughes and T. Pinch, 83–103. Cambridge, MA: MIT Press.

Carney, T. 2019. Robo-debt illegality: The seven veils of failed guarantees of the rule of law? *Alternative Law Journal*, 44 (1): 4–10.

Clay, S. 2018. The (neo) tribal nature of Grindr. In *Neo-Tribes: Consumption, leisure and tourism*, edited by A. Hardy, A. Bennett and B. Robards, 235–251. Basingstoke: Palgrave Macmillan.

Danaher, J. 2016. The threat of algocracy. *Philosophy & Technology*, 29 (3): 245–268.

Dare, T. and E. Gambrill. 2016. Ethical analysis: Predictive risk models at call screening for Allegheny County. https://www.alleghenycountyanalytics.us/wp-content/uploads/2019/05/Ethical-Analysis-16-ACDHS-26_PredictiveRisk_Package_050119_FINAL-2.pdf.

Dastin, J. 2018, October 10. Amazon scraps secret AI recruiting tool that showed bias against women. *Reuters*. https://www.reuters.com/article/us-amazon-com-jobs-automation-insight/amazon-scraps-secret-ai-recruiting-tool-that-showed-bias-against-women-idUSKCN1MK08G.

Davis, J.L. and J.B. Chouinard. 2016. Theorizing affordances: From request to refuse. *Bulletin of Science, Technology and Society*, 36 (4): 241–248.

Dean, M. 2010. *Governmentality* (2nd edition). London: Sage.

Deleuze, G. 1992. Postscript on the societies of control. October, 59: 3–7.

Diallo, I. 2018. *The machine fired me: No human could do a thing about it!* idiallo.com/blog/when-a-machine-fired-me.

Ericson, R. V. and K.D. Haggerty. 1997. *Policing the risk society*. Oxford: Clarendon Press.

Eubanks, V. 2018. *Automating inequality*. New York: St. Martin's Press.

Ewald, F. 1991. Insurance and risk. In *The Foucault effect: Studies in governmentality*, edited by G. Burchell, C. Gordon and P. Miller, 197–210. London: Harvester Wheatsheaf.

Feuz, M., M. Fuller and F. Stalder. 2011. Personal web searching in the age of semantic capitalism: Diagnosing the mechanisms of personalisation. *First Monday*, 16 (2): 1–8.

Fjeld, J., N. Achten, H. Hilligoss, A. Nagy and M. Srikumar. 2020. *Principled artificial intelligence: mapping consensus in ethical and rights-based approaches to principles for AI*. https://ssrn.com/abstract=3518482.

Foucault, M. 1978. *The history of sexuality, volume 1: An introduction*. Harmondsworth: Penguin.

Foucault, M. 1981. Omnes et singulatim: towards a criticism of political reason. *The Tanner Lectures on Human Values*, 2: 223–254.

Foucault, M. 1982. The subject and power: afterword. In *Michel Foucault: Beyond structuralism and hermeneutics*, edited by H.L. Dreyfus and P. Rabinow, 208–226. Sussex: Harvester Press.

Foucault, M. 1991. Governmentality. In *The Foucault effect: Studies in governmentality*, edited by G. Burchell, C. Gordon and P. Miller, 87–104. Chicago, IL: The University of Chicago Press.

Foucault, M. 2007. *Security, territory, population: Lectures at the College de France 1977–78* (G. Burchell, Trans.). Hampshire: Palgrave Macmillan.

Foucault, M. 2008. *The birth of biopolitics: Lectures at the College de France 1978–79* (G. Burchell, Trans.). Hampshire: Palgrave Macmillan.

Gillespie, T. 2014. The relevance of algorithms. In *Media technologies: Essays on communication, materiality, and society*, edited by T. Gillespie, P.J. Boczkowski and K.A. Foot, 167–194. Cambridge, MA: MIT Press.

Gillingham, P. 2006. Risk assessment in child protection: Problem rather than solution? *Australian Social Work*, 59 (1): 86–98.

Gillingham, P. 2019. Decision support systems, social justice and algorithmic accountability in social work: A new challenge. *Practice*, 31 (4): 277–290.

Gomez-Uribe, C.A. and N. Hunt. 2015. The netflix recommender system: Algorithms, business value, and innovation. *ACM Transactions on Management Information Systems*, 6 (4): 1–19.

Gordon, C. 1991. Governmental rationality: An introduction. In *The Foucault . Studies in governmentality, effect*edited by G. Burchell, C. Gordon and P. Miller, 1–52. Chicago, IL: University of Chicago Press.

Graham, T. 2018. Platforms and hyper-choice on the world wide web. *Big Data & Society*, 5 (1): 1–12.

Graham, T. and P. Henman. 2019. Affording choice: How website designs create and constrain 'choice'. *Information, Communication & Society*, 22 (13): 2007–2023.

Hannah-Moffat, K. 2019. Algorithmic risk governance: Big data analytics, race and information activism in criminal justice debates. *Theoretical Criminology*, 23 (4): 453–470.

Harcourt, B.E. 2008. *Against prediction: Profiling, policing, and punishing in an actuarial age*. Chicago, IL: University of Chicago Press.

Henman, P. 1995. The role of computers in texturing the micro-social environment. *Australian and New Zealand Journal of Sociology*, 31 (1): 49–63.

Henman, P. 2004. Targeted!: Population segmentation, electronic surveillance and governing the unemployed in Australia. *International Sociology*, 19 (2): 173–191.

Henman, P. 2005. E-government, targeting and data profiling: policy and ethical issues of differential treatment. *Journal of E-government*, 2 (1): 79–98.

Henman, P. 2007. Governing individuality. In *Contested individualization*, edited by C. Howard, 171–185. New York: Palgrave Macmillan.

Henman, P. 2010. *Governing electronically*. Basingstoke: Palgrave.

Hoang Ngan Le, T., Y. Zheng, C. Zhu, K. Luu and M. Savvides. 2016. *Multiple scale faster-rcnn approach to driver's cell-phone usage and hands on steering wheel detection*. Paper presented at the *Proceedings of the IEEE Conference on Computer Vision and Pattern Recognition Workshops*, Las Vegas.

Hossain, N., T. Hu, R. Feizi, A.M. White, J. Luo and H. Kautz. 2016. *Precise localization of homes and activities: Detecting drinking-while-tweeting patterns in communities.* Paper presented at the *Tenth International AAAI Conference on Web and Social Media*, Cologne.

Høybye-Mortensen, M. 2013. Decision-making tools and their influence on caseworkers' room for discretion. *The British Journal of Social Work*, 45 (2): 600–615.

Hu, L. and Q. Ni. 2017. IoT-driven automated object detection algorithm for urban surveillance systems in smart cities. *IEEE Internet of Things Journal*, 5 (2): 747–754.

Huq, A.Z. 2018. Racial equity in algorithmic criminal justice. *Duke LJ*, 68: 1043.

Introna, L.D. 2016. Algorithms, governance, and governmentality: On governing academic writing. *Science, Technology & Human Values*, 41 (1): 17–49.

Koopman, C. 2019. *How we became our data: A genealogy of the informational person.* Chicago: University of Chicago Press.

Lanier, J. 2010. *You are not a gadget: A manifesto.* New York: Vintage Books.

Latour, B. 1988. Mixing humans and Nnonhumans together: The sociology of a door-closer. *Social Problems*, 35 (3): 298–310.

Latour, B. 2005. *Reassembling the social: An introduction to actor-network-theory.* New York: Oxford University Press.

Law, J. 1992. Notes on the theory of the actor-network: Ordering, strategy, and heterogeneity systems practice. *Systems Practice*, 5 (4): 379–393.

Lemke, T. 2015a. *Foucault, governmentality, and critique.* London: Routledge.

Lemke, T. 2015b. New materialisms: Foucault and the 'government of things'. *Theory, Culture & Society*, 32 (4): 3–25.

Lomell, H.M. 2004. Targeting the unwanted: Video surveillance and categorical exclusion in Oslo, Norway. *Surveillance & Society*, 2 (2/3): 346–360.

Lyon, D. (Ed.) 2003. *Surveillance as social sorting.* London: Routledge.

Miller, P. and N. Rose. 2008. *Governing the present.* Cambridge: Polity.

Mittelstadt, B.D., P. Allo, M. Taddeo, S. Wachter and L. Floridi. 2016. The ethics of algorithms: Mapping the debate. *Big Data & Society*, 3 (2): 1–21.

Neff, G. and Nagy, P. 2016. Automation, algorithms, and politics talking to bots: Symbiotic agency and the case of Tay. *International Journal of Communication*, 10: 4915–4931.

Noble, S.U. 2018. *Algorithms of oppression.* New York: New York University Press.

Northpointe. 2015. Practitioner's guide to COMPAS core. equivant.com: http://www.north-pointeinc.com/downloads/compas/Practitioners-Guide-COMPAS-Core-_031915.pdf

O'Malley, P. 2004. *Risk, uncertainty and government.* London: Glasshouse Press.

Oosterlinck, D., D.F. Benoit, P. Baecke and N. van de Weghe. 2017. Bluetooth tracking of humans in an indoor environment: An application to shopping mall visits. *Applied Geography*, 78: 55–65.

Palmer, D., I. Warren and P. Miller. 2013. ID scanners in the night-time economy: Social sorting or social order? *Trends and Issues in Crime and Criminal Justice*, 466: 1.

Peeters, R. 2013. *The preventive gaze.* The Hague: Eleven International Publishing.

Peeters, R. and M. Schuilenburg. 2018. Machine justice: Governing security through the bureaucracy of algorithms. *Information Polity*, 23 (3): 267–280.

Perry, M. 2014. *iDecide: the legal implications of automated decision-making.* Paper presented at the *Cambridge Centre for Public Law Conference*, Cambridge.

Perry, W.L. 2013. *Predictive policing: The role of crime forecasting in law enforcement operations.* Washington, DC: Rand Corporation.

Powers, E. 2017a. My news feed is filtered? Awareness of news personalization among college students. *Digital Journalism*, 5 (10): 1315–1335.

Powers, T.M. (Ed.) 2017b. *Philosophy and Computing.* Cham: Springer.

Rader, E. and R. Gray. 2015. *Understanding user beliefs about algorithmic curation in the Facebook news feed*. Paper presented at the *Proceedings of the 33rd Annual ACM Conference on Human Factors in Computing Systems*, Seoul.

Ren, Y., M. Tomko, F.D. Salim, K. Ong and M. Sanderson. 2017. Analyzing web behavior in indoor retail spaces. *Journal of the Association for Information Science Technology*, 68 (1): 62–76.

Rodrigues, N. 2016. Algorithmic governmentality, Smart Cities and spatial justice. https://halshs.archives-ouvertes.fr/halshs-01507099/

Rose, N. 1999. *Powers of Freedom*. Cambridge: Cambridge University Press.

Rosenblat, A. 2018. *Uberland: How algorithms are rewriting the rules of work*. Oakland: University of California Press.

Rouvroy, A. 2013. The end (s) of critique: Data behaviourism versus due process. In *Privacy, due process and the computational turn: The philosophy of law meets the philosophy of technology*, edited by M. Hildebrandt and K. de Vries, 157–182. London: Routledge.

Rouvroy, A. and T. Berns. 2013. Algorithmic governmentality and prospects of emancipation. *Réseaux*, 1: 163–196.

Rouvroy, A. and B. Stiegler. 2016. The digital regime of truth: from the algorithmic governmentality to a new rule of law. *La Deleuziana: Online Journal of Philosophy*, 3: 6–29.

Scott, D. 2005. Colonial governmentality. *Anthropologies of Modernity*, 23–49.

Slobogin, C. 2008. Government data mining and the fourth amendment. *The University of Chicago Law Review*, 75 (1): 317–341.

Spohr, D. 2017. Fake news and ideological polarization: Filter bubbles and selective exposure on social media. *Business Information Review*, 34 (3): 150–160.

Steiner, C. 2012. *Automate this*. New York: Penguin.

Totaro, P. and D. Ninno. 2014. The concept of algorithm as an interpretative key of modern rationality. *Theory, Culture & Society*, 31 (4): 29–49.

Trottier, D. 2016. *Social media as surveillance: Rethinking visibility in a converging world*. Farnham, UK: Routledge.

Tsiptsis, K.K. and A. Chorianopoulos. 2011. *Data mining techniques in CRM: inside customer segmentation*. New York: John Wiley & Sons.

Turing, A. 1936. On computable numbers, with an application to the Entscheidungsproblem. *Proceedings of the London Mathematical Society*, 2 (42): 230–265.

Vámos, T. 2010. *Knowledge and computing: A course on computer epistemology*. Budapest: Central European University Press.

Walters, W. 2012. *Governmentality: Critical encounters*. London: Routledge.

Washington, A.L. 2018. How to argue with an algorithm: Lessons from the COMPAS-ProPublica debate. *The Colorado Technology Law Journal*, 17: 131.

Weizenbaum, J. 1984. *Computer power and human reason*. London: Penguin.

White House. 2015. Big data and differential pricing. https://obamawhitehouse.archives.gov/sites/default/files/whitehouse_files/docs/Big_Data_Report_Nonembargo_v2.pdf

Zarsky, T. Z. 2011. Governmental data mining and its alternatives. *Penn State Law Review*, 116: 285.

Chapter 3

Algorithmic regulation
Machine learning as a governance tool

Cary Coglianese

Introduction

Throughout history, humans have made all the critical decisions that govern society. But today, new algorithmic tools are beginning to emerge that could augment or replace human decision-making to fulfil many important governance functions. Governments are increasingly turning to – or at least are investigating – the application of artificial intelligence tools to find more effective and administratively efficient ways of maintaining social order (Coglianese & Lehr, 2017). Algorithms, it is now apparent, can be deployed in digital systems that help make decisions about allocating regulatory oversight resources, applying enforcement penalties, and even creating rules in the first place.

When used responsibly by government officials, new algorithmic tools promise to deliver considerable advantages in terms of making smarter, faster, and more consistent decisions, thereby facilitating outcomes that are better for society and potentially of lower cost to government. Yet, as with any new type of policy or tool, machine learning will deliver its benefits with accompanying costs. In this chapter, I highlight not merely the potential benefits of algorithmic regulation – that is, of the governmental use of machine-learning tools – but I also consider a series of concerns that scholars and activists have raised about machine learning, including those of accountability, equality, due process, privacy, transparency, and abuse of power (O'Neil, 2016; Eubanks, 2017). Although these concerns are genuine, I will show that they are not inherently problems with machine-learning technology itself – instead, they depend ultimately on human decision-making about how algorithmic technologies are designed and used. The risks of algorithmic regulation are sufficiently avoidable that responsible and just governments should be able to design and monitor algorithmic systems so that their benefits will outweigh their costs and will not trample protected rights.

But even though algorithmic regulation should not face inherent challenges of the kind that many scholars and activists have raised to date, machine-learning technology will need confront other limitations. Perhaps the biggest constraint on machine learning as a governance tool will stem from humans' inability to achieve clear social consensus around the trade-offs that regulatory algorithms will need specified with precision. For machine-learning algorithms to work, they must be constructed at the outset with well-defined mathematically stated objectives. As such, widespread reliance on algorithmic regulation is likely to encounter the same kind of pitfalls that can plague performance-based regulation (Coglianese, 2017) – which is, like a machine learning, a type of 'algorithm' that is defined in terms of objectives. Moreover, algorithmic regulation is unlikely to replace humans in fulfilling highly consequential governance functions to perform any task in which human collective decision-making is unable to yield sufficient precision over normative values and their trade-offs.

In the end, I suggest in this chapter that the most serious limitations on algorithmic regulation will stem not so much from the technology itself but from the humans that seek to use these new tools. This does not mean that governments necessarily need to shy away altogether from research on and experimentation with the regulatory use of machine-learning tools. But they do need to approach the prospects of algorithmic regulation with eyes wide open to the technology's risks and limitations, and they should prepare now to develop the human capabilities within the public sector that will be necessary for governments to use algorithms responsibly.

The promise of algorithmic regulation

The private sector currently deploys machine-learning algorithms to drive an increasing variety of uses, including Internet search, medical screening, autonomous driving, digital marketing, and the processing of loan applications. For many of these uses, algorithms perform better than human beings in terms of speed and accuracy, which helps to explain their increasing attraction to governments. These same advantages can make machine-learning algorithms of considerable potential value in performing governmental functions.

To see how machine-learning technology could be deployed to help carry out regulatory and other governance tasks currently conducted by humans using less sophisticated analytic tools, consider the following three possibilities:

-   The US Environmental Protection Agency (EPA) must oversee hundreds of thousands of industrial facilities to ensure that they comply with water pollution regulations. But EPA has limited inspection staff. It can decide by random draw which facilities to send its limited inspectors to visit. Or it can instead develop a machine-learning algorithm that forecasts which facilities are most likely to be out of compliance, and then use those results to direct the limited number of inspectors toward those facilities. A machine-learning tool could actually allow EPA to identify as many as 600% more violators than the random approach (Hino, Benami & Brooks, 2018).
-   The rules governing disbursement of government benefits for individuals with disabilities currently call for human administrative judges at the US Social Security Administration (SSA) to make determinations about whether any particular applicant qualifies for such benefits. But concerns exist that, under this human-driven system, racial minorities may tend to receive less

favourable benefit determinations (Godtland et al., 2007). Irrespective of race, human decision-making is highly inconsistent, with one study showing that some SSA judges grant benefits 90 percent of the time, while others grant them in only 10 percent of the time (TRAC, 2011). The government agency responsible for administering these benefits has developed an algorithmic tool to help check the quality of decision-making (Ray & Lubbers, 2015), identifying possible errors in human decisions. Further use of an algorithmic system might help streamline and improve the overall process, not only clearing backlogs but making more accurate and consistent decisions.

- One aspect of social ordering in large cities centres on the management of traffic flow. Traditional roadway signalling systems are set to change traffic lights on predetermined time intervals or to follow simple rules programmed by human engineers. But instead, the rules of the road could be determined automatically by an artificial intelligence system that adapts in real time to inputs from sensors embedded in the roads. These sensors could feed information about current traffic conditions to a machine learning algorithm that would autonomously operate the traffic signals to minimise traffic congestion. This type of algorithmic ordering of city traffic is more than just a thought experiment. The city of Pittsburgh has already installed such a system that has reportedly reduced by 25% the amount of time that residents sit in traffic (Snow, 2017).

Decision systems like these can replace slower, less accurate, or inconsistent human judgements, leading to smarter and faster governance-related decisions.

Other examples of governmental use of machine learning include the allocation and assignment of police personnel and building inspectors in major cities such as New York and Los Angeles (Coglianese & Ben Dor, 2020). In Pennsylvania, a machine-learning system helps one county's officials decide which complaints of possible child abuse merit follow up from limited social services staff (Vaithianathan et al., 2019). A study of 142 different federal administrative agencies in the United States found that 45% of them had initiated at least one project using machine-learning algorithms to try to improve their agencies' performance (Engstrom et al., 2020). Examples of such projects include the use of machine learning by the Securities and Exchange Commission to identify possible cases of securities fraud and by the Internal Revenue Service to identify likely instances of incomplete or inaccurate income tax filings (Coglianese & Lehr, 2017). Over time, the use of artificial intelligence by governmental authorities throughout the United States and around the world is only likely to grow, especially as the promise of machine learning becomes more evident and accepted in an increasing number of other applications.

How algorithmic regulation is different

As anyone can attest who has typed a Google search or observed how accurately Amazon and Netflix make automatic recommendations for their customers, machine-learning algorithms can produce highly accurate predictions. Although machine-learning algorithms come in different varieties, what sets them apart from traditional statistical analytic methods is the way that learning algorithms process large volumes of data and autonomously find patterns in the data. Human technicians do still need to be involved in specifying the learning algorithm's 'objective function' – that is, telling the algorithm what to search for and optimise. Humans must also specify the type of machine-learning algorithm to deploy and typically they must also be involved in training, tweaking, and evaluating the performance of these algorithms. But what truly sets machine-learning algorithms apart is that they can essentially roam through vast quantities of data on their own in search of patterns. They try out, essentially on their own accord, different combinations of data variables and different mathematical relationships between these variables, seeking to find – or 'learn' – the best combinations of variables and mathematical relationships between them to yield accurate predictions (Lehr & Ohm, 2017).

Unlike traditional multivariate regression analysis, machine learning does not depend on humans to specify which variables to test and whether to apply a specific mathematical function to those variables. As a result, exactly how these algorithms reach the predictions that they yield can be hard for any human to discern or explain in a clear, intuitive manner – hence, machine-learning algorithms are sometimes called 'black box' tools. Moreover, although machine learning generates highly accurate forecasts, it does not typically support causal claims of the kind that can be ordinarily provided by traditional statistical tools. This means that, although users of machine-learning algorithms can have confidence that their results amount to accurate predictions, they cannot easily understand exactly why these algorithms generate the specific results that they do (Coglianese & Lehr, 2019).

When algorithmic tools are used by government to promote social order, these distinctive features of machine-learning algorithms – namely, their opacity and relative autonomy – raise concerns, especially if these algorithms might potentially replace human-directed analysis and decision-making. For many members of the public, governmental decisions made by humans can seem more legitimate than rule by robot. It is one thing to use algorithms in ways that still keep a human 'in the loop', as when, for example, algorithms merely guide the allocation of human inspectors or auditors who then independently determine whether fraud or tax evasion has occurred (Coglianese & Lehr, 2017). It is another matter altogether for humans to take a back seat – to be taken 'out of the loop' altogether. Yet we get closer each day to a human-out-of-the-loop world of robotic regulation and algorithmic adjudication in which previously human-driven governance can be fully automated.

Of course, anyone who is reminded of humans' foibles – their myriad cognitive biases and group dysfunctionalities – might be forgiven for thinking that at least some governmental functions would be better if humans were removed from the loop, at least when well-calibrated, demonstrably superior digital machines could take their place. But public acceptance of the use of algorithmic tools by governments – at least for consequential decisions – appears likely to be halting at best. That degree of acceptance is likely to depend on both the consequences associated with the degree to which humans are removed from decision-making and the use to which machine learning is put. Few members of the public seem concerned that machine-learning algorithms have been used for years to make decisions related to sorting postal mail (Coglianese & Lehr, 2017). Similarly, members of the public may also be relatively unconcerned about governmental reliance on algorithms to decide what tax returns to audit or where to send workplace safety inspectors, as long as the key decisions about whether to penalise taxpayers or businesses still depend on what a human auditor or inspector finds upon an individualised review. Even when algorithms are given the authority to generate simple rules – as automated, algorithmic traffic signalling systems effectively do – they seem unlikely to raise serious public concern because the stakes seem rather low.

But it is a different matter altogether when it comes to an algorithmic system used to determine how much time a convicted defendant will spend in jail. Even though algorithmic systems used by courts have in reality yet to rely on machine learning per se, and even though human judges still remain in the loop with the traditional algorithms they do use, advocacy groups have nevertheless mobilised to challenge governmental use of algorithms in the court system (Coglianese & Ben Dor, 2020). In 2016, the advocacy organisation ProPublica released a widely circulated report that criticised a risk assessment tool called COMPAS that has been used widely by state courts in making criminal sentencing decisions (Angwin et al., 2016). The tool purportedly relied on a proprietary algorithm – albeit not one based on machine learning – to forecast a defendant's risk of recidivism. Judges were simply given the COMPAS risk ranking for each defendant and allowed to take it into account in making their sentencing decisions. Not only did the ProPublica report receive extensive media coverage, but the COMPAS tool later found itself under legal attack in a case that eventually reached the Wisconsin Supreme Court. In *State* v. *Loomis*, the defendant, Loomis, challenged his high risk score generated by COMPAS and argued that the Wisconsin trial judge's reliance on the tool deprived him of a fundamentally fair trial – both because the precise source code for the COMPAS tool was proprietary (and thus secret), and because the risk forecasts were biased against men.

The Wisconsin Supreme Court rejected Loomis's arguments and upheld the decision of the trial judge to take the COMPAS risk rating into account. But the litigation in *Loomis* will not be the last to challenge governmental reliance on algorithms – and black-box, machine-learning systems, especially when they take humans out of the loop, seem particularly vulnerable to legal challenge on a variety of grounds, including legal concerns over accountability, due process, equal protection, privacy, transparency, and abuse of power. Yet, as I have explained in greater detail elsewhere (Coglianese & Lehr, 2017, 2019), as long as governmental officials exercise reasonable care in developing machine-learning systems, most legal challenges would appear likely to end up like the *Loomis* decision, with the government prevailing.

As I explain in the next five sections of this chapter, the main criticisms that have been levelled at the governmental use of machine learning can probably be adequately addressed by responsible decisions made by human officials. Despite its distinctive 'black-box' features, machine learning actually does not raise any truly novel challenges and should prove no more legally or even morally problematic than other more traditional technologies that have been incorporated into governmental use. After all, when a traditional governmental regulation imposes a requirement that regulated entities such as food processors keep items at a specified temperature, it hardly offends legal or moral norms for government to rely on a thermometer to enforce that regulatory goal. A machine-learning algorithm is ultimately a lot like a thermometer or any other machine which regulators and other government officials rely on all the time. This is not to dismiss the concerns addressed in the sections to follow, but to say that they do not pose any *inherent* or *insuperable* barriers to the use of machine-learning algorithms. With careful planning and thoughtful decision-making, governments should be able to deploy algorithmic tools responsibly without producing significant problems of accountability, due process, equal protection, privacy, transparency, and abuse of power.

Algorithmic accountability

As already indicated, machine learning's relative autonomy makes salient the question of what governmental accountability would mean in a world of algorithmic regulation. Do citizens have a right to expect that humans will make all regulatory and other governmental decisions (Huq, 2020)? The answer might intuitively seem to be 'yes'. After all, accountability typically demands that a clearly identifiable governmental official or set of officials bear responsibility for rules made and other actions taken by government. The desire for accountability is reflected both in the chain of command within governmental organisations as well as in the democratic processes that holds public officials electorally accountable. But when governmental officials who possess authority to establish rules and carry out policies simply pass off their authority to others, they abdicate their responsibility and accountability breaks down.

In US constitutional law, this desire for accountability is reflected in a doctrine known as the non-delegation doctrine, which in principle constrains the degree to which the US Congress can delegate rulemaking authority to regulatory agencies. The prevailing understanding allows Congress to authorise such agencies to exercise rulemaking power, but only if the legislation making such an authorisation imposes an 'intelligible principle' to guide and constrain agencies exercise of rulemaking autonomy. In fact, the Supreme Court has approved almost every delegation of rulemaking authority Congress has made, even those supposedly constrained by principles no more intelligible than 'public interest, convenience, and necessity' (Breyer et al., 2017: 50–84).

At least under this notion of accountability, regulatory robots driven by machine-learning algorithms should pose few accountability problems because the algorithms need mathematically precise objective functions if they are to work at all. Rather than possessing a license to roam and regulate at will, algorithmic regulation will be remarkably accountable because humans have to tell the algorithms what objectives to optimise. Machine-learning algorithms possess autonomy only in how they go about processing and analysing data to achieve their clearly specified optimisations – a mathematical necessity that will fully satisfy any intelligible-principle test of accountability.

Even with an intelligible principle, still another reason exists to worry about governmental accountability: namely, the desire for laws and policies to be motivated by public values, not private interests. Outside the context of algorithms, after all, it would be troubling if government officials passed off their responsibilities to private actors who would then be likely to adopt laws and take policy actions that advance their own private interests to the exclusion of the broader public interest. Yet even under this notion of accountability, algorithmic regulation will likely pose only the most minimal of risk. Algorithms, after all, possess no independent interests of their own; they will work as they are programmed to work, to yield the predictions they are designed to generate. As long as an algorithm's designers are sufficiently accountable to the public, and an algorithm's objective function is defined in publicly interested ways, then algorithmic regulation should pose virtually no risk of corruption or conflict of interest. Indeed, well-designed algorithmic systems could even prove more resistant to corruption and conflicts of interest than human systems.

Black-box algorithms and governmental transparency

A common way to hold human officials accountable is to demand that they conduct public affairs in the open for all to see and that they provide reasons for their decisions. Sunlight, it has been said, is the best disinfectant (Brandeis, 1914). Against this understanding of accountability through transparency, any 'black-box' digital tool that replaces human decision-making might intuitively be viewed with some suspicion. If algorithmic regulation were to be designed in secret, with no ability for the public to understand what they are used for or how they are built, then this would be a serious problem – just as it would be for any non-machine-learning algorithmic tool. But beyond deliberately secretive systems, worries about algorithmic explainability create no insuperable barriers to the governmental use of machine learning judged by conventional standards (Coglianese & Lehr, 2019).

It is true, of course, that machine learning does not support intuitive causal reasoning, such as 'A is regulated to reduce problem B because A causes B'. Machine-learning algorithms make correlative predictions rather than produce results that can support statement such as 'A causes B'. But the inability to produce easily intuited causal explanations need not generate blanket disapproval of machine learning.

For one thing, societies do not now demand anything close to full explainability or perfect transparency. For example, even though the US Freedom of Information Act otherwise requires openness about much government information, the law still exempts from public disclosure much governmental information, such as information related to law enforcement or personnel or information that is protected by trade secrets (Coglianese & Lehr, 2017: 1210). It was hardly surprising that the Wisconsin Supreme Court, in the *Loomis* case, rejected the defendant's claim that the trial judge should have ordered that he be given more details about the algorithm used by the judge in sentencing. The court not only honoured the proprietary rights of the private firm that created the algorithm under contract with the state, but it also held that procedural due process only necessitated that the state allow the defendant to confirm the accuracy of his own personal information processed by the algorithm, not to be able to access the tool's full underlying source code.

Furthermore, although individual human judges may be capable of coming up with cogent-sounding reasons for certain decisions, this does not mean that they are the *real* reasons for individual decisions. When it comes to group decision-making by humans – the kind that dominates many administrative organisations of government – economists and organisational theorists have long recognised that it is difficult, if not impossible, to ascribe clear explanations for collective decision-making. Arrow's Impossibility Theorem, for instance, teaches that when decision-making preferences are arrayed across multiple dimensions, collective decisions may have effectively no stable explanation whatsoever (Arrow, 1963).

Perhaps in the future transparency norms will change to apply more stringently to machine-learning tools. But absent such a change, government officials will likely be able to meet reasonable demands for explanations of algorithmic regulation by simply describing in general terms how the algorithm has been structured to work, validating its performance, and showing that it works as intended (Coglianese & Lehr, 2019). After all, this is mainly what is expected of any machine or instrument – such as a thermometer – on which governmental bodies often rely. The information needed to provide such a basic explanation should be readily available and releasable, even though the intricate inner workings of a machine-learning algorithm might remain obscure.

Finally, although machine-learning algorithms are opaque compared with traditional analytic tools, computer scientists are currently hard at work in developing technical ways to make available more information about how they function (Kearns & Roth, 2019). As a result, whatever valid concerns may exist today about the explainability of algorithmic regulation, they can be expected to diminish over time as the technology advances and becomes more understandable.

Algorithms and procedural fairness

Reasoned decision-making not only provides a source of accountability, it also provides a hallmark of a fair decision-making process. Other characteristics of a fair process include decision-making by a neutral decision-maker and an opportunity for those affected by a decision to provide input before a final decision is made. Nothing about machine learning precludes the provision of public input. Quite the contrary, machine-learning algorithms are currently being used to help federal regulators in the United States digest vast quantities of public comments submitted on proposed regulations (Engstrom et al., 2020). It is hardly difficult to imagine a fully automated rulemaking system that integrates machine-learning analysis of public comments with the processing of other relevant data used by the system to generate rules (Coglianese & Lehr, 2017). Moreover, when it comes to a neutral decision-maker, I have already noted that algorithms might provide a greater degree of neutrality than human decision-makers, who can bring with them a host of biases and produce inconsistent results. For these reasons, it hardly seems like algorithmic regulation would necessarily lead to a denial of procedural fairness; it might actually enhance fairness.

This conclusion is only reinforced by a consideration of the prevailing test for procedural fairness under US constitutional law. Under this test, a governmental decision-making process is judged with three factors in mind: 1) the private stakes in the decision; 2) the accuracy of the decision-making process; and 3) the costs and administrative burdens demanded of the process (*Mathews* v. *Eldridge*, 1976). Algorithmic regulation would seem to quite easily pass this three-part balancing test. The private stakes will, of course, be exogenous to algorithmic decision tools, but such tools should rate favourably under the other two factors of the test. After all, the main attraction of an algorithmic system is that it can reduce decision-making error and lower administrative costs.

Although the use of algorithms will likely prove readily justifiable in terms of fairness, it should be noted that the development and design of an algorithmic system will also implicate procedural fairness. It only seems fair that affected members of the public should be given some opportunity to scrutinise the design of machine-learning tools that will directly affect their interests. For this reason, integral design choices should be developed through open processes whenever possible, with opportunities for public and expert input via advisory committees, public hearings, or public comment periods when feasible. When the city of Boston used machine learning to propose a reconfiguration of its school bus schedules, for example, it afforded residents a number of opportunities to provide input (Goodman, 2019). Public engagement will surely always be a good practice for any algorithmic system affecting members of the public. Indeed, for many governments, such opportunities for public input already represent business as usual for other important policy and management decisions, so it should not necessitate special steps merely because a new system will be based on machine learning. In the end, procedural fairness should not pose any distinctive or significant barriers to the development of algorithmic regulation.

Algorithmic bias

What about bias? Human decision-making, of course, already reflects a host of biases. Some of these represent the kinds of cognitive errors that psychologists and behavioural economists have documented extensively, such as hindsight bias or loss aversion (Kahneman, 2011). Others reflect implicit or explicit prejudices based on race, gender, and other personal characteristics (Eberhardt, 2019). A shift from human-based systems to machine-learning systems offers the possibility of overcoming these human biases. Yet machine learning also poses the risk of entrenching human biases still further if an algorithmic system relies unthinkingly on data with human biases built into them. Unless for some reason the algorithm itself is intentionally designed in a biased manner, the data will be the source of the bias, not the algorithm. The underlying data used to train and test the algorithm (at least initially) will have been generated by humans and will reflect the biases of human systems.

Uncovering such biases baked into the data may seem at first glance as challenging with machine-learning systems as it is with human-based decision-making. The autonomous, black-box nature of machine-learning algorithms means that, even if underlying data used by the system include variables for race, gender, or other personal characteristic, it will not be obvious whether or how the algorithm's outputs are affected by the inclusion of such data. Even if data on specific variables such as race and gender are excluded from the data set, as long as the remaining variables have been influenced by or are correlated with humans' racial or gender biases, then an algorithm's output could still be affected by race or gender.

When governmental entities use algorithms as tools to achieve specific goals, such as to identify tax evasion or determine eligibility for financial benefits, the algorithm will seek to optimise on the basis of that goal – not to discriminate on the basis of a personal characteristic. Absent separate evidence of actual animus by the designers or users of an algorithmic system, then, it will neither be easy or straightforward to discern whether such discrimination has occurred. When an algorithm generates an output that is averse to an individual with a particular racial or other personal characteristic, it will not be readily apparent from that single instance whether the algorithm in general produces outputs that are averse to the entire group of individuals with the same characteristic. Even when the outputs for the wider group can be reviewed, it may not be readily knowable whether or how the characteristic of interest enters into the algorithm's computation.

In instances where the US Supreme Court has held that governmental entities have unconstitutionally discriminated based on race, those entities had categorically used race in their decision-making as a consistent factor to favour (or disfavour) individuals (Coglianese & Lehr, 2017). Such categorical discrimination will seldom, if ever arise when governments use algorithmic tools, simply because the algorithm is processing a mix of different variables to optimise an objective function not defined in terms of race. Moreover, even if an algorithm can be shown to have disparate effects based on race, when the algorithm's objective function is defined in terms of an important governmental purpose, a court may well conclude that the algorithm advances a compelling state interest that nevertheless justifies its continued use.

Of course, even if courts do sometimes excuse algorithmic bias in the name of some other important governmental objective, this does not mean that the bias should escape public disapproval, any more than should the persistent, if not endemic, bias that currently pervades human decision-making. Indeed, that very persistence of unjustified human bias suggests a strong reason why government should consider adopting machine-learning systems. Even if these systems do rely on biased data, it is much easier to identify bias when data are being statistically analysed and then to make mathematical adjustments to an algorithm that can reduce such bias (Miller, 2018; Mullainathan, 2019). Some promising research suggests that such adjustments may be able to be made to offset substantially, if not entirely, the biases contained within existing data sets without sacrificing much accuracy in algorithmic outputs (Berk et al., 2018). Ultimately, it is almost certainly easier to adjust algorithms to reduce biases in their outputs than it is to retool human beings so as to decrease the effects of deeply seated, implicit biases in their decision-making.

Big data and individual privacy

Machine-learning algorithms run on large volumes of data – so-called big data – and they seek out patterns in these data that even humans cannot discern. Some of the data analysed by machine-learning algorithms will contain personal or other sensitive information about individuals or businesses, and thus they will present potential privacy concerns related to how these data are stored and used. As with the other values we have discussed in this chapter, the privacy implications of machine learning are hardly unique to this technology. Protecting privacy with machine learning will involve the same steps that government officials and analysts take for any type of statistical analysis that draws on personal or confidential information.

One potentially distinctive privacy challenge with machine learning arises from its ability to make accurate predictions. Through machine learning, government analysts could find out sensitive or secret aspects of people's lives just by using seemingly benign, non-sensitive data sources. A now-famous example of this ability to reverse-engineer data to reveal personal information comes from the private sector, when a major department store chain in the United States used data on purchases made by female customers to make chillingly accurate predictions of which women were pregnant – and then used those predictions to target customers with marketing information geared toward expectant mothers (Duhigg, 2012). Government officials could in like fashion potentially exploit algorithms' power to identify characteristics that individuals deem private, such as their political affiliations or sexual orientations, and then use that knowledge to discriminate against those individuals. But again, this harm is not inherent in the technology but rather stems from how people use it. Discriminatory actions by government officials are already illegal in many countries independent of machine learning.

Algorithms and the abuse of power

Up to this point, I have argued that as long as government designs and deploys algorithmic tools responsibly, their use can fit comfortably within prevailing norms that make it acceptable for governments to rely on other kinds of statistical tool or automated systems. If machine-learning algorithms can be shown to help government make better, faster, and less costly decisions, they are unlikely to encounter insuperable barriers to their use on the grounds of accountability, transparency, procedural fairness, and equality. Furthermore, if the advantages of using machine learning for particular tasks justify or outweigh the disadvantages, governmental use of this technology would seem more than just acceptable; its use would be positively recommended by any standard of good government.

Yet as much as algorithmic regulation promises performance advantages when used responsibly, it can also better enable unjust governments to engage in oppressive or intentionally harmful actions. In an important sense, I suspect that it is machine learning's overall potential for facilitating the abuse of power that probably animates much of the criticism it receives. There is no denying that unjust governments could use algorithmic tools to enhance their power to evade accountability, invade privacy, and discriminate against minorities, political opponents, or any disfavoured group.

A particular worry surrounds the surveillance functions on which unjust regimes usually depend and how these functions can be enhanced by machine learning. Regimes bent on monitoring their citizens' every move need a tool that can help make sense of the mountains of data available from phone calls, social media and other electronic communications, and mobile phone GPS signals (Mayer-Schönberger & Cukier, 2013). In this sense, machine-learning tools could well prove to be one of dictators' best friends.

Anyone concerned about liberty and human flourishing will rightly oppose the use of machine learning to enable or reinforce oppression. But it is possible to oppose such unjust uses while still seeing the value that machine learning can bring when deployed responsibly. After all, the potential for abuse is a reality with any tool of governance. Law itself – at least in the sense meant by legal positivists – has been, and will continue to be used, as a weapon in the hands of unjust regimes.

Even though machine learning could be a similarly dangerous weapon in the hands of authoritarian rulers, this does not make it a danger inherent in algorithmic technology. It is yet another threat posed by the human beings in government who could design and use the technology to support unjust and illegitimate regimes. Consequently, it will fall to human systems of legal oversight and democratic accountability to ensure that the people who occupy positions of governmental power do not abuse the power of machine learning.

Machine learning will need adequate oversight by independent auditors, legislators, and judges. Such oversight may not need to be any different than that given to other governance tools in countries with sufficiently robust systems of administrative law. But to ensure adequate oversight, special care may need to be taken when governments develop new machine-learning systems to document their goals, key design choices, underlying data sources, and efforts undertaken to validate them (Coglianese & Lehr, 2019). To the extent that governments rely on private contractors in building, training, tuning, or operating algorithmic systems, they should also ensure during the procurement process that government contracts are drafted to make such essential information publicly available – something which is possible to do without undermining private contractors' legitimate claims to protect the confidentiality of underlying intellectual work product (Coglianese & Lampmann, 2020).

Social values and the human limits of algorithmic regulation

Just as humans ultimately determine whether machine learning is used for legitimate or illegitimate purposes, humans also ultimately present what will likely prove to be the most significant practical constraint on the extent to which governments will be able to make use of machine learning. For machine-learning algorithms to work, they must be constructed with well-defined objective functions that tell each algorithm exactly what to optimise and what trade-offs should be made between different values. This technical necessity gives rise to two practical problems that will vex government officials seeking to rely on human-out-of-the-loop algorithmic systems and will likely serve as the most substantial limitation on their use. The first is a problem of value completeness; the second is a problem of value precision.

With *value completeness*, the problem is identifying and coming to agreement on the full range of values at stake in any policy decision or governance system. It will often be easy to identify some values – namely, those reflected in the primary goal of a policy or system – but harder to identify the full range of all relevant values. To illustrate this problem, consider the fact that most people would probably agree that environmental regulations should protect human health. But should other values also be considered in setting actual environmental standards? Should environmental standards take account of compliance costs as well as health risks? If an algorithm is to substitute for human officials at an environmental regulatory agency, designers will need to incorporate into the algorithm's objective function a full set of all relevant social values.

Unfortunately, humans' track record with value completeness is far from stellar. Decades' worth of experience with so-called performance-based regulation provides example after example of value incompleteness when regulators focus on a single objective – the main problem they are seeking to solve – but are blinded to other important concerns (Coglianese & Nash, 2017). For example, when consumer safety regulators in the United States first established standards for child-resistant packaging for medicines and household cleaners, they rightly focused on the problem of children getting poisoned by being able to open containers of dangerous products. Although the initial standards did keep children from opening medicine bottles and cleaner containers, they also kept adults from easily opening these items as well. As a result, adults who finally managed to get their medicine bottles and cleaning containers opened would often left these containers uncapped or would transfer them to other containers that were not child resistant. The dangerous products were then even more accessible to children than they had been before. It took years before the regulations were changed to optimise along two dimensions instead of one, incorporating into the regulation a standard both for child resistance and for adult accessibility (Coglianese, 2017).

Algorithmic regulation shares much in common with performance-based regulation because both demand the specification of objectives. Most of the time, even when people are focused on a specific problem, they actually care about more than just one objective. They do care about solving the problem of childhood poisonings, but they also care about adults opening them too. They care about environmental protection, but also about not imposing too many costs on small businesses. They care about banks avoiding insolvency, but they also want them to take some risks in loaning money to businesses. As a result, whenever government officials develop algorithmic systems, they need to be attentive to multiple, and at times competing, values at stake – and make sure that these values are incorporated into their systems' design. By providing adequate opportunities for public consultation and input early in the development of algorithmic systems, government officials can minimise the possibility of overlooking one or more important values.

Once government officials have identified a complete set of values, they next need to grapple with what may be the greatest challenge of all: *value precision*. To rely on algorithms as effective regulatory tools, the designers of such systems must specify the relevant value choices and trade-offs with mathematical precision and build those mathematical relationships into an algorithm's objective function. If an algorithmic system were designed to set standards for health and safety protection, for instance, it would need to be told exactly how safe is safe enough. It will also need to know how precisely to make any trade-offs between protecting public health and avoiding undue financial burdens on business activity. But social planners and lawmakers are frequently unable to provide such precision, either because individuals themselves cannot specify it or because no social consensus exists at the required level of precision.

Lacking clear answers, the designers of legal rules have for centuries opted instead for broad terms such as 'reasonable', 'practicable', and 'appropriate'. Section 304(b)(1) of the Clean Water Act, for example, provides that EPA shall establish certain water pollution standards based on the 'best practicable control technology currently available', which the agency determines based on a loosely specified multi-factor test that includes a catch-all 'other factors as EPA deems appropriate' (EPA, 2020). But what really does 'practicable' or 'appropriate' mean?

Law often relies on spongy terms because of uncertainty, confusion, and disagreement over value preferences. American legal scholar Cass Sunstein captures well the challenge of value precision with his concept of 'incompletely theorized agreements' (Sunstein, 1995). Even if people can agree on what to do in a particular case, Sunstein notes, they often cannot agree on exactly why:

> [W]hether set down by judges, legislators, or administrators… [l]egal rules are typically incompletely theorized in the sense that they can be accepted by people who disagree on many general issues… A key social function of rules is to allow people to agree on the meaning, authority, and even the soundness of a governing legal provision in the face of disagreements about much else. Much the same can be said about other devices found in the legal culture, including standards, factors, and emphatically analogical reasoning. Indeed, all of the lawyer's conventional tools can allow the achievement of incompletely

theorized agreements on particular outcomes, though in interestingly different ways.

(1995: 1741–1742)

Yet machine-learning algorithms will indeed need precision if they are to substitute for judges, legislators, and administrators as the drivers of regulatory decisions.

An important task of value precision will involve the specification of trade-offs. Once a complete set of the substantive values at stake have been identified, the question will become one of what precise weights should be given to each. There will arise a range of other common questions about trade-offs too, such as how a system is to deal with false positives versus false negatives. How many guilty people should be allowed to go free to prevent a single innocent person from spending time in jail? A similar question will arise whenever a desire to ensure that algorithms minimise disparate treatment of different racial groups if doing so presents a trade-off in terms of predictive accuracy: Exactly how much forecasting accuracy should be sacrificed for how much equality protection? These and other kinds of trade-offs will be endemic to algorithmic regulation, and they will demand clarity from the humans that develop and design machine-learning governance tools, at least if these tools are to have more than random or arbitrary value weightings built into them. Where humans are unable to provide answers to key questions about values and trade-offs, then reliance on an algorithmic system may simply be unsuitable until greater clarity can be provided.

Building human capacity to deploy algorithmic tools

It should be clear by now that, to develop effective tools of algorithmic regulation, governments will need more than just computing technology and access to large data sets. They will also need human capacity to design these tools responsibly and to evaluate them to ensure they work as intended (Coglianese, 2018). This human capacity will need to be multifaceted and multidisciplinary.

Government personnel will be needed who possess the requisite technical skills in data analytics. Governments have always faced competition with the private sector for top talent, but now they will need to compete for personnel who possess a new type of skill. Admittedly, some of the technical work needed to build algorithmic systems can be performed by private contractors, but contractors may not be sufficiently sensitive to the particular demands on government for explainability, due process, or avoidance of bias. Government agencies will still need to ensure they have the in-house capacity needed to oversee contractors in an intelligent manner than ensure systems are designed in ways that will meet the distinctive accountability and fairness demands placed on governmental entities.

But governmental organisations will also need to build algorithmic regulatory teams with a variety of additional skillsets. In addition, data scientists and subject matter experts, government agencies will need Renaissance decision-makers. These will be team members who can think carefully about the governance problems that algorithmic systems aim to solve, the values and trade-offs at stake, and the kinds of problems such as bias, due process, transparency that can arise when systems are not built and operated with care. These higher-level system thinkers will need to understand the technical issues sufficiently well to provide a necessary translational bridge between the public and political leaders and the data analysts and system developers.

Government agencies will also need experts who can effectively facilitate public engagement processes to ensure that interested members of the public and relevant outside experts provide needed input into the specification of an algorithm's objective, including which values and weights on values align with a shared social expectations. Designers can benefit from public input into how a range of other critical features of an algorithmic system are designed. The backlash that has occurred in recent years against criminal courts' reliance on risk management tools in sentencing should provide a wake-up call to officials in any part of government about the value of sincerely and empathically seeking early public input into algorithmic design.

Governments will also need human expertise to conduct rigorous pilot testing that can give designers additional feedback about how their systems will work when implemented fully (Chien, 2019). Relatedly, once algorithmic systems have been implemented, they should be periodically subjected to evaluation to ensure that they are being operated as intended and are in fact achieving improvements over the status quo (Coglianese, 2011). Initially this may necessitate running some parallel testing of the performance of a new system against the human decision-making system it has replaced (Engstrom et al., 2020). Over time, similar evaluations of new system upgrades and refinements should be made against older versions of the system to ensure that performance improvement is being achieved.

In the end, perhaps it seems somewhat ironic, but governments seeking to build digital systems that effectively take humans out-of-the-loop will actually need to make deliberate investments in building the human capital essential to these systems' success. To ensure that machine-learning systems work effectively as well as satisfy fairness, transparency, equality, and accountability criteria, humans will continue to be needed to steer the design process and make the key normative choices upon which these systems depend (Coglianese, 2015).

Conclusion

As the tools of artificial intelligence continue to diffuse throughout business, medicine, and, increasingly, government, alarm bells will continue to sound over the possible dangers of a world increasingly dominated by algorithms. Those alarm bells can serve an important function if they make the human officials who develop and use machine-learning algorithms more deliberate and careful about how they design and use algorithms. In the end, it will be these humans who determine whether algorithms can achieve their full promise of overcoming the flaws in existing governmental processes.

A world of algorithmic regulation need not be one of danger, for there is nothing inherently dangerous in machine-learning algorithms per se. The uncomfortable truth is that the dangers stem from the humans who design and use these algorithms. Machine learning, at its core, is really quite much like any machine. It can be deployed for evil or for good; it can be used carelessly or deliberately. The future of algorithmic regulation holds great promise for a government that is smarter, fairer, more consistent. But whether government achieves that promise ultimately rests in human hands.

References

Angwin, J., J. Larson, S. Mattu and L. Kirchner. 2016. Machine bias. *ProPublica*. https://www.propublica.org/article/machine-bias-risk-assessments-in-criminal-sentencing.

Arrow, K.J. 1963. *Social choice and individual values*. New Haven, CT: Yale University Press.

Berk, R., H. Heidari, S. Jabbari, M. Kearns and A. Roth. 2018. Fairness in criminal justice risk assessments: The state of the art. *Sociological Methods & Research*. doi.org/10.1177/0049124118782533

Brandeis, L.D. 1914. *Other people's money*. New York: Frederick A. Stokes Co.

Breyer, S. et al. 2017. *Administrative law and regulatory policy: Problems, text, and cases*, 8th ed. New York: Wolters Kluwer.

Chien, C.V. 2019. Rigorous policy pilots: Experimentation in the administration of the law. *Iowa Law Review*, 104: 2313–2350.

Coglianese, C. 2011. Evaluating the performance of regulation and regulatory policy. Organization for Economic Cooperation and Development. https://www.oecd.org/gov/regulatory-policy/1_coglianese%20web.pdf

Coglianese, C. 2015. Regulatory excellence as 'people excellence'. *The Regulatory Review*, Oct. 23, https://www.theregreview.org/2015/10/23/coglianese-people-excellence/.

Coglianese, C. 2017. The limits of performance-based regulation. *University of Michigan Journal of Law Reform*, 50: 525–563

Coglianese, C. 2018. Optimizing regulation for an optimizing economy. *University of Pennsylvania Journal of Law and Public Affairs*, 4: 1–13.

Coglianese, C. and L. Ben-Dor. 2020. AI in adjudication and administration. *Brooklyn Law Review*, forthcoming.

Coglianese, C. and E. Lampmann. 2020. Contracting for algorithmic accountability. *Administrative Law Review Accord*, forthcoming.

Coglianese, C. and D. Lehr. 2017. Regulating by robot: Administrative decision making in the machine-learning era. *Georgetown Law Journal*, 10: 1147–1223.

Coglianese, C. and D. Lehr. 2019. Transparency and algorithmic governance. *Administrative Law Review*, 71: 1–56.

Coglianese, C. and J. Nash. 2017. The law of the test: Performance-based regulation and diesel emissions control. *Yale Journal on Regulation*, 34: 33–90.

Duhigg, C. 2012. How companies learn your secrets. *New York Times* (Feb. 16). https://www.nytimes.com/2012/02/19/magazine/shopping-habits.html.

Eberhardt, J.L. 2019. *Biased: Uncovering the hidden prejudice that shapes what we see, think, and do*. New York: Viking.

Engstrom, D.F., D.E. Ho, C.M. Sharkey and M.-F. Cuéllar. 2020. *Government by algorithm: artificial intelligence in federal administrative agencies. Administrative Conference of the United States*, Washington, DC. https://www-cdn.law.stanford.edu/wp-content/uploads/2020/02/ACUS-AI-Report.pdf

Eubanks, V. 2017. *Automating inequality: How high-tech tools profile, police, and punish the poor.* New York: St. Martin's.

Godtland, E.M., M. Grgich, C.D. Petersen, D.M. Sloane and A.T. Walker. 2007. Racial disparities in federal disability benefits. *Contemporary Economic Policy*, 25 (1): 27–45. doi:10.1111/j.1465-7287.2006.00031.x.

Goodman, E. 2019. The challenge of equitable algorithmic change. *The Regulatory Review* (Feb. 11). https://www.theregreview.org/wp-content/uploads/2019/02/Goodman-The-Challenge-of-Equitable-Algorithmic-Change.pdf.

Hino, M., E. Benami and N. Brooks. 2018. Machine learning for environmental monitoring. *Nature Sustainability*, 1: 583–588. doi.org/10.1038/s41893-018-0142-9.

Huq, A.Z. 2020. A right to a human decision. *Virginia Law Review*, 105: 611–688.

Kahneman, D. 2011. *Thinking fast and slow.* New York: Farrar, Straus and Giroux.

Kearns, M. and A. Roth. 2019. *The ethical algorithm: The science of socially aware algorithm design.* Oxford: Oxford University Press.

Lehr, D. and P. Ohm. 2017. Playing with the data: What legal scholars should learn about machine learning. *University of California Davis Law Review*, 51:653–717.

Mathews v. Eldridge, 424 U.S. 319 1976.

Mayer-Schönberger, V. and K. Cukier. 2013. *Big data: A revolution that will transform how we live, work, and think.* London: John Murray.

Miller, A.P. 2018. Want less-biased decisions? Use algorithms. *Harvard Business Review* (July 26). https://hbr.org/2018/07/want-less-biased-decisions-use-algorithms.

Mullainathan, S. 2019. Biased algorithms are easier to fix than biased people. *New York Times* (Dec. 6). https://www.nytimes.com/2019/12/06/business/algorithm-bias-fix.html.

O'Neil, C. 2016. *Weapons of math destruction: How big data increases inequality and threatens democracy.* New York: Crown.

Ray, G.K. and J.S. Lubbers. 2015. A government success story: How data analysis by the Social Security Appeals Council (with a push from the Administrative Conference of the United States) is transforming social security disability adjudication. *George Washington Law Review*, 83: 1575–1608.

State v. Loomis, 881 N.W.2d 749 Wis. 2016.

Snow, J. 2017. This AI traffic system in Pittsburgh has reduced travel time by 25%. https://www.smartcitiesdive.com/news/this-ai-traffic-system-in-pittsburgh-has-reduced-travel-time-by-25/447494/

Sunstein, C.R. 1995. Incompletely theorized agreements. *Harvard Law Review*, 108: 1733–1772.

Transactional Records Access Clearinghouse (TRAC). 2011. Social security awards depend more on judge than facts. https://trac.syr.edu/tracreports/ssa/254/.

US Environmental Protection Agency (EPA). 2020. Learn about effluent guidelines. https://www.epa.gov/eg/learn-about-effluent-guidelines.

Vaithianathan, R., N. Jiang, T. Maloney, P. Nand and E. Putnam-Hornstein. 2019. Developing predictive risk models to support child maltreatment hotline screening decisions. https://www.alleghenycountyanalytics.us/wp-content/uploads/2019/05/16-ACDHS-26_PredictiveRisk_Package_050119_FINAL-2.pdf.

Chapter 4

Responsible and accountable algorithmization

How to generate citizen trust in governmental usage of algorithms

Albert Meijer and Stephan Grimmelikhuijsen

Introduction

Algorithms are increasingly popular in the public sector in countries all around the world: they are used to provide services (Pencheva, Esteve & Mikhaylov, 2018) but also to, for instance, support decision-making (Van der Voort et al., 2019) and predict recidivism (Kleinberg et al., 2017). Furthermore, the police use algorithms to predict crime patterns (Meijer & Wessels, 2019), tax departments use algorithms to detect tax fraud (Zouridis, Van Eck & Bovens, 2020) and local governments use algorithms to make garbage collection more efficient (Ramalho, Rossetti & Cacho, 2017). The current wave of algorithms uses relatively new techniques, such as machine-learning and deep learning, to transform organizational processes (Brynjolfsson & McAfee, 2014; Burrell, 2016).

The 'magic' of these new technologies is appealing to governments since they promise to bring us more effective processes, better informed decisions and more insights in complex realities through informative and seamless interfaces. At the same time, the 'magic' of these new technologies is also risky since the use of algorithms can produce bias and even discriminatory practices; it can result in errors in the implementation of policies and it can also hamper the interactions between governments and citizens. Therefore, various authors stress that we need to step back and reflect on how algorithms can be applied to realize desirable outcomes (O'Neil, 2016; Eubanks, 2018; Gerards, 2019). For instance, various municipal governments in the Netherlands used a machine-learning algorithm (*Systeem Risicoindicatie, SyRI*) to detect welfare fraud amongst citizens. While at the beginning there was widespread support for this system among government officials, in early 2020 the system was judged 'discriminatory' and 'not transparent', not only by civil rights activists, but also by the District Court. Vulnerable citizens, often those from a migrant background, were unfairly profiled to be a suspect of welfare fraud.

The example of SyRI in the Netherlands illustrates an issue of wider significance: there is an urgent societal need to not only focus on issues of effectiveness and efficiency but also identify how governments can avoid negative unintended consequences of the use of algorithms – such as bias and problems of fairness – to maintain the trust of citizens (Hoffman, 2019). How can we expect citizens to trust government if this system works with an algorithm that is both opaque and discriminatory? Various concerns have been raised regarding the impacts of these systems on privacy but also on discrimination of different groups in society and its neglect of human contact. It is still unclear how government organizations will deal with issues such as interpreting big data in a non-discriminatory manner, handling privacy fairly, using means proportional to the objectives and ensuring human contact (Dencik et al., 2019).

We argue that these concerns go beyond the mere implementation of algorithms; they also relate to how organizations transform and change to enable the use of algorithms. In this chapter, we will label this process *algorithmization*: an organization that transforms its working routines around the use of algorithms for its actions and decisions. We highlight that an analysis of algorithmization requires a focus not only on the technology but also on its organizational implementation in terms of the expertise of employees, information resources, organizational structure, organizational policy and monitoring & evaluation to understand why the use of algorithms does or does not produce citizen trust.

In this chapter we link algorithmization to a crucial concept in contemporary governance: *citizen trust in government*. Trust in government is regarded as an essential element in developed societies. It has been found, for example, that if government institutions are not trusted by the citizens they serve, they are unable to function properly (Fukuyama, 1995; Inglehart, 1999; Levi & Stoker, 2000). Given the rapid algorithmization of government, we need to identify desirable forms of algorithmization in the public sector. Two preconditions for maintaining citizen trust have been proposed in the literature: (1) incorporating values in the design of algorithms as a precondition for organizational *responsibility* (e.g. Friedman, Kahn & Borning, 2008; Van den Hoven, 2013) and (2) demonstrating the correct usage of algorithms to the public as a precondition for *accountability* (e.g. Diakopoulos, 2016). In this chapter we argue that algorithmization in the public sector can only sustain citizen trust when it is based on both preconditions.

To this end, we first discuss what we understand by citizen trust and we outline why trust is so important in the public sector. We then offer a discussion of algorithmization as an organizational process and we stress that this organizational process, rather than the technology in itself, demands our attention if we want to strengthen citizen trust. The next sections discuss how two preconditions – responsible and accountable algorithmization – can contribute to citizen trust. We end this chapter by presenting a model for responsible and accountable algorithmization in the public sector.

The fundamental role of trust in government

Although many scholars have emphasized the importance of trust, we start off with a note that trust in government as such is not strictly necessary. People can 'accept' and obey an oppressive government, not because they trust it but because they fear the consequences of disobedience. According to political scientist Russell Hardin (1999, 2002), trust in government is 'only' needed under relatively benign circumstances, such as can be found in democratic regimes. Hardin further argues that government functions well as long as it not actively distrusted by people.

A certain degree of trust makes governing much easier and more benign. Many scholars argue that if government is perceived to be trustworthy, citizens tend to comply more often with its demands, laws and regulations without coercion (Tyler, 2006). For instance, Tom Tyler and Peter Degoey (1996) found that people's evaluations of the trustworthiness of organizational authorities shape their willingness to accept the decisions of authorities and influence their feelings of obligation to follow organizational rules and laws. Indeed, trust can be viewed as an important component of government legitimacy (Tyler, 2006).

Furthermore, Marc Hetherington (1998) highlights the relevance of political trust. Political trust concerns citizens' trust in their political leaders, which translates into more support for politicians and political institutions. This gives leaders more leeway to govern effectively and offers institutions more support and legitimacy. Furthermore, without public support for solutions, problems tend to linger and become more acute; if not resolved, this becomes the foundation for discontent.

Citizen trust is not a necessity, but it is still regarded as highly important for government. But what exactly is trust in government? To better understand citizen trust in government we have to turn to a variety of scholarly disciplines. Understanding why and how people trust has been a central focus of research by psychologists, sociologists, political scientists, economists and organizational scientists (Grimmelikhuijsen, 2012). Across and even within disciplines, countless definitions, concepts and operationalizations are being used. In an attempt to find cross-disciplinary agreement about the concept of trust, Denise Rousseau, Sim Sitkin, Ronald Burt, and Colin Camerer (1998) developed a definition that is frequently cited in the social sciences. According to them, trust is 'a psychological state comprising the intention to accept vulnerability based upon positive expectations of the intentions or behaviour of another'.

According to Rousseau and colleagues, all definitions of trust assume the presence of some form of positive expectation regarding the intentions and behaviour of the object of trust. The object of trust in this chapter is government. An element of this definition that requires more elaboration is 'positive expectations of the intentions or behaviour of another'. Of what, in the context of government, are these positive expectations comprised?

Trustworthiness concerns the characteristics of the object of trust as perceived by an individual (Mayer, Davis & Schoorman, 1995). A large body of literature has attempted to identify specific elements that might influence an individual's perceptions of trustworthy behaviours and intentions (see, for an overview, McKnight, Choudhury & Kacmar, 2002; McEvily & Tortoriello, 2011; Grimmelikhuijsen & Knies, 2017). Generally, the importance of the various elements tends to differ according to the discipline in question, yet some degree of commonality can be found.

The three most commonly cited elements are perceived competence, perceived benevolence and perceived integrity (also sometimes called honesty) (Grimmelikhuijsen, 2012). Perceived competence is the extent to which a citizen perceives government to be capable, effective, skillful, and professional; perceived benevolence refers to the extent to which a citizen perceives government to care about the welfare of the public and to be motivated to act in the public interest; perceived integrity is whether a citizen perceives government to be sincere, truthful, and to fulfil its promises. It should be noted that benevolence and integrity are of a different nature than competence, as they reflect ethical traits rather than some kind of capability. Benevolence reflects the trustee's motives and is based on altruism. In contrast, competence is a utilitarian dimension of trust, as it refers to the actual functioning of government organizations.

This section discussed the fundamental role of trust in government and how it can be conceptualized. We highlighted that trust should be understood as a multidimensional concept that consists of citizens' perceptions of government competence, benevolence and integrity. In the next section, we outline what we mean by algorithmization of government.

Algorithmization in the public sector

Many academic debates focus on the characteristics and features of algorithms as a technological artifact. This perspective focuses on the design of these algorithms to prevent biases and prejudices. We acknowledge the importance of value-sensitive design of algorithms but also stress that it is not only about the design. We know from decades of studies of information and communication technologies in the public sector that we need to study organizational practices to understand the effects of the use of algorithms. This is why we use the term 'algorithmization' as an organizational process rather than algorithm as a technological artifact. Building upon earlier work on informatization in government (Zuurmond, 1994: 42–48), we distinguish the following components of algorithmization:

1   *Technology*. The process of algorithmization starts with the introduction of a technology into organizational processes. The algorithm can be a stand-alone decision-support system but also a system that is well integrated in the organization's infrastructure.
2   *Expertise*. The use of algorithms in an organization requires a variety of expertise. Experts that know how to work with the system are needed but also experts that maintain the algorithm and ensure that it is properly installed in the organization's information environment.
3   *Information relations*. Algorithmic applications will generally build upon existing information in the organization but also produce new types of information. This means that the algorithm has an effect on the information relations within the organization and often also outside of the organization if information from other actors is used.
4   *Organizational structure*. The use of algorithms often leads to new collaborations between different departments. Algorithmic applications can also lead to new forms of organizational control if they dictate the implementation of processes.

5   *Organizational policy*. Organizations develop policies for the use of an algorithm in the organization. These policies touch upon issues such as the transparency of the algorithm, responsibilities for usage, maintenance, etc.

6   *Monitoring and evaluation*. Organizations develop methods and systems for monitoring and evaluating the foreseen and unforeseen outcomes of the use of algorithms in terms of output and effects.

These six elements form the cornerstones of a conceptual understanding of algorithmization and help us to sharpen our perspective when we study how algorithms are used in the public sector. They also provide starting points for thinking about strengthening citizen trust in the use of algorithms. This trust does not only depend on the nature of the technology but also on the experts that guide the use of the algorithm, the information that is used by the algorithm to provide its output, the organizational control over the algorithm, and the policies that organizations have developed to guide the usage and maintenance of the algorithm.

In an empirical study of the Berlin Police, Lukas Lorenz (2019) used this organizational perspective on algorithms to rethink the nature of bureaucratic organizations. Building upon Max Weber's classic work on bureaucratic organizations and Arre Zuurmond's (1998) work on infocratic organizations, Lorenz sketches the contours of a new type of organization: the algocracy. He conceptualizes the algocracy as new ideal type of rational-legal authority that helps to understand and explain how algorithmic systems shape public organizations. He characterizes the algocracy as a further rationalized organizational configuration of the professional bureaucracy rather than of the machine bureaucracy: the standardization of skills is replaced by automated advice.

This discussion highlights that we need to think about the organizational processes surrounding the introduction of new technologies in organizations – the emerging algocratic organizations – to develop ways to strengthen citizen trust in the public sector. To this end, we emphasize two classical approaches to strengthening trust in government organizations: responsibility and accountability.

Responsible algorithmization

A first route for strengthening citizen trust in algorithmization is provided by the notion of responsibility. Responsibility is one of the key concepts in ethical theory and its roots can be traced back to Aristotle. He emphasized that moral responsibility grows out of an ability to reason, an awareness of action and consequences, and a willingness to act free from external compulsion (Roberts, 1989). Responsibility refers to the idea that persons have moral obligations and duties to others, such as their well-being and their health, and to larger ethical and moral traditions such as freedom and empowerment, and that persons, thus, need to consider these obligations and duties in their individual decisions and actions.

More recently, the notion of responsibility has been applied to public organizations. Political scientist Herman van Gunsteren (1976) highlights that we should strive to embed responsibility in (complex) organizations rather than emphasize the need to control the activities of all individual members of organizations. His approach stresses the need to acknowledge the limitations of bureaucratic control mechanisms such as hierarchy and formal rules and to place more emphasis on the responsibility of individuals in the organization. According to Van Gunsteren, the notion of responsibility is needed when rigid moral norms – embedded in organizational standard procedures – cannot keep up with rapidly changing circumstances and more flexibility is required to apply sound moral judgement. At the same time, this does not mean that 'anything goes': judgement needs to be made based on ethically respectable values and reasonable perceptions of relevant facts (Van Gunsteren, 2015: 318). 'Responsibility forums' where individual judgement needs to be explained can play a key role in strengthening the responsibility of individuals in organizations.

Furthermore, the notion of responsibility has been used to think about innovation. In the context of the European Union, the notion of responsible innovation has come to play an important role in funding for technology development. The key idea is that innovation traditionally focuses only on gains in efficiency and effectiveness. Other considerations are often regarded as barriers to the innovation process. The notion of responsible innovation reconceptualizes these barriers and stresses that other values need to play a role in the way the innovation process is structured and implemented. In our understanding of responsible algorithmization, we build upon the broader notion of responsible innovation, which Richard Owen, Phil Macnaghten and Jack Stilgoe define as 'a collective duty of care, first to rethink what we want from innovation and then how we can make its pathways responsive in the face of uncertainty' (2012: 757–758).

These general notions about responsibility in organizations and responsible innovation can be used as a basis for ideas about the responsible use of algorithms in public organizations. Key elements in this conceptualization are (1) ethical judgement, (2) based on values, (3) and perceptions of relevant facts, (4) to enact a duty of care (5) through responsive pathways. Based on these elements, we formulate the following conceptualization of responsible algorithmization:

> Responsible algorithmization refers to the adequate weighing of ethical dilemmas involved in the organizational use of algorithms based on knowledge about the (possible) impacts to ensure that the algorithmization respects moral obligations to others and to moral traditions through methods that are responsive to the various other actors involved.

Responsibility for algorithmization can be operationalized by building upon the notion of value-sensitive design, which can be defined as 'a theoretically grounded approach to the design of technology that accounts for human values in a principled and comprehensive manner throughout the design process' (Friedman, Kahn & Borning, 2008: 69). For a value-sensitive algorithmization of government, a comprehensive understanding of the values at stake in a specific process of algorithmic decision-making and of how these values are incorporated in the organizational use of the algorithm is needed (Mingers & Walsham, 2010). Thus, we apply value-sensitivity not only to the design of the technology but also to the other elements of algorithmization (expertise, information resources, organizational structure, organizational policy). The questions that can help guide organizations towards responsible algorithmization are presented in Table 4.1.

How will responsible algorithmization affect citizen trust in government? In the above, we identified value-sensitivity as a core component of responsible algorithmization. This relates directly to the benevolence and integrity dimension of trust in government. Benevolence refers to the expectations by citizens that government is acting benign and in the interest of citizens; integrity refers to expectations of honesty and truthfulness (Mayer, Davis & Schoorman, 1995; Grimmelikhuijsen & Knies, 2017). If algorithmization is done with consideration of relevant values – e.g. algorithms are used in a fair and unbiased manner – this will likely positively affect citizens' perceptions of the honesty and benevolence of government. Conversely, when citizens, for instance, feel a welfare fraud algorithm targets them unfairly, this is likely to cause a decline in perceived honesty and benevolence.

The different organizational policy components – organizational policy and monitoring & evaluation – are also likely to contribute to citizen trust in government competence. The basic argument here is that well-considered choices in terms of how the algorithm is to be used in the organization and a consistent monitoring and evaluation of the desired and undesired outcomes contribute to

Table 4.1 Assessment questions for value-sensitivity as a precondition for responsible algorithmization

Dimension of algorithmization	Assessment question
Technology	How are the different values at stake identified and embedded in the design of the algorithm?
Expertise	Are the experts that develop, support and maintain the algorithm aware of relevant ethical considerations and can they make value-sensitive choices?
Information relations	Have the value choices in the datasets used by the algorithm been analysed and are the values that follow from new combinations of data acknowledged?
Organizational structure	Has the overall responsibility for a value-sensitive use of the algorithm in organizational practices been clearly allocated?
Organizational policy	Does the organization have a policy for ensuring value-sensitivity in the organizational use of the algorithm?
Monitoring and evaluation	Does the organization have a system for monitoring and evaluating outcomes in terms of the various values at stake in the use of the algorithm?

the perception that government is using these algorithms in a rational manner. There is a reason for caution here, however. If citizens expect governments to perform much better than they actually do, this can also result in a decline of perceived competence (Grimmelikhuijsen, 2012).

In sum, the first condition that we have identified for maintaining the trust of citizens in an organization that uses algorithms is responsible algorithmization. We have argued that value-sensitivity is the basis for responsible algorithmization and we listed six questions that can help organizations assess their level of responsible algorithmization.

Accountable algorithmization

A second route to strengthening citizen trust in algorithmization is provided by the notion of accountability. This notion builds upon the concept of public accountability which political scientist Mark Bovens defines as 'a relationship between an actor and a forum, in which the actor has an obligation to explain and to justify his or her conduct, the forum can pose questions and pass judgement, and the actor may face consequences' (2007: 450). Based on this general definition, we can provide a specific definition (see Wieringa, 2020, for an in-depth analysis) of algorithmic accountability:

> Accountable algorithmization can be defined as the justification of the organizational usage of an algorithm and explanations for its outcomes to an accountability forum that can ask questions, pass judgement and impose consequences.

Transparency is an important condition for realizing public accountability, although scholars have noted that transparency does not automatically lead to more accountability (Hood, 2010). Albert Meijer (2014) indicates that transparency facilitates accountability if it presents an actual and significant increase in the available information, if there are actors capable of processing the information, and if exposure has a direct or indirect impact on the government or public agency. Without transparency, accountability is difficult to realize since relevant facts that need to be assessed are not available.

Lack of transparency is a key concern regarding the use of algorithms in the public sector (e.g. Lepri et al., 2018). Machine-learning algorithms that use various internal and external data sets are so complicated that the logic of decision-making – and possible biases – are difficult to detect (Janssen & Van den Hoven, 2015). In addition, the lack of transparency may concern the responsibilities, procedures and practices of algorithmic usage in the organization. In response to these concerns, algorithmic transparency has been proposed as a key element of accountable algorithms applications in the public sector (Diakopoulos, 2016; Lepri et al., 2018). We extend this concept to transparency and apply it not only to the algorithm as a technology but also to its organizational use.

The basic idea is that algorithmic decision-making by government should be accessible and explainable (Kroll et al., 2017). Accessibility implies providing clear information about the input, throughput and output of a decision-making process: which data has been used, which decision rules have been applied and what was the outcome? Explainability concerns the substantive reasons for a decision: on what grounds was the decision made and how does this relate to legislation and other formal rules and policies? In short, accountable algorithmization means that algorithmic decision-making needs to be accessible and explainable. Following these considerations, we define a set of questions to guide organizations (see Table 4.2).

Procedural fairness theory offers valuable insights in how transparency – in terms of accessibility and explicability – may affect trust. Procedural justice theory (e.g. Tyler, 2006) posits that individuals can be satisfied with negative decisions as long as they consider the decision procedure to be fair. Accordingly, accessible and explainable algorithmization helps foster fair procedures and eventually more trust in a decision-maker (i.e. government) (Grootelaar & Van den Bos, 2018; Porumbescu & Grimmelikhuijsen, 2018).

Table 4.2 Assessment questions for transparency as a precondition for accountable algorithmization

Dimension of algorithmization	Assessment question for accessibility	Assessment question for explainability
Technology	Is there access to the code to scrutinize design choices?	Does the algorithm provide substantive reasons for decisions or advice?
Expertise	Are the function characteristics of the experts involved in algorithmization transparent?	Are reasons provided for the expertise involved in algorithmization?
Information relations	Is there access to the key features of the data sets used by the algorithm?	Does the organization explain which datasets are used by the algorithm, why and how?
Organizational structure	Are organizational responsibilities for the algorithmization transparent?	Are choices regarding organizational responsibilities for algorithmization explained?
Organizational policy	Is the organizational policy for algorithmization accessible?	Is the organizational policy for algorithmization explained?
Monitoring and evaluation	Is there access to the results of the algorithmization in terms of foreseen and unforeseen effects?	Are the foreseen and unforeseen effects of algorithmization explained?

More specifically, explicability is a core component of procedural fairness. Explaining citizens how an algorithm functions is expected to have a positive impact on levels of trust (cf. Grimmelikhuijsen et al., 2019). A second component of procedural fairness is the neutrality of the decision-maker (Van den Bos, Vermunt & Wilke, 1997). Core elements of Table 4.2, such as the accessibility of datasets, algorithms and organizational policies indicate that, in an optimistic scenario, decisions based on algorithmization are neutral and unbiased. Eventually, similar to value-sensitivity, this relates to how citizens perceive the benevolence and integrity of government.

Transparency regarding the foreseen and unforeseen effects of algorithmization may contribute to the perceived competence of government. If citizens see that algorithmization actually leads to desired outcomes while the undesired outcomes are limited, their trust in government's ability to realize better outcomes may increase. The monitoring and evaluation of algorithmization is also expected to play a key role in contributing to perceived competence.

In sum, the second condition that we have identified for maintaining the trust of citizens in an organization that uses algorithms is accountable algorithmization. Using transparency as a proxy for accountable algorithmization, we have listed 12 questions that organizations can use to assess their level of accountable algorithmization.

Conclusion

In this chapter, we have discussed how 'algorithmization' has become a potent force, changing traditional bureaucracies into algocracies. The new generation of algorithms that are now finding their way to governments across the globe are more than a change of technology: they trigger a range of organizational changes that eventually transform bureaucratic decision-making. In this context, machine-learning algorithms are often portrayed as problematic for accountable and responsible decision-making. We argue that both accountable and responsible algorithmization are needed to sustain citizen trust in the use of these algorithms. The argument we developed in this chapter is summarized in Table 4.3.

The two preconditions of value-sensitivity and transparency are a starting point for realizing responsible and accountable algorithmization. However, this does not resolve all issues. A first issue is that algorithmization is not limited to the use of merely one technological system in an organization. There are entire ecosystems of algorithms that use data from various sources and that are implemented in networks of organizations (Cicirelli et al., 2019). The 'problem of many hands' is compounded by these developments and it is not easy to indicate who is responsible and accountable. In that sense, further work on the assessment questions formulated here is needed to test and re-develop them for ecosystems of algorithms.

A second issue that demands more attention is the fact that machine-learning algorithms change over time. This raises questions about the dynamics of values: value-sensitivity may be ensured at the start but a machine-learning algorithm can, over time, develop patterns that conflict with key values. In addition, transparency

Table 4.3 Potential relations between algorithmization and trust in government

Dimension of trust	Value-sensitivity as a precondition for responsible algorithmization	Transparency as a precondition for accountable algorithmization
Competence	Value-sensitive algorithmization may strengthen perceived competence if the organization demonstrates that various values are measured and its policy focuses on realizing value.	Explicable and accessible monitoring and evaluation of algorithmization provides insights in the outcomes, which is expected to increase perceived competence.
Benevolence	Value-sensitive algorithmization ensures that values important to citizens (e.g. fairness) are not overlooked, which is expected to increase perceived benevolence.	Explicable and accessible algorithmization ensures that government works in the interest of citizens, which is expected to increase perceived benevolence.
Integrity	Value-sensitive algorithmization ensures that decision-makers are more value-sensitive and thus act more ethically; this is expected to increase perceived integrity.	Explicable and accessible algorithmization ensures that external stakeholders have access, which contributes to more open and truthful algorithmization.

may be ensured at the start, but after a process of machine-learning the algorithm can have become opaque because its decision rules have changed following learning processes. This means that the questions formulated here may need to be applied iteratively to ensure that responsibility and accountability persist over time. Further research is needed to provide an understanding of these dynamics of responsible and accountable algorithmization.

In sum, this chapter provides a basic understanding of the importance of responsibility and accountability in producing citizen trust in algorithmization. The key message is that organizations should not only look at designers of algorithms and expect that they will bring the solution: public organizations need to take action to organize responsible and accountable use of algorithms in their organizational processes.

References

Bovens, M. 2007. Analysing and assessing accountability: A conceptual framework. *European Law Journal*, 13 (4): 447–468. doi: 10.1111/j.1468-0386.2007.00378.x

Brynjolfsson, E. and A. McAfee. 2014. *The second machine age: Work, progress, and prosperity in a time of brilliant technologies*. New York: WW Norton & Company.

Burrell, J. 2016. How the machine 'thinks': Understanding opacity in machine learning algorithms. *Big Data & Society*, 3 (1): 1–12. doi: 10.1177/2053951715622512

Cicirelli, F., A. Guerrieri, C. Mastroianni, G. Spezzano and A. Vinci. (Eds.). 2019. *The internet of things for smart urban ecosystems*. Cham: Springer.

Dencik, L., Redden, J., Hintz, A. and H. Warne. 2019. The 'golden view': Data-driven governance in the scoring society. *Internet Policy Review*, 8 (2): 1–24. doi: 10.14763/2019.2.1413

Diakopoulos, N. 2016. Accountability in algorithmic decision making. *Communications of the ACM*, 59 (2): 56–62. doi: 10.1145/2844110

Eubanks, V. 2018. *Automating inequality: How high-tech tools profile, police, and punish the poor*. New York: St. Martin's Press.

Friedman, B., P.H. Kahn and A. Borning. 2008. Value sensitive design and information systems. In *The handbook of information and computer ethics*, edited by K. Himma and H. Travani, 69–102. New Jersey: John Wiley & Sons Inc.

Fukuyama, F. 1995. *Trust: The social virtues and the creation of prosperity*. New York: Simon and Schuster.

Gerards, J. 2019. The fundamental rights challenges of algorithms. *Netherlands Quarterly of Human Rights*, 37 (3): 205–209. doi: 10.1177/0924051919861773

Grimmelikhuijsen, S. 2012. *Transparency and trust: An experimental study of online disclosure and trust in government*. Doctoral dissertation. Utrecht: University Utrecht.

Grimmelikhuijsen, S. and E. Knies. 2017. Validating a scale for citizen trust in government organizations. *International Review of Administrative Sciences*, 83 (3): 583–601. doi: 10.1177/0020852315585950

Grimmelikhuijsen, S., F. Herkes, I. Leistikow, J. Verkroost, F. de Vries and W.G. Zijlstra. 2019. Can decision transparency increase citizen trust in regulatory agencies? Evidence from a representative survey experiment. *Regulation & Governance*. doi: 10.1111/rego.12278

Grootelaar, H.A. and K. van den Bos. 2018. How litigants in Dutch courtrooms come to trust judges: the role of perceived procedural justice, outcome favorability, and other sociolegal moderators. *Law & Society Review*, 52 (1): 234–268. doi: 10.1111/lasr.12315

Hardin, R. 1999. Do we want trust in government? In *Democracy and trust*, edited by M.E. Warren, 22–41. Cambridge: Cambridge University Press.

Hardin, R. 2002. *Trust and trustworthiness*. New York: Russell Sage Foundation.

Hetherington, M.J. 1998. The political relevance of political trust. *The American Political Science Review*, 92 (4): 791–808. doi: 10.2307/2586304

Hoffman, A.L. 2019. Where fairness fails: Data algorithms, and the limits of the antidiscrimination discourse. *Information, Communication & Society*, 22 (7): 900–915. doi: 10.1080/1369118X.2019.1573912

Hood, C. 2010. Accountability and transparency: Siamese twins, matching parts, awkward couple?. *West European Politics*, 33 (5): 989–1009. doi: 10.1080/01402382.2010.486122

Inglehart, R. 1999. Trust, well-being and democracy. In *Democracy and trust*, edited by M.E. Warren, 88–120. Cambridge: Cambridge University Press.

Janssen, M. and J. Van den Hoven. 2015. Big and open linked data (BOLD) in government: A challenge to transparency and privacy?. *Government Information Quarterly*, 32 (4): 363–368. doi: 10.1016/j.giq.2015.11.007

Kleinberg, J., H. Lakkaraju, J. Leskovec, J. Ludwig and S. Mullainathan. 2017. Human decisions and machine predictions. *The Quarterly Journal of Economics*, 133 (1): 237–293. doi: 10.1093/qje/qjx032

Kroll, J.A., S. Barocas, E.W. Felten, J.R. Reidenberg, D.G. Robinson and H. Yu. 2017. Accountable algorithms. *University of Pennsylvania Law Review*, 165 (3): 633–706.

Lepri, B., N. Oliver, E. Letouzé, A. Pentland and P.Vinck. 2018. Fair, transparent, and accountable algorithmic decision-making processes. *Philosophy & Technology*, 31 (4): 611–627. doi: 10.1007/s13347-017-0279-x

Levi, M. and L. Stoker. 2000. Political trust and trustworthiness. *Annual Review of Political Science*, 3: 375–507. doi: 10.1146/annurev.polisci.3.1.475

Lorenz, L. 2019. *The algocracy: Understanding and explaining how public organizations are shaped by algorithmic systems.* MSc Thesis, Utrecht University.

Mayer, R., J.H. Davis and F.D. Schoorman. 1995. An integrative model of organizational trust. *Academy of Management Review*, 20 (3): 709–734. doi: 10.5465/amr.1995.9508080335

McEvily, B. and M. Tortoriello. 2011. Measuring trust in organisational research: Review and recommendations. *Journal of Trust Research*, 1 (1): 23–63. doi: 10.1080/21515581.2011.552424

McKnight, D.H., V. Choudhury and C. Kacmar. 2002. Developing and validating trust measures for e-commerce: An integrative typology. *Information Systems Research*, 13 (3): 334–359. doi: 10.1287/isre.13.3.334.81

Meijer, A. 2014. Transparency. In *The Oxford handbook of public accountability*, edited by M. Bovens, R.E. Goodin and T. Schillemans, 507–524. Oxford: Oxford University Press.

Meijer, A. and M. Wessels. 2019. Predictive policing: Review of benefits and drawbacks. *International Journal of Public Administration*, 42 (12): 1–9. doi: 10.1080/01900692.2019.1575664

Mingers, J. and G. Walsham. 2010. Toward ethical information systems: the contribution of discourse ethics. *MIS Quarterly*, 34 (4): 833–854. doi: 10.5555.2017496.2917505

O'Neil, C. 2016. *Weapons of math destruction. How big data increases inequality and threatens democracy.* New York: Crown.

Owen, R., P. Macnaghten and J. Stilgoe. 2012. Responsible research and innovation: From science in society to science for society, with society. *Science and Public Policy*, 39 (6), 751–760. doi: 10.1093/scipol/scs093

Pencheva, I., M. Esteve and S.J. Mikhaylov. 2018. Big data and AI: A transformational shift for government: So, what next for research?. *Public Policy and Administration*, 35 (1): 24–44. doi: 10.1177/0952076718780537

Porumbescu, G.A. and S. Grimmelikhuijsen. 2018. Linking decision-making procedures to decision acceptance and citizen voice: Evidence from two studies. *The American Review of Public Administration*, 48 (8): 902–914. doi: 10.1177/0275074017734642

Ramalho, M.A., R.J. Rossetti and N. Cacho. (2017). *Towards an architecture for smart garbage collection in urban settings.* Presented at the *2017 International Smart Cities Conference (ISC2)*, Wuxi, September 1–6.

Roberts, J. 1989. Aristotle on responsibility for action and character. *Ancient Philosophy*, 9 (1): 23–36. doi: 10.5840/ancientphil19899123

Rousseau, D.M., S.B. Sitkin, R.S. Burt and C. Camerer. 1998. Not so different after all: a cross-discipline view of trust. *Academy of Management Review*, 23 (3): 393- 404. doi: 10.5465/amr.1998.926617

Tyler, T.R. 2006. *Why people obey the law.* Princeton: Princeton University Press.

Tyler, T.R. and P. Degoey. 1996. Trust in organizational authorities: The influence of motive attributions on willingness to accept decisions. In *Trust in organizations: Frontiers of theory and research*, edited by R. Kramer and T. Yler, 331–356. Thousand Oaks, CA: Sage Publications.

Van den Bos, K., R.Vermunt and H.A.Wilke. 1997. Procedural and distributive justice: What is fair depends more on what comes first than on what comes next. *Journal of Personality and Social Psychology*, 72 (1), 95.

Van Gunsteren, H.R. 1976. *The quest for control: A critique of the rational-central-rule approach in public affairs*. London: John Wiley & Sons.

Van Gunsteren, H.R. 2015. The ethical context of bureaucracy and performance analysis. In *The public sector: Challenge for coordination and learning*, edited by F.-X. Kaufmann, chapter 15. Berlin: Walter de Gruyter.

Van den Hoven, J. 2013. Value sensitive design and responsible innovation. In *Responsible innovation*, edited by R. Owen, J. Bessant and M. Heintz, 75–84. Chichester, UK: Wiley.

Van der Voort, H.G., A.J. Klievink, M. Arnaboldi and A.J. Meijer. 2019. Rationality and politics of algorithms. Will the promise of big data survive the dynamics of public decision making? *Government Information Quarterly*, 36 (1): 27–38. doi: 10.1016/j.giq.2018.10.011

Wieringa, M. 2020. *What to account for when accounting for algorithms. A systematic literature review on algorithmic accountability*. Paper presented at *ACM Conference on Fairness, Accountability, and Transparency (ACM FAT*)*, Barcelona. ACM, New York, NY, USA, January 27–30.

Zouridis, S., M. van Eck and M. Bovens. 2020. Automated discretion. *In Discretion and the quest for controlled freedom*, edited by T. Evans and P. Hupe, chapter 20. London: Palgrave Macmillan.

Zuurmond, A. 1994. *De infocratie. Een theoretische en empirische heroriëntatie op Weber's ideaaltype in het informatietijdperk*. Den Haag: Phaedrus.

Zuurmond, A. 1998. From bureaucracy to infocracy: Are democratic institutions lagging behind? In: *Public administration in an information age: A handbook*, edited by I.Th.M. Snellen and W.B.H.J. van de Donk, chapter 16. Amsterdam: IOS Press.

Chapter 5

Towards principles of good digital administration

Fairness, accountability and proportionality in automated decision-making

Arjan Widlak, Marlies van Eck and Rik Peeters

Introduction

Automated decision-making is gaining ground in public administration and funda-mentally changing core bureaucratic procedures and mechanisms. We are already seeing applications in the delivery of social services, in data sharing among govern-ment organizations, in tackling welfare fraud, in regulatory practices, in risk assess-ments, in evaluation of professionals and in determining eligibility for social programmes or taxation (e.g. Bovens & Zouridis, 2002; Berk & Bleich, 2013; Harcourt, 2015; O'Neil, 2016; Smith & O'Malley, 2017; Peeters & Schuilenburg, 2018; Peeters & Widlak, 2018; Van Eck, 2018; Yeung, 2018). There is little doubt that in the near future the automation of decision-making procedures will expand to more areas and practices. Organizational efficiency is usually the main argument in favour of automated decision-making. Its consequences, however, extend far beyond that – and are, in part, still unforeseen. The implementation of new tech-nology is not a neutral intervention, nor something that merely affects the means through which decisions are made (Verbeek, 2006). In analogy with Marshall McLuhan's (1964) adage that 'the medium is the message', the characteristics of a medium or a technology are – perhaps even more so than the content it transmits – key to understanding its social, political and administrative consequences.

Without disregarding potential benefits, we take as a starting point the increasing amount of literature that shows how algorithms and automated decision-making trigger concerns regarding the fair treatment of citizens in governmental decision-making (Grimmelikhuijsen & Meijer, 2014; Rehavi & Starr, 2014; Smith, Bennett Moses & Chan, 2017). Furthermore, we underscore the argument that the use of these new technologies is essentially a tool for further rationalization and standard-ization (e.g. Pasquale, 2015; Peeters & Schuilenburg, 2018). Instead of applying general rules to individual cases through bureaucratic procedures and case assess-ment, algorithms are used to automatically generate decisions, determine what cases are handled automatically or not (Zouridis, Van Eck & Bovens, 2020: 16) and generate predictions based on statistics that direct attention, provide a default for human decision-makers (Hamilton, 2015: 49) or both.

Discretion, regulated by principles of good administration, and the design of administrative procedures have long been the two most important mechanisms to find balance the need for universal and predictable rules that allow us to build systems – whether organizational or algorithmic – with the need to sometimes deviate from those rules on the basis of principles such as fairness, proportionality and accountability that allow us to do justice when the rules fall short. Both these mechanisms are changing because of the automation of street-level discretion (Zouridis, Van Eck & Bovens, 2020) and the black-boxing of algorithmic procedures (Peeters & Widlak, 2018).

A discussion about the legitimacy and fairness of automated decision-making requires an inquiry of two main questions. First, an empirical question is the comparison of values institutionally safeguarded earlier by classic bureaucratic procedures and now by automated decision-making. This is relevant because our understanding of the impact of this technology is far from complete. Technological innovation not only changes discretion or procedural transparency, but also shifts power, administrative burdens, bias and more. Second, a normative question is what government should do to materialize principles of good administration that safeguard these values in this new situation. This may require complementary institutional arrangements.

In this contribution, we use these two elements as a starting point. We argue that the balance between them is threatened by automated decision-making and that, in response, a more principle-based approach of automated decision-making is required. This issue has been raised in various recent studies (Danaher, 2016; Kool, Timmer & Van Est, 2017; Van Eck, 2018; Widlak & Peeters, 2018; Meijer, Schafer & Branderhorst, 2019), but requires further elaboration. In the following, we first analyse how automated decision-making threatens to usurp key principles of good administration. Second, we present a preliminary shared set of established principles in advanced democracies that govern administrative decision-making and apply these principles to automated decision-making. Third, we move from positive law to an inductive analysis of the specific nature of automated decision-making to assess where additional safeguards need to be developed. We conclude this contribution by reflecting on the meaning of algorithms for the way governments provide citizens with access to rights and services.

Automated decision-making and good administration

Automated decision-making in government

Automated decision-making, also known as its near-synonyms of autonomous decision-making, algorithmic decision-making and data-driven decision-making, refers to administrative decisions issued by a government organization to affect the relation between government and citizen. It involves breaking down a decision in a set of 'if then' rules and criteria through algorithms (a sequence of reasoning) that make selections from predetermined alternatives (Le Sueur, 2016: 2). By using the word automated, we mean that a computer reaches a conclusion by itself based on data, without human interference (Larus et al., 2018: 2), based on either a pre-programmed algorithm or on an algorithm that adapts itself through machine learning. The absence of human interference in decision-making can be understood as a continuum (Citron & Pasquale, 2014; Binns, 2016; Danaher, 2016) – ranging from automated decisions that leave virtually no space for human agency (Peeters & Widlak, 2018) to automated decisions that provide a default for human decision-makers, which may be overruled (Hamilton, 2015: 49).

An important distinction should be made between automated individual decisions and automated prediction (EU, 2016). The former refers to decisions that affect individual citizens in their status as either eligible for services or rights or as eligible for enforcement of obligations (such as taxation). The latter is a form of statistical analysis used to identify individuals from a broader group based on specific characteristics that justify the singling out of individuals for further attention. This can be attention in a positive way – the provision of better public services based on profiles; however, profiling is mostly used for enforcement purposes, such as tackling welfare fraud or sorting out citizens that are more likely to show deviant behaviour. The 'automated' part is the risk analysis, which is commonly followed up by human decision-makers (Houser & Sanders, 2017: 13).[1]

Another key distinction is whether automated decision-making is limited to a single organization or affects the operations and decisions of multiple organizations. The latter implies that data used to make automated decisions might come from a different organization than the one that makes the actual administrative decision regarding a citizen's rights or obligations, or that decisions made by one organization also impact the administrative decisions other organizations make. The automatic exchange of data leads to chain-decisions (Van Eck, 2018) or automated network decisions. We speak of a 'chain' if several hierarchically independent organizations cooperate in a sequential process towards a collective result (Grijpink, 1997; Borst, 2019: 24), such as the police and the public prosecutor in criminal law. In such cases, there usually is a shared legal framework and (data-)definitions are harmonized.

However, the analogy with a supply chain is lost when there is no sequential process, no collective objective or no harmonized definitions. In such cases, it is better to speak of automated network decisions. A good example are the so-called 'basis registrations' that the Dutch government uses to digitize and centralize vital data on citizens, businesses, geographical locations, buildings, vehicles, and so on (Peeters & Widlak, 2018). The authentic data contained in these vital registrations as well as changes in that data are automatically shared among a large variety of public and semi-public organizations to allow for the execution of their primary processes. This improves efficiency and reduces double registrations and obsoleteness of the data object. However, it also reduces technical transparency for citizens and user organizations, because the source of data as well as the procedures followed in the use of data often remain unclear (Van Eck, 2018).

Principles of good administration

Automated decision-making, in its various forms, profoundly alters the way government organizations make decisions regarding the access to rights and services of citizens. These decisions – administrative decisions – are subjected to norms and principles to ensure the protection of citizens' rights and weigh values in concrete situations and decisions. Given the 'absence' of the legislator in the day-to-day execution of the law by administrative bodies, guidelines for administrative decision-making have developed over centuries (Ostrom, 1996: 1) and are, especially in civil law countries, commonly incorporated in formal administrative law to govern (1) the legality and procedures of administrative decisions; and (2) the protection of citizens against breaches of those legal norms (Van der Heijden, 2001). Jurisprudence and Ombudsmen are additional sources of norm setting. In some cases, such as in Dutch administrative law, the EU's Code of Good Administrative Behaviour, and article 41 of the EU Charter of Fundamental Rights ('the right to good administration'), these norms are codified. Their purpose is to guarantee administrative justice and protect citizens against unreasonable or unmotivated administrative decisions – thereby going further than merely guaranteeing the legality of decisions and procedures.[2]

In the Western legal tradition, where the citizen enjoys legal protection against state intervention and any such intervention needs to be legally justified, principles of good administration are a cornerstone of the rule of law (Mashaw, 2007: 99; Van Hout, 2019) – despite clear differences between national legal traditions. It can be safely argued that administrative decisions made by computers instead of human agents should be covered by the same norms or guidelines as traditional man-made decisions. The Danish case provides a good illustration. Here, the Principle of Administrative Law by Design was developed to ensure that legislation and unwritten principles of administrative law are to be embedded in the technology, practices and organizational structure (Motzfeld & Naesborg-Andersen, 2018: 139–140). The underlying idea is to prevent the violation of administrative law due to impetuous design of technologies. This is also reflected in the European Union's General Data Protection Regulation, which seeks the protection of natural persons with regard to the processing of personal data (EU, 2016).

Principles of good administration regulate the use of discretion in individual administrative decisions as well as the design of fair and transparent administrative procedures. These are the two prime mechanisms through which rules of law balance universal and predictable rules with the specifics of individual cases. Crucially, these are also the two mechanisms primarily affected by the introduction of automated decision-making. First, processing decisions or predictions through computer-programmed algorithms leads to a 'hiddenness concern' (Danaher, 2016): it is unknown which data are collected, data are often used without consent and the procedures through which data is analysed are not transparent (Grimmelikhuijsen & Meijer, 2014; Hannah-Moffat, 2019), thereby hiding ethical dimensions of analysis and classification from sight (Kallinikos, 2005; Cordella & Tempini, 2015; Peeters & Widlak, 2018). Second, automated decision-making reduces discretionary space at street-level (Bovens & Zouridis, 2002; Landsbergen, 2004; Zouridis, Van Eck & Bovens, 2020) – anywhere on a continuum from creating a default or advice for human decision-makers to full automation in which algorithms decide without human oversight or override (Citron & Pasquale, 2014; Peeters & Schuilenburg, 2018).

Towards principles for digital administrative decisions

In the following, we apply existing principles of good administration to automated decision-making and analyse whether additional safeguards need to be formulated. First, we distil three principles from an analysis of positive law. Even though every country's specific legal tradition has given rise to a wide variety of principles for good administration, we argue that principles of due process, accountability and proportionality are widely shared. These three principles are applied to automated decision-making to demonstrate their relevance and usefulness. An important limitation of this strategy, however, is that it does not take into account the specific logic of automated decision-making and the consequences it can have for citizens. According to legal scholar Jurgen van der Heijden (2001), drawing on the works of Ronald Dworkin and Jürgen Habermas, principles of good administration set requirements for 'the action situation'. An action situation is an abstraction of concrete situations where citizens' access to rights and services is at stake and 'where participants […] interact […], solve problems, dominate one another or fight' (Ostrom, 2005: 14). Therefore, we use a second, inductive strategy to analyse how automated decision-making changes this action situation. Through three short case studies, we demonstrate possible undesirable consequences of automated decision-making for a citizen's legal position. This allows us to identify additional norms to ensure good automated administrative decision-making.

Principles in positive law

In the following, three internationally well-established principles of good administration are applied to automated decision-making and automated predictions: (1) due process (which focuses on the procedure of a decision); (2) accountability (which focuses on the allocation of responsibility); and (3) proportionality (which focuses on the material fairness of a decision). The selection of these principles is an attempt to capture a minimum level of shared norms in the variety of national legal traditions in advanced democracies.

Principle of due process

Due process obliges administrative organizations to demonstrate and make explicit what steps have been taken during the entire decision-making procedure. This principle is, therefore, closely related to the issue of algorithmic transparency (Grimmelikhuijsen & Meijer, 2014; Mittelstadt et al., 2016), which is concerned with the throughput legitimacy of automated decision-making (Schmidt, 2013). Though due process clauses have a different emphasis and impact in different countries, we can say that one essential part of due process is the ability of the citizen to defend himself against an adverse decision by government (Ponce, 2005: 582). This is, for instance, codified as part of the right to good administration in the EU Charter of Fundamental Rights (article 41, sub 1 and 2), which states that every person has the right to have his or her affairs handled impartially, fairly and within a reasonable timeframe, including the right of every person to be heard before any adverse individual measure is taken (EU, 2012). Applied to automated decision-making, due process means that the black box of algorithms should be opened up to give citizens insights into the criteria used and the steps taken to reach a decision.

Guaranteeing due process is also relevant for automated prediction (Citron & Pasquale, 2014). Both individual automated decisions and automated prediction have the characteristic that a person is described by data in databases. However, where individual decisions work with business rules programmed by a team of human programmers combined with facts represented by individual data, automated predictions rely on probability derived from statistics, rating and classification (ibid.). Governments mine personal information to make predictions about individuals on questions such as 'which individuals will be more likely to own crypto currencies and might not report these – either by mistake or intent – to the Tax Authority?' Essentially different from individual data processing is the addition of an inference based on probability. It is a score that indicates if a citizen looks like a terrorist, fraud or hooligan. Introduction of the principle of due process implies at least that the quality of the process can be audited (what steps were taken and were they legitimate?) in all the different stages of the scoring process.

Principle of accountability

Every organization that makes administrative decisions is responsible for them, 'owns' them and can be held accountable for them (Bovens, 2010). Public organizations cannot simply hide behind general rules and claim they are 'merely implementing them', nor divert responsibility for administrative decisions to individual civil servants. Automated decision-making can raise the same instinctive administrative reaction – 'the computer says no' (Van Eck, 2018) – signalling a lack of willingness or capability to take responsibility for individual administrative decisions. Availability of data or lack thereof does not remove the responsibility to verify if these data reflect the actual relevant facts. And technological complexity or poor information management are not a reason to remove administrative accountability (Fosch-Villaronga, 2019). Some authors consider accountability the twin-sister of transparency. Even if full transparency is not possible, the accountability of the decision-making process as a whole still needs to be ensured (Zalnieriute, Moses & Williams, 2019). However, as political scientist Mark Bovens (2010) warns, the principle of accountability may, in its institutional implementation, lead to proceduralism that hampers reflexivity, efficiency and effectiveness of administrative organizations and lead to goal displacement.

Every administrative organization that uses automated decision-making and automated predictions can be held accountable for the system, its flaws (glitches), the use of the system (such as function creep), and the outcomes in individual cases. This includes issues that may be organized beyond the direct control of the administration, such as problems with the code of an outsourced information system. No matter what technology does, or how the contract works between the company that sold the technology and the government, the administrative organization is accountable for using the technology and accountable for any actions aimed at individuals. This includes automated network decisions, where organizations make decisions based on data gathered and administrated by other organizations. The organization that makes the decision is accountable for the data it uses – for its correctness and for the consequences of the decisions made based on that data. In other words, the responsibility for automated decisions cannot be transferred to other organizations or to the information system that 'generated' the decision.

The principle of accountability affects both data and procedures. When data is no longer provided by the citizen or to the citizen on paper, the administration must be able to provide the source, the date and content of the data on which a decision was based (Widlak & Peeters, 2018: 111–117). When procedures are no longer (practically) accessible, the administration must be able to organize a procedural review in its professional community and professional discourse. Consequently, correction of erroneous decisions must be a possibility. Data and software cannot be interwoven in a way that makes this a practical impossibility (ibid.: 117–120). Keeping 'humans in-the-loop' does not mean that individual civil servants should constantly verify automated decisions, but the principle of accountability does imply a right to a 'human eye', that allows for comparison of data with the facts in real life and for a meaningful intervention in individual cases (see also article 22 of the EU's General Data Protection Regulation; EU, 2016).

Principle of proportionality

The exclusion of human agency in decision-making begs the question if an organization can still guarantee that the decisions it makes lead to fair results and do not affect citizens excessively or unnecessarily (cf. Ranchordás & De Waard, 2016). The principle of proportionality can be aimed at the legislator when it wants to intervene in human rights (such as Article 8 of the European Convention of Human Rights and Fundamental Freedoms), but it can also be used to guide the behaviour of civil servants (see article 6, section 1 of the European Code of Good Administrative Behaviour; EU, 2002). In automated decision-making, proportionality also needs to be guaranteed at both levels. However, given the fact that a single set of data may now be used for a myriad of administrative decisions, the legislator should assess proportionality at the level of information architecture as well: are all governmental interventions combined aimed at one citizen still in balance? Or should strategies be developed to mitigate possible disproportional consequences?

At an individual level, proportionality first and foremost requires the possibility to overrule an automated decision when circumstances are unforeseen or errors have been made. Generally, the use of automated decision-making has shifted human judgement from the core of the decision-making process to the phase of objection and complaints, thereby also shifting the responsibility to observe the need for judgement and to monitor for errors from the administration to the citizen. The issue of proportionality is especially relevant in cases of automated network decisions. In the execution of tasks, administrations use data that is provided by other agencies for their own primary decision-making processes. For instance, the aforementioned 'basis registrations' require Dutch governmental agencies to use data already available in designated governmental databases. Other countries are also working on implementing the 'single registration, multiple use' principle as an essential part of their e-government strategies (e.g. Government of Flanders, 2015: 4, 17–18; Digital Government Factsheet Norway, 2019: 7). A downside of these strategies is that user organizations often have little interest in carefully monitoring the quality of the data they receive. Furthermore, data are not always interoperable – the definitions in the different applicable laws are not the same, but their databases are used to compile the decisions nevertheless (Van Eck, 2018: 447). Another issue in this respect is that the consequences of a change in vital records for an individual citizen cannot be fully foreseen (Peeters & Widlak, 2018), which complicates the assessment of the proportionality of such an administrative decision.

Good digital administration in changing action situations

In this section, we present three short cases of citizens that have been negatively affected by automated administrative decisions. More specifically, all cases involve automated network decisions, in which algorithms govern the exchange of data from vital public records and, thereby, impact the capability of organizations to guarantee fairness, accountability and proportionality in their individual administrative decisions. The objective of this inductive approach is to assess the need for additional or more specific norms to ensure good digital administration. All cases involve an administrative error, because errors made by the administration are the most undisputed examples of specific circumstances that justify use of discretion and deviation from the rules. The first two cases are based on original data gathered through document analysis and interviews in 2018 and 2019 in the Netherlands. The third case (see also Widlak & Peeters, 2020) has been studied since 2014.[3]

Buy one house, pay property tax for two

When Simone bought a house in Amsterdam, she soon received a property tax assessment. Strangely enough, she also received a second assessment for a house a bit further down the street. She files a formal complaint, which is only handled by the municipality fourteen months later – two months after the legally established maximum period. According to the municipality, research by the municipal department of vital record registries has demonstrated that she is registered as the owner of the second house and, therefore, is required to pay the corresponding property tax. In order to prove the municipal data is incorrect, Simone obtains an extract from the land registry office which shows that the owner of the second house is an investment fund. Records also show that the property has exchanged hands multiple times during the past few years. Eventually, proof is retrieved of the ownership at the time the municipality sent Simone the tax assessment. She sends the documents to the municipal ombudsman and not long after she receives notice that the mistake will be corrected.

Simone's case is resolved in her favour, but not after a lengthy and complicated procedure in which the burden of proof of *not* owning a house was placed on her. Analysis of this case shows that the problems can be traced back to the reproduction of an administrative error through automated network decisions. Amsterdam's municipal property tax is determined by linking three types of data: the land registry's data of ownership is linked to data on addresses and buildings, which, in turn, is linked to the residence registry. This data is updated frequently and stored in a municipal data pool. In Simone's case, a human error was made in this process and ownership of a property was incorrectly assigned to her. When Simone filed her complaint, municipal employees reviewed their own data instead of looking at the original data sources or at the evidence presented by Simone. In the land registry, they could have seen that Simone was not the owner of the second house. However, employees trusted the municipal data to be correct and proceeded accordingly. Algorithms provided them with a default that they did not question.

Paying for unreceived care

Piet is the legal administrator for his father, who is hospitalized and receives geriatric care rehabilitation. Months before termination of the treatment, it is clear that Piet's father will require permanent care. The hospital suggests him to file a request for long-term care at the Care Assessment Centre ('CIZ'). This is publicly funded, but also involves a personal contribution. A month *after* Piet's request, he receives an indication of eligibility pre-dated a month *before* the date of his request. Another month later, the actual long-term care starts. A different administrative body, the Central Administration Office ('CAK'), determines Piet's monthly personal contribution. Basing itself on data obtained from the Care Assessment Centre, the amount is set at 850 euros – starting three months *before* the start of the actual treatment. This would mean that Piet has to pay for three months in which no actual care was received. After an unsuccessful complaint, Piet starts a lawsuit against the Central Administration Office claiming that he should not pay for the three months identified incorrectly as part of the long-term care.

The judge rules that the Central Administration Office may trust the information it automatically receives from the Care Assessment Centre regarding the effective starting date of a personal contribution (Rechtbank Midden-Nederland, 2018). The reasoning is that the Central Administration Office cannot be made responsible for verifying if the assessment centre's decisions are correct and if the care provided by hospitals and other institutions is in accordance with the information provided. The Central Administration Office's responsibility is merely to provide the funding for the institutions providing the long-term care and to collect a patient's personal contribution. While this makes sense form an organizational perspective, it also means that an error made by the assessment centre or care institution is, therefore, reproduced without any form of control and that the burden of correction it falls on the citizen – if such a correction is practically possible at all. Automated network decisions facilitate the spread of errors and set a default that is not questioned by user organizations.

A stolen car

On April 30, 1998, Saskia's car is stolen. The same day she reports this to the police. On August 20, Saskia receives a letter to remind her to have her car tested. Initially, she thinks her police report has not been processed yet. However, soon after that she starts receiving tax forms from the Dutch tax authority. A complaint by Saskia leads to nothing as the tax authority says that data from the vehicle registration authority confirms she is the owner of a car. The vehicle registration authority claims its records to be correct despite Saskia's police report of her stolen car. Therefore, she remains liable for motor vehicle tax and vehicle safety tests. Saskia is a single mother and over the years her financial problems accumulate and she has trouble paying her taxes – which she does to avoid legal problems, even though she is convinced she should not have to pay for a car she does not own anymore. When she loses her job, she is no longer able to pay and the judicial collection agency comes into action to collect her debts. This agency also claims the fines are justified based on the data provided by the vehicle registration authority. In 2011, Saskia finally succeeds in striking the title of ownership from the vehicle registration. From now on, no new taxes and fines are added. However, this does not automatically lead to a nullification of all outstanding bills, nor to a refund of all unjustly paid fines and taxes.

Desperately, Saskia sends a handwritten letter to the mayor of Rotterdam in March 2014. This triggers an unofficial investigation, which shows that the vehicle registration authority received an 'end date of theft' by the police the day after Saskia's car was stolen in 1998. Subsequently, the authority reinstated Saskia as owner of a vehicle. After some pressure from the mayor's office, the police look into the case as well. It turns out that the car was found the day after Saskia had reported it as stolen – the police had simply failed to inform her about this. On September 4, 2014, the police offer a letter of apology to Saskia. Based on that letter, the tax authority is willing to nullify all outstanding taxes. However, the tax authority is unable to look back in their records more than five years nor is able to provide a record of road tax settled with other taxes. The vehicle registration authority will not retroactively change Saskia's registration because this 'would severely harm the integrity of the registry'. And the judicial collection agency informs Saskia that she is no longer registered in their system and, moreover, that they cannot reimburse the fines she paid because 'we already sent the money to The Hague years ago'.[4] As a result, Saskia still has debts. Automated decision-making not only causes a simple error to spread throughout an entire system, it also proves highly complex in practice to identify the source of an error and to make organizations assume responsibility for the consequences of an error.

Analysis

In all cases, the combination of an administrative error and automated network decisions triggers enormous problems for individual citizens. Specifically for network decisions – in which data is automatically shared among organizations – the previously described three principles for good digital administration seem to fall short of providing adequate protection for citizens. The main issue here is that an organization makes administrative decisions based on information coming from other organizations. An organization may formally 'own' a decision and bear responsibility for it, but in practice this responsibility is evaded by two mechanisms:

1   Design problem: bureaucratic barriers often impede an organization in both formal and practical terms from verifying the source of the information upon which it depends to make its own administrative decisions. This is perhaps best exemplified by the second case, in which a judge rules that an administrative organization may trust the information it receives from another organization. Crucial elements of a decision-making procedure are obscured for both the 'owner' of the data and the 'owner' of the administrative decision: the former cannot assess or control the applications and consequences of the data it collects and distributes, whereas the latter cannot verify the data upon which it makes a decision that impacts the life of a citizen. Algorithms govern these processes and blindside all parties involved.

2   Discretion problem: even if algorithms allow for human oversight and override, they may create a behavioural default for civil servants to trust the presumed objectivity of data and hide behind the complexity of an information architecture instead of using their discretion for individual case assessment. As the first case shows, civil servants are inclined to trust municipal data over the arguments presented by an individual citizen. 'Hard facts' are preferred over 'real-life' evidence – a strong argument is needed for *not* following what automated processes present as the truth. Moreover, in its current implementation, it often requires an enormous practical and analytical effort to uncover all data sources, links and algorithms behind an automated decision. And as the third case shows, data and the information architecture that produces and distributes it are not designed to allow for correction, and especially not for retroactive correction. Hence, they are treated as sacrosanct institutions not to be meddled with at the price of 'loss of integrity' or as immovable objects that defy any attempt of human intervention.

Complementary principles for automated network decisions

The logic of automated network decisions complicates compliance with, above all, the principle of accountability. This principle demands organizations to take full responsibility for the decisions they make. The way an administrative system or information architecture is designed cannot be an excuse to avoid accountability. Yet this is exactly the reality of many automated network decisions: data collected by other organizations is either inaccessible for citizens, by default presumed correct or impossible to correct in case of an error. This, by definition, also affects the two other identified principals for good digital administration. Due process cannot be guaranteed because data collection and data sharing are not made fully transparent for neither the decision-making organization nor the affected citizen. Of particular concern is the difficulty citizens face when trying to identify where and by whom an error has been made. Furthermore, proportionality is at stake for two reasons: (1) the organization that collects and shares data cannot guarantee that decisions made by other organizations will be reasonable; and (2) the organization that makes a decision based on erroneous data shifts the burden of proof for detecting errors and correcting their consequences for multiple organizations to the citizen.

In light of our analysis, we argue that automated decision-making places a considerable strain on the ability of an administrative organization to ensure accountability, due process and proportionality in administrative decisions. Therefore, we suggest the introduction of additional elements to the previously identified principles in order to mitigate the specific risks that automated network decisions pose to good digital administration:

1   *Procedural completeness* to complement the principle of due process. The citizens in the three cases presented above face an information problem. The inability to identify the source of administrative errors can be traced back to a lack of insight in what data is used for decision-making, who owns these data and whether these data are complete, contextually relevant, correct and up-to-date. In traditional decision-making, the organization that owned the decision also owned the data. This unity is severed in automated network decisions. Completeness in the process of decision-making means that an administrative organization must be able to provide a citizen with information about both elements of the procedure. This goes beyond traditional calls for algorithmic transparency, because these do not address the division of labour between data collection and sharing on the one hand and individual administrative decisions on the other hand. Both procedures may be transparent individually, but still add up to an opaque system from the perspective of the citizen and the decision-maker.

2   *Factual assessment* to complement the principle of accountability. Administrative organizations avoid responsibility for their decisions because they tend to treat data as unquestionable facts and the information architecture as an untouchable entity. Trusting the algorithms is the default option for decision-making. To prevent organizations from hiding their responsibility, the possibility of a human assessment of administrative decisions must be guaranteed. It is crucial, however, that this assessment is fact-based instead of data-based: instead of reviewing databases, a citizen's factual situation should be the focus of the assessment.

3   *Central correction* to complement the principle of proportionality. Automated decisions based on erroneous information can lead to disproportional consequences for affected citizens. The burden of proof for administrative errors is placed on the citizen. This is often also the case with traditional paper-based decisions, but an important difference is that correction not only needs to

take place in the organization that made the individual administrative decision, but also in the organization that collects and shares the data. Moreover, the consequences of erroneous data increase if this data is shared with other organizations. To prevent citizens from being disproportionally burdened with erroneous or unfair administrative decisions, a central correction of the error must be guaranteed.

Conclusion

The classic Weberian bureaucracy in which civil servants individually apply general rules to individual cases is a thing of the past for a long time already. Especially since the 1990s, databases and computers have steadily taken over tasks originally entrusted to paper files and human assessment. The 'infocracy' (Zuurmond, 1994) is an important touchstone in the digitalization of administrative decisions. The increasingly widespread use of algorithms marks a new phase in which data is not only digitalized but entire decisions-making procedures are automated. Moreover, automated network decisions combine the 'algocracy' (Aneesh, 2006) with the 'system-level bureaucracy' (Bovens & Zouridis, 2002). Every technological transformation in administrative decision-making begs the question how this affects citizens in their rights and obligations. The main concerns regarding automation of processes are that it reduces an organization's capacity to assess individual cases because of automated discretion (Zouridis, Van Eck & Bovens, 2020) as well as reduces an organization's control over the fairness and transparency of its procedures (Grimmelikhuijsen & Meijer, 2014; Peeters & Widlak, 2018).

Whether we are talking about rights and obligations determined by individual automated decisions, about risks and profiles identified through automated prediction, or about vital public records shared among multiple organizations in automated network decisions – the principles that govern good administrative decision-making are at risk of being usurped by a technology that fundamentally transforms the way administrative organizations make decisions. Due process is at risk because data collection and data sharing are not transparent, accountability is complicated because organizations pass responsibility for the correctness of data on to other organizations, and proportionality is jeopardized because the responsibility for detecting errors and correcting their consequences for multiple organizations is placed on citizens. In response, we have identified three specifications of these principles to mitigate the specific risks that automated decision-making, and especially automated network decisions, pose.

However, formulating principles for good digital administration on paper is something else than safeguarding them in practice. Three challenges need to be tackled. Algorithms pose, first, a design problem because they complicate oversight or 'reviewability' (Danaher, 2016) by organizations and affected citizens. Here, a key issue is to design algorithms that keep humans in-the-loop and organize the possibility of oversight and override (Citron & Pasquale, 2014). Second, algorithms trigger a behavioural problem because they set a default for action which – despite having humans 'in-the-loop' – is likely to be unquestioned (Peeters & Schuilenburg, 2018). Both problems can only be tackled through a thorough institutionalization of principles of good digital administration. Much work remains to be done to ensure a principle-based design of automated decision-making.

There is, however, also a third, epistemological problem in the input, throughput and output of automated decisions. The issue here is not that algorithms are in some way hidden, but that they might be inherently opaque or incomprehensible to human reason (Danaher, 2016). At the level of input, this translates into unknowability of the data used and their origin to reach a decision – especially if 'big data' and network decisions are involved. At the level of throughput, algorithms can be relatively simple and 'interpretable' but they might also, as is often the case with machine learning algorithms or predictive algorithms, be 'non-interpretable' and impossible to 'reduce to a human language explanation' (Zarsky, 2011: 293). Finally, at the level of output, a decision generated by algorithms may equal a 'fait accompli' for both citizen and human decision-maker, which can only be questioned ex-post. Merely keeping a human in-the-loop is, therefore, not enough. The question is how this can be done in a meaningful way. How can we organize the analytical tools for humans to assess whether an automated decision was based on correct and unbiased data and whether it was reached according to fair criteria? How can an automated decision and its consequences can be overturned? And how can human decision-makers identify the exact cases from the massive daily flow of automated decisions in which specific circumstances caused unreasonable outcomes? This shows that the challenge goes beyond forcing automated decision-making into the templates of classic 'analogue' decision-making. The key challenge lies in developing the mechanisms that are responsive to changing action situations.

Notes

1 There are, beyond the scope of this contribution, many more government tasks that involve automation, such as digital monitoring of water management systems or managing traffic flows.
2 Furthermore, principles for administrative decisions can also be seen as an instrument to facilitate application of legal frameworks to changing social circumstances (Van der Heijden, 2001). Principles differ from rules in the sense that rules, applied to facts, imply an imperative for action, whereas principles have an open character and allow for interpretation in concrete situations (Dworkin, 1985). Thereby, principles – even if they are codified in positive law – allow for law to remain open for change and adaptation to new circumstances or to specific situations that cannot be captured in general rules.
3 A more detailed methodological justification is available upon request and available in Widlak & Peeters, 2020, for the third case.
4 'The Hague' refers to the seat of Dutch government, where the Ministry of Justice is located.

References

Aneesh, A. 2006. *Virtual migration*. Durham, NC: Duke University Press.
Berk, R.A. and J. Bleich. 2013. Statistical procedures for forecasting criminal behavior. *Criminology & Public Policy*, 12 (3): 513–544.

Binns, R. 2016. Algorithmic accountability and public reason. *Philosophy & Technology*, 31 (4): 543–556.

Borst, W. 2019. *De verdachte in de keten*. Den Haag: Boom.

Bovens, M. 2010. Two concepts of accountability: Accountability as a virtue and as a mechanism. *West European Politics*, 33 (5): 946–967.

Bovens, M. and S. Zouridis. 2002. From street-level to system-level bureaucracies: How information and communication technology is transforming administrative discretion and constitutional control. *Public Administration Review*, 62: 174–184.

Citron, D.K. and F. Pasquale. 2014. The scored society: Due process for automated predictions. *Washington Law Review*, 89: 1–33.

Cordella, A. and N. Tempini. 2015. E-government and organizational change: Reappraising the role of ICT and bureaucracy in public service delivery. *Government Information Quarterly*, 32 (3): 279–286.

Danaher, J. 2016. The threat of algocracy: Reality, resistance and accommodation. *Philosophy & Technology*, 29 (3): 245–268.

Digital Government Factsheet. 2019. *Norway*. https://joinup.ec.europa.eu/sites/default/files/inline-files/Digital_Government_Factsheets_Norway_2019.pdf, accessed 10-12-2019.

Dworkin, R. 1985. *A matter of principle*. Cambridge: Harvard University Press.

EU. 2002. The European code of good administrative behaviour. https://www.ombudsman.europa.eu/es/publication/en/3510, accessed 10-12-2019.

EU. 2012. EU charter of fundamental rights. https://ec.europa.eu/info/aid-development-cooperation-fundamental-rights/your-rights-eu/eu-charter-fundamental-rights_en, accessed 10-12-2019.

EU. 2016. General data protection regulation. https://gdpr-info.eu/, accessed 10-12-2019.

Fosch-Villaronga, E. 2019. Responsibility in robot and AI environments. Working Paper eLaw 2019/02.

Government of Flanders. 2015. Vlaanderen radicaal digitaal. https://overheid.vlaanderen.be/sites/default/files/Conceptnota%20Vlaanderen%20Radicaal%20digitaal.pdf, accessed 10-12-2019.

Grijpink, J.H.A.M. 1997. *Keteninformatisering met toepassing op de justitiële bedrijfsketen*. Den Haag: SDU.

Grimmelikhuijsen, S.G. and A.J. Meijer. 2014. Effects of transparency on the perceived trustworthiness of a government organization: Evidence from an online experiment. *Journal of Public Administration Research and Theory*, 24 (1): 137–157.

Hamilton, M. 2015. Adventures in risk: Predicting violent and sexual recidivism in sentencing law. *Arizona State Law Journal*, 47 (1): 1–62.

Hannah-Moffat, K. 2019. Algorithmic risk governance: Big data analytics, race and information activism in criminal justice debates. *Theoretical Criminology*, 23 (4): 453–470.

Harcourt, B.E. 2015. *Exposed: Desire and disobedience in the digital age*. Cambridge: Harvard University Press.

Houser, K. and D. Sanders. 2017. The use of big data analytics by the IRS: Efficient solutions or the end of privacy as we know it?. *Vanderbilt Journal of Entertainment and Technology Law*, 19 (4): 817–872.

Kallinikos, J. 2005. The order of technology: Complexity and control in a connected world. *Information and Organization*, 15: 185–202.

Kool, L., J. Timmer and R. van Est, 2017. *Opwaarderen. Borgen van publieke waarden in de digitale samenleving*. Den Haag: Rathenau Instituut.

Landsbergen, D. 2004. Screen level bureaucracy: Databases as public records. *Government Information Quarterly*, 21 (1): 24–50.

Larus, J., C. Hankin, S.G. Carson, M. Christen, S. Crafa, O. Grau, C. Kirchner, B. Knowles, A. McGettrick, D.A. Tamburri and H. Werthner. 2018. When computers decide: European recommendations on machine-learned automated decision making. *Technical Report*. New York: ACM.

Le Sueur, A. 2016. Robot government: Automated decision-making and its implications for parliament. In *Parliament: Legislation and accountability*, edited by A. Horne and A. Le Sueur, Oxford: Hart Publishing.

Mashaw, J.L. 2007. Reasoned administration: The European Union, the United States, and the project of democratic governance. *The George Washington Law Review*, 76 (1): 99–124.

McLuhan, M. 1964. *Understanding media: The extensions of man*. New York: Signet Books.

Meijer, A., M.T. Schafer and M. Branderhorst. 2019. Principes voor goed lokaal bestuur in de digitale samenleving. Een aanzet tot een normatief kader. *Bestuurswetenschappen*, 73 (4): 8–23.

Mittelstadt, B.D., P. Allo, M. Taddeo, S. Wachter and L. Floridi. 2016. The ethics of algorithms: Mapping the debate. *Big Data & Society*, 3 (2): 1–21.

Motzfeld, H.M. and A. Naesborg-Andersen. 2018. Developing administrative law into handling the challenges of digital government in Denmark. *The Electronic Journal of e-Government*, 16 (2): 136–146.

O'Neil, C. 2016. *Weapons of math destruction: How big data increases inequality and threatens democracy*. New York: Penguin Random House.

Ostrom, V. 1996. Faustian bargains. *Constitutional Political Economy*, 7: 303–308.

Ostrom, E. 2005. *Understanding institutional diversity*. Princeton, NJ: Princeton University Press.

Pasquale, F. 2015. *The black box society: The secret algorithms that control money and information*. Boston: Harvard University Press.

Peeters, R. and M. Schuilenburg. 2018. Machine justice: Governing security through the bureaucracy of algorithms. *Information Polity*, 23 (3): 267–280.

Peeters, R. and A.C. Widlak. 2018. The digital cage: Administrative exclusion through information architecture – the case of the Dutch civil registry's master data management system. *Government Information Quarterly*, 35 (2): 175–183.

Ponce, J. 2005. Good administration and administrative procedures. *Indiana Journal of Global Legal Studies*, 12 (2): 551–588.

Ranchordás, S. and B. Waard (Eds.). 2016. *The judge and the proportionate use of discretion: A comparative study*. London: Routledge.

Rechtbank Midden-Nederland. 2018. ECLI:NL:RBMNE:2018:4574, Case number UTR 18/1169.

Rehavi, M.M. and S.B. Starr. 2014. Racial disparity in federal criminal sentences. *Journal of Political Economy*, 122 (6): 1320–1354.

Schmidt, V.A. 2013. Democracy and legitimacy in the European Union revisited: Input, output and 'throughput'. *Political Studies*, 61 (1): 2–22.

Smith, G.J.D., L. Bennett Moses and J. Chan. 2017. The challenges of doing criminology in the big data era: Towards a digital and data-driven approach. *The British Journal of Criminology*, 57 (2): 259–274.

Smith, G.J.D. and P. O'Malley. 2017. Driving politics: Data-driven governance and resistance. *The British Journal of Criminology*, 57 (2): 275–298.

Van Eck, M. 2018. *Geautomatiseerde ketenbesluiten & rechtsbescherming: Een onderzoek naar de praktijk van geautomatiseerde ketenbesluiten over een financieel belang in relatie tot rechtsbescherming* (dissertation). Tilburg: Tilburg University.

Verbeek, P.P. 2006. Materializing morality: Design ethics and technological mediation. *Science, Technology, & Human Values*, 3: 361–380.

Van der Heijden, J. 2001. *Een filosofie van behoorlijk bestuur. Een verklaring voor de juridische en de maatschappelijke functie van de beginselen van behoorlijk bestuur* (dissertation). Deventer: W.E.J. Tjeenk Willink.

Van Hout, M.B.A. 2019. *Algemene beginselen van een binair bestuur*. Den Haag: SDU.

Widlak, A.C. and R. Peeters. 2018. *De digitale kooi*. Den Haag: Boom bestuurskunde.

Widlak, A. and R. Peeters. 2020. Administrative errors and the burden of correction and consequence: How information technology exacerbates the consequences of bureaucratic mistakes for citizens. *International Journal of Electronic Governance*, 12(1): 40–56.

Yeung, K. 2018. Algorithmic regulation: A critical interrogation. *Regulation & Governance*, 12 (4): 505–523.

Zalnieriute, M., L.B. Moses and G. Williams. 2019. The rule of law and automation of government decision-making. *The Modern Law Review*, 82: 425–455.

Zarsky, T.Z. 2011. Governmental data-mining and its alternatives. *Penn State Law Review*, 116: 285–330.

Zouridis, S., M. van Eck and M. Bovens. 2020. Automated discretion. In *Discretion and the quest for controlled freedom*, edited by T. Evans and P. Hupe. London: Palgrave Macmillan.

Zuurmond, A. 1994. *De infocratie. Een theoretische en empirische heroriëntatie op Weber's ideaaltype in het informatietijdperk*. Den Haag: Phaedrus.

Part II

Algorithmic justice

Chapter 6

The seductiveness of fairness

Is machine learning the answer? – Algorithmic fairness in criminal justice systems

Fernando Ávila, Kelly Hannah-Moffat and Paula Maurutto

Introduction

Criminal justice agencies are increasingly experimenting with and adopting big data technologies and predictive algorithmic tools to produce more defensible, objective, efficient, and fair decisions. Legal and criminal justice decision-makers are turning to algorithmic tools to sentence offenders, determine pretrial or immigration detention, and manage penal populations (Feeley & Simon, 1992; Kemshall, 2003; O'Malley, 2004, 2010a; Harcourt, 2007; Hannah-Moffat & Maurutto, 2010; Hannah-Moffat, 2013, 2016; Hyatt & Chanenson, 2016; Van Eijk, 2017). The increasing infusion of predictive tools in the justice system is shifting institutional practices. It has been described as ushering in new forms of 'automated justice' (Marks, Bowling & Keenan, 2017), 'algorithmic justice' (Završnik, 2019), 'simulated justice' (O'Malley, 2010b), and 'algorithmic governmentality' (Hannah-Moffat, 2019). Understanding the potential impact on criminal procedure and justice decision-making is critical since machine learning risk algorithms influence configurations of punishment. The incorporation of new forms of algorithmic justice and risk assessment calculations is also raising legal and justice concerns about equity, equality, fairness and discrimination.

Actuarial risk assessment tools and predictive analytics have been commonly used since the 1980s and are now firmly embedded in criminal justice practices (Feeley & Simon, 1992; Kemshall, 2003; O'Malley, 2004, 2010a; Harcourt, 2007; Hannah-Moffat & Maurutto, 2010; Hannah-Moffat, 2013; Hyatt & Chanenson, 2016; Van Eijk, 2017). In this chapter, we distinguish between commonly used 'traditional risk assessments' and 'machine learning assessments'. The actuarial tools that we refer to as 'traditional risk assessments' are predominately psychologically informed and use statistical calculations to pinpoint variables that predict recidivism and enable evidence-based scores that are portrayed as more accurate and objective methods of assessment than clinical ones. These 'traditional' tools share a common logic and structure. They are premised on aggregate statistical calculations (using multiple regressions, correlations and meta-analyses) that predict an offender's likelihood of future recidivism. Examples include the Salient Factor Score and the Correctional Offender Management Profiling for Alternative Sanctions (COMPAS, used in the United States), the Risk of Reconviction (used in the

United Kingdom) and the Level of Service Inventory (LSI, used internationally). Traditional risk assessment tools have faced a sustained academic critique arguing that they reproduce bias through 'black boxes' that rely on sets of variables that are proxies for race, gender inequality and marginalization (Maurutto & Hannah-Moffat, 2006; Harcourt, 2007; Hannah-Moffat, 2009; Hannah-Moffat & Maurutto, 2010; O'Neil, 2016; Noble, 2018; Tonry, 2019). This body of research has shown how risk-based practices and assessments embed and exacerbate inequalities, thereby generating various forms of systemic discrimination (Hudson & Bramhall, 2005; Fass et al., 2008; Gavazzi et al., 2008; Vose, Cullen & Smith, 2008; Hannah-Moffat & Maurutto, 2010; Hannah-Moffat & Struthers Montford, 2019).

In response to this critique, a new cadre of experts has entered the field of criminal risk prediction. These experts, primarily from the fields of computer science, statistics, and engineering, are leading innovative research designed to incorporate sophisticated big data analytics and machine learning algorithms to produce less-biased risk assessment algorithms. We refer to these emerging developments in risk assessment as 'machine learning risk assessments'. These models use advanced statistical techniques to produce classification systems that target and reduce overall bias. One of the fundamental differences between traditional and machine learning assessment techniques is that the latter assumes rather than ignores bias. Certain machine learning assessments, those informed by fair representation models,[1] are deliberately designed to target bias and control for gendered and racial artifacts in the data (Dwork et al., 2011; Kamishima et al., 2012; Kusner et al., 2017; Madras, Pitassi & Zemel, 2017; Wadsworth, Vera & Piech, 2018). Data experts in this field see themselves as responding to leftist critiques and as acknowledging discrimination in traditional approaches. They are seeking to design models that offer 'fairer' calculations that reduce the 'data harms' produced by less sophisticated traditional risk algorithms.

We argue that despite advances introduced by machine learning algorithms, these models continue to reproduce the limitations inherent in traditional risk assessments. Notwithstanding the sophistication of big data analytics and machine learning, the mathematical design of assessment instruments combined with the type of data they rely on, make it difficult to create 'new' tools that are both bias-free and accurate. The new generation of risk assessments increasingly relies on data that inescapably mirrors social inequality, and on data extraction processes that reinforce and introduce new biases to the model, thereby recreating disadvantage. We will explore how machine learning algorithms reproduce the illusion of objectivity while obscuring how trade-offs between accuracy and fairness are hidden in the algorithms. Moreover, this illusion of fairness and ambiguity is exacerbated by a lack of multidisciplinary dialogue and the ongoing conceptual gaps that exist across knowledge fields. Although data scientists seek to produce 'fairer', less-biased algorithms, critical scholars have demonstrated that machine learning algorithms reproduce forms of algorithmic oppression (Pasquale, 2015; Eubanks, 2017; Ferguson, 2017; Noble, 2018; Benjamin, 2019). Critical race scholars have developed concepts like 'the New Jim Code' to refer to how big data algorithms 'reproduce existing inequities', yet they continue to be perceived as 'more objective or progressive than the discriminatory systems of a previous era' (Benjamin, 2019: 5–6).

As the criminal justice system embraces the big data revolution, it is vital to clarify the computational and legal complexities, logics, and shifts in configurations of punishment that arise from the incorporation of big data risk logics. We argue for more analysis of how the new forms of algorithmic governance and risk assessments can affect criminal procedures and constitutional protections. We show how growing sophistication and reliance on big data analytics can further the 'black-box' phenomenon and obscure how data and calculations reproduce inequities. This opacity may operate to undermine the due process rights of defendants and the ability of researchers to test these models. Additionally, we illustrate how the concepts of 'fairness' and 'bias' promoted by computer sciences through machine learning algorithms not only differ and conflict with social scientists' conceptualizations and analyses of (in)equality, equity, discrimination, and criminal law procedure, but also overlook the political and social dimensions of data. To do so, we deconstruct some of the assumptions embedded in actuarial risk assessments, and particularly in the new frameworks introduced by machine learning algorithms. The goal is to cultivate cross-disciplinary dialogues about the use of machine learning risk-based algorithms and their legal implications and to deconstruct some of the claims made by well-intentioned developers.

Algorithmic justice and traditional risk assessments

The calculation and application of actuarial or algorithmic risk in law and criminal justice increased dramatically, with significant advances in probability models during the 20th century. Although risk assessments were initially developed in the 1920s, they did not become commonplace until the mid-1980s, when many criminal justice sectors actively embraced risk logics and technologies (Feeley & Simon, 1992, 1994). Criminological literature typically classifies the evolution of risk assessments into four generations, from clinical judgement to more statistical calculus of static and dynamic risk prediction (Bonta, 1996). First-generation risk models include clinical assessments that rely on analyses by skilled practitioners, most often psychologists, who use psychological tools and personality inventories to identify risk. These approaches adopt a more holistic approach to survey a broad spectrum of individual needs, characteristics, and traits. By the 1980s, these clinical approaches were increasingly being replaced with evidence-based actuarial assessments. The widespread use of traditional risk assessments coincided with the prison boom in the United States, which ushered in efficient and cost-effective approaches to prison management (O'Malley, 2004). Actuarial assessments appealed to correctional administrators because they could be quickly scored by correctional staff, thereby reducing the need for expensive laborious assessments by professionally trained clinicians.

These actuarial risk assessments replaced first-generation clinical assessments and are described as evolving over three generations. Second-generation assessments rely primarily on static measures of risk such as the age of first offence or criminal history, yielding a fixed risk score that is rigid and cannot be altered (Andrews, 1989). Third-generation risk scores, developed in the early 1990s, integrate static variables with dynamic criminogenic risk factors that allow for mutable risk scores, where correctional interventions and treatment can reduce the overall risk level (Brennan, Dieterich & Ehret, 2009). For example, criminogenic needs include variables such as education, employment, family relations and attitudes, all of which are highly correlated with recidivism but also amenable to intervention and change. Fourth-generation risk scores integrate responsibility measures that match treatment interventions to the learning style and motivation to streamline appropriate interventions (Motiuk, 1997a, 1997b, 1998; Andrews & Bonta, 2010). All these generations can be referred to collectively as traditional risk assessments because they all rely on statistical calculations of risk of recidivism. Examples of these actuarial tools include COMPAS, Risk of Reconviction and the LSI.

These traditional risk assessments claim to inform and guide decision-makers with objective evidence-based criteria that are theoretically bias-free, and by extension, fair. They apply a systematic assessment whereby all defendants and offenders are classified according to a standard set of variables. They purportedly treat each case alike by using the same set of variables that are statistically correlated with recidivism, whether static or dynamic. The variables included in these assessment tools are statistically significant and correlate with recidivism based on a general offender population. Practitioners or probation officers score the tool by checking off each variable that pertains to a specific defendant or offender. The relevant variables are tallied to produce a final risk score that classifies the individual as low, medium, or high risk. The classification is based on how closely an individual matches the risk variables and recidivism rates of the general offender population. This type of traditional risk assessment is modelled on Ernest Burgess' (1928) 0/1 binary non-weighted scoring method, which was initially developed in the 1920s to predict reoffending among those released on parole.

These tools were popularized because they reportedly rely on evidence-based, objective criteria that were promoted as fairer than other forms of assessment. However, several scholars have shown how predictive algorithms can reproduce data harms by entrenching forms of systemic discrimination. This research argues that instead of producing objective and neutral outcomes, actuarial risk assessments embed overt and nuanced forms of systemic discrimination that reproduce class, gendered, and racialized forms of oppression (Bhui, 1999; Pridemore, 2004; Hudson & Bramhall, 2005; Harcourt, 2007; Hannah-Moffat & O'Malley, 2007; Mayson, 2019). Specifically, it is argued that the statistical variables correlated and used to predict recidivism – such as education, finances, acquittances, aptitudes, family relations, and leisure pursuits – are also highly correlated with marginalization in terms of gender, race, class, and other forms of social disadvantage. As a result, they rely on data and correlations that serve as proxies for race and gender, and thereby indirectly embed legally prohibited criteria (Horn & Evans, 2000; Shaw & Hannah-Moffat, 2000; Harcourt, 2007, 2015). The algorithm treats each variable as an indicator of individual criminogenic risk, decontextualized from broader social, political, economic and historical disadvantage. What the calculations ignore is how an offender's 'exposure to risk' in society is often the result of histories of disadvantage and discrimination that are often correlated with risk variables, thereby resulting in 'higher' risk scores, particularly for marginalized populations (Hannah-Moffat & Maurutto, 2010). For example, financial difficulties, often arising from poverty, are correlated with higher rates of recidivism; those on social assistance are regularly assessed as a higher risk.

In contrast, middle-class offenders, who may have committed similar or more severe offences, are less likely to score high on measures of financial difficulty. These tools include multiple variables related to socioeconomic status, many of which are correlated with race and gender, such as education, consistent housing, and family relations. As a result, they can reproduce and magnify bias. Risk variables are also criticized for their normative evaluations of morality, which is reflected in the inclusion of variables such as personal and familial relationships, associations with organized religion, and leisure activities which are subject to high degrees of discretionary evaluation (Hudson & Bramhall, 2005; Hannah-Moffat, Maurutto & Turnbull, 2009).

Arguably, gendered and racialized norms, experiences and knowledge shape what behaviours are viewed by assessors as a risk. Bias also extends beyond calculations and to the subsequent interpretation of results by the courts. Factors associated with marginalization and need are often used in the scoring of risk, wherein those 'at risk and high need' become 'high risk'. A designation of high risk can lead to a greater likelihood of detention and more stringent conditions that cause individuals to be more vulnerable to breaches, increased surveillance, and further criminalization. For this reason, critical scholars have argued that traditional risk assessments are 'algorithms of oppression' that offer a veneer of objectivity and alternatively produce/reproduce racism, sexism, and 'technological redlining' (O'Neil, 2016; Noble, 2018; Benjamin, 2019). In so doing, these tools undermine due process and constitutional protections.

Recent advancements in the field of big data analytics, along with increases in public open-source data, have created new avenues for testing and exposing the level of discriminatory outcomes produced through traditional risk assessments. Data scientists can now merge multiple and large datasets and have a greater capacity to test predictive outcomes. Propriety laws often mean that researchers are not able to access the datasets used to produce and test the outcomes of traditional risk assessment for bias. More recently, open-source data protocols have meant that governments are making data – including criminal justice data – publicly available. The authors of the article 'Machine Bias' used big data analytics to integrate several public online criminal justice data sources obtained through a Freedom of Information request to analyse more than 7000 risk scores produced by the COMPAS risk assessment (Angwin et al., 2016). They were the first to incorporate big data analytics and merge multiple datasets and data points to identify and disclose levels and percentages of bias in COMPAS. They compared predicted scores to actual recidivism among criminal defendants in Broward County, Florida, over two years. The results demonstrated that black accused were almost twice as likely as white defendants to be incorrectly scored as at a higher risk of recidivism. Conversely, white defendants were more likely to be incorrectly flagged as low risk. The results revealed an even more significant disparity when predicting violent recidivism: black defendants were 77% more likely to be misidentified as higher risk. These discriminatory findings catalysed researchers to develop new ways of producing fairer assessment models.

Machine learning algorithms

The sustained international critique of traditional risk assessments inspired artificial intelligence and machine learning data scientists to develop fairer and more accurate algorithms for predicting recidivism. A new cadre of scientists from fields including computer science, mathematics, statistics, and engineering has entered the field of criminal risk prediction. These data scientists use machine learning algorithms to experiment with different measures of statistical fairness. Here, we refer to these broad innovations as 'machine learning algorithms' because they seek to introduce different models of statistical fairness to reduce the bias inherent in commonly used risk assessments. Some scholars have described these as fifth-generation risk assessment tools (Taxman & Dezember, 2016; Garrett & Monahan, 2020). Data scientists use large datasets and machine learning techniques to test their models. In this context, machine learning is a form of artificial intelligence used by algorithms to automatically detect and reduce bias without the explicit need for programming. Rather than ignore discrimination, machine learning algorithms assume bias in the data and seek to identify and sanitize the bias through enhanced statistical modelling. Many who work in this field are concerned with instilling ethics in big data analytics. They view themselves as responding to left critiques by acknowledging the limitations of earlier risk assessment models. They claim to be able to produce responsible, ethical designs that will inject algorithms with solutions for problems of discrimination (Greene, Hoffmann & Stark, 2019).

In contrast to traditional risk assessments, machine learning algorithms are not grounded in a theoretical understanding of criminal behaviour. The predictive models are built using patterns extracted from big data and the use of sophisticated, automated statistical methods like random forests (Breiman, 2001). The datasets used to create these predictive models are immense, and they have the potential to include infinite data points. This feature distinguishes them from the limited and smaller datasets (generally obtained from analyses of a prison population or subset of offenders) relied on by traditional risk assessments. Additionally, machine learning risk models are not static: they are adaptive. They dynamically self-adjust to new data over time in undetermined and unanticipated ways through sophisticated algorithms and artificial intelligence techniques (Pasquale, 2015). In this context, the term 'dynamic' refers to models that continuously learn and self-correct following the parameters of the program; this differs from traditional risk tools (e.g. COMPAS), where a 'dynamic' factor refers to specific types of criminogenic behaviour that can be altered. Overall, proponents of applying machine learning argue that by letting the data speak for itself, it is possible to achieve an exhaustive unveiling of factors that can be statistically related to an outcome but beyond the reach of human actors or traditional techniques of data analysis (Dwork et al., 2011;

Chouldechova, 2016; Berk et al., 2017; Kleinberg, Mullainathan & Raghavan, 2017; Kusner et al., 2017; Verma & Rubin, 2018).

Scholars working on machine learning models position questions of fairness at the centre of their research. They acknowledge that algorithms learn patterns from vast amounts of training data from the real world, which include biased data (Barocas & Selbst, 2016). Hence, machine learning models specifically attempt to operationalize fairness. However, fairness is an abstract idea; it is not a straightforward mathematical calculation. Statistical models of fairness typically involve a trade-off between accuracy and fairness. In other words, to reduce biases arising from gender, racial, or other forms of discrimination embedded in the data, these models often have lower accuracy in terms of predicted scores. How best to address this trade-off has led to a plethora of scientific research focusing on leveraging fair representations: the goal is to optimize the trade-off, but how best to do this remains the subject of much debate.

Currently, there are about 20 different definitions of fairness explored in this area (Kleinberg, Mullainathan & Raghavan, 2017; Gajane & Pechenizkiy, 2018; Verma & Rubin, 2018; Mehrabi et al., 2019). For example, one simple formalization of fairness in machine learning is *fairness through unawareness*, where training data exclude sensitive attributes such as gender, race, or another minority status (Dwork et al., 2011). Other definitions, such as *demographic parity, equalized odds,* and *predictive rate parity*, can be classified as 'group' fairness definitions because they are used in models that divide a given population into different groups, typically protected and unprotected, and include checks to determine whether each group is balanced considering a given classification rate and statistic metric (Dwork et al., 2011; Corbett-Davies et al., 2017; Johndrow & Lum, 2017). In contrast, 'individual' fairness definitions require that similar individuals be treated similarly (Dwork et al., 2011). Still other models rely on *counterfactual fairness*, where a decision is considered fair if it would be the same in a counterfactual scenario where the individual belonged to a different demographic group (Kusner et al., 2017). As demonstrated by this wide range of definitions, scholars have a diverse range of choices for how they conceptualize when designing a machine learning algorithm.

There is no consensus on how to balance accuracy and fairness in an algorithm. Research has shown that a single model cannot simultaneously satisfy all definitions of group fairness and that the required trade-offs are statistically impossible to reconcile (Chouldechova, 2016; Kleinberg, Mullainathan & Raghavan, 2017; Courtland, 2018). For example, the big data study of COMPAS scores illustrated the extant trade-offs that occur when balancing fairness and accuracy (Angwin et al., 2016). Northpointe, the company that created COMPAS, claims that their tool is valid because it satisfies predictive rate parity and is equally adept at predicting whether a white or black defendant classified as high risk would re-offend. In contrast, Angwin and others argued that the COMPAS tool is discriminatory because it does not satisfy the equalized odds test, and it yields a disproportionate number of false positives among black defendants. Each model frames fairness differently.

Advances in artificial intelligence have also resulted in innovations at various stages of the machine learning process: from the initial data mining (pre-processing) and model training (in processing) to the final prediction (post-processing). Machine learning algorithms can be programmed to learn bias in the data and automatically adjust for disparate effects without the need for reprogramming. In other words, they are designed to scan data, detect bias, and automatically develop different algorithms for subsets of populations to reduce bias without a programmer consistently updating the code. One example is *learning fairness representation* (Zemel et al., 2013), where the goal is to achieve group and individual fairness through a good representation of data that obfuscates protected data. The assumption is that algorithms can detect bias and cleanse it from the output before producing an assessment. A model that applies *fairness through unawareness* calculates and identifies sensitive attributes and automatically learns to exclude their use in the decision-making process (Kusner et al., 2017). One of the most recent innovations in machine learning is the *learning to defer* approach (Madras, Pitassi & Zemel, 2017); it can detect when an algorithm's prediction is less robust and notify a decision-maker. In this case, the algorithm works adaptively with decision-makers about whether to override a score based on the strength of the prediction. Decision-makers are notified when a prediction is not sufficiently robust; they can then assess whether it is best to bypass the algorithm and rely on their own expertise. Overall, these models are all designed to produce outcomes that reduce social, racial, and gender bias.

Notwithstanding advances in machine learning technologies, scholars continue to debate traits in data and the extent to which algorithms will continue to reproduce discriminatory outcomes. Studies involving big data have demonstrated that while tools relying on mathematical and statistical modelling provide the allure and illusion of objectivity, they mask embedded forms of discrimination that reproduce gender, racial, ethnic, and other forms of inequality (Eubanks, 2017; Noble, 2018) in a manner that is similar to the traditional risk assessment. Machine learning risk assessment tools still tend to decontextualize data, overstate their mathematical correction, obfuscate the significance of their ethical/social effects, and thereby risk reproducing discriminatory effects or 'data harms'. These tools require a more nuanced understanding of how inequality can be embedded in insidious and unanticipated ways (Eubanks, 2017; Noble, 2018; Benjamin, 2019). The data entered into a machine learning system, and the calculations on which they are based, continue to be abstracted from broader socio-political, economic and historical relations that embed discrimination into algorithms.

For example, the developers of these machine learning risk tools are often unfamiliar with the considerable body of criminological research related to discriminatory practices, policies and histories of race relations, gender inequality, and colonialism and how these can be embedded in all forms of data and algorithms. There is presently insufficient understanding of and ability to 'clean' and neutralize data to control for discrimination. Criminal justice systems involve chained and sequential trajectories (e.g. from policing, stop and frisk, arrest, bail, sentencing, parole), but data scientists have yet to fully consider how biases and discriminatory decisions at each of those stages can influence predictive outcomes. For example, one of the most accessible forms of data used in algorithms are police reports on arrests. However, arrest data often reflect municipal priorities, such as the desire for increased revenues that can be generated from fines imposed on those arrested – and increases in arrests to create municipal profits are often conflated with actual crime (Ferguson, 2017).

Moreover, marginalized neighbourhoods are more frequently targeted, increasing the arrests of racial and other marginalized individuals, especially given racial profiling and hot-spot policing. Charging and arrest data are decontextualized from the War on Drugs that has driven mass incarceration rates (Western & Wildeman, 2009; Alexander, 2010). Together, these practices disproportionally affect black and marginalized communities and lead to bias in data. When these data become embedded in an algorithm, the resulting probability score is more reflective of select policies than actual criminal behaviour. Consequently, machine learning algorithms purportedly improve prediction accuracy and fairness, but predictors of risk continue to reproduce and magnify markers of inequality and discriminatory practices.

Algorithmic governance and legal considerations of fairness

While the sophisticated mathematical calculations and use of big data analytics provide the allure of objectivity and neutrality, machine learning algorithms reproduce the same problems inherent in earlier risk assessments. As such, it is essential to question how machine learning algorithms may be integrated into criminal justice and how predictive algorithms may conflict with protected rights and criminal law procedure. In legal and criminal justice contexts, the concept of fairness extends beyond mathematical calculations or definitions typically used in computer and statistical science (Kleinberg, Mullainathan & Raghavan, 2017; Gajane & Pechenizkiy, 2018; Verma & Rubin, 2018; Mehrabi et al., 2019). It requires and involves judgements about formal and substantive equality that may conflict with machine learning modelling.

Legal jurisprudence balances formal equality premised on equal treatment with substantive equality, which is predicated on a recognition of the need to treat groups differently to address discrimination, and to ensure equity and equal benefit of the law. Algorithms that use different criteria or modelling for subsets of populations can produce a form of substantive equality. However, in a legal context, differential treatment produces disparity because different criteria are used to assess defendants committing similar offences. Concerns about equal treatment emerge when and if different assessment tools with specific algorithmic sequences that are tailored to group differences are used to predict a common outcome like recidivism. To reduce bias, fairness models may introduce different calculations for subsets of populations to ensure equitable outcomes. In so doing, they fundamentally alter the premise of traditional risk assessments that provided consistent, standardized evaluations of individuals. It is unclear to what extent a different calculus for different minority groups will be accepted in a court of law. Inevitably, machine learning algorithms will need to be reconciled with the legal principles of equality and parity.

A second problem related to formal equality that arises from the use of machine learning refers to the dynamic and adaptive nature of automated predictive models. Some machine learning algorithms operate through a continuous process of feedback and learning from new data, mostly in an unsupervised manner, resulting in perennial unfinished predictive models. In other words, the algorithm updates itself as it learns bias in the data; it does not follow a standard static program. As a result, risk scores for an individual and the variable used in the calculus can change over time as the algorithms detect and adjust for bias. In a legal context, these uncontrolled variations raise questions about equality and the validity of an offender's risk score. If the risk assessment tool produces different scores for similarly situated individuals, or even for the same individual in different moments, to what extent can it be reliably used to make concrete and legitimate decisions about punishment?

The proprietary nature of risk assessments is also problematic. Risk assessment is a million-dollar industry where developers are quick to patent their products and protect them from public scrutiny. Machine learning algorithms increasingly introduce inscrutable 'black boxes' in terms of their complexity and opacity – as well as their propriety ownership. The average person does not know how an algorithm works, and algorithms are increasingly being copyrighted and protected through propriety laws that restrict access to the data and the calculations used to produce a risk assessment. For example, in *Loomis* v. *Wisconsin* (2016), Eric Loomis was sentenced based on the results of the standard COMPAS. His attorneys argued that the use of the software had violated his due process rights because the proprietary rights of the parent company, Northpointe, prevented the disclosure of how the algorithm produced the score. Northpointe successfully argued that COMPAS was a trade secret: it was deemed a proprietary product protected by copyright, and hence there was no obligation to disclose the psychometric properties of the tool or how the risk score was calculated. This precedent-setting case raises questions about how the proprietary right to algorithms can erode the transparency of decisions. If tool developers are protected from disclosing the data points that are used in a model, the measures fairness and trade-offs in accuracy that were selected, and whether subgroups were evaluated equally, courts would not be able to adequately evaluate the risk score. The lack of access to risk assessment calculations undermines the due process rights of those appearing before the law, and it makes it even more challenging to contest discriminatory calculations that become embedded in the tools.

Finally, risk algorithms often conflate correlation with causation. Rather than interpreting a risk score correctly as a mere correlation that predicts the probability of reoffending, legal professionals often misinterpret the score. Risk scores are often assumed to be indices of dangerousness rather than recidivism. This conflation can heavily influence how courts understand an offender's risk and can, thereby, affect the type, length, and conditions attached to a sentence (Cole & Angus, 2002; Bonta, 2005; Hannah-Moffat & Maurutto, 2010). Studies investigating recommendations in pre-sentence reports and how they affect sentences imposed by judges have consistently revealed high concordance rates: 92% in the United States (Norman &

Wadman, 2000); 80% in Canada (Boldt et al., 1983); 78% in England and Wales (Thorpe & Pease, 1976); and 77%–80% in New Zealand (Deane, 2000). Although the specific effects of risk assessment on sentencing are contested, highly nuanced, and challenging to unravel empirically (Tata et al., 2008; Haines & Morgan, 2013), this evidence suggests that risk information provided through sentencing reports or by court and probation officers do influence sentencing and judicial decision-making (Tata, 2010; Wandall, 2010). As mentioned above, some legal professionals interpret higher risk scores as indices of dangerousness, which can result in more stringent conditions and forms of punishment (Hannah-Moffat & Maurutto, 2010). However, risk scores cannot differentiate between types of recidivism: they are not designed to assess between, for example, whether a defendant is likely to breach a probation order or commit an assault. Risk scores are also poor at predicting violent recidivism and have proven to be better predictors of low-level criminal behaviour (Campbell & Gendreay, 2008). Overall, machine learning risk assessments that 'black box' and, thereby, obscure risk calculations can reproduce and magnify the conflation between causation and correlation.

Conclusion

Scholars have identified a movement away from a mode of adjudicative justice and toward a mode of justice that can be called preventive or managerial justice (Ashworth & Zedner, 2014; Kohler-Hausmann, 2014; Tonry, 2019). This shift illustrates how the tension between two duties of the state – the duty to provide security and prevent crime and the 'duty to respect the rights of individuals' (Ashworth & Zedner, 2014: 257) – is increasingly resolved in favour of preventive justice. Some scholars have argued that risk assessments based on machine learning should not be used to predict risk scores, but rather to mitigate risk or respond to risk with support rather than restraint (Barabas et al., 2018; Mayson, 2019). Others have acknowledged that the prevailing context of emotionalism can make the elimination of preventive justice unlikely, and call for the development of mechanisms to guide and limit the use of machine learning algorithms (Tonry, 2019).

Our analysis shows how the recent experimentation with machine learning risk assessments can reproduce the problems and limitations inherent in traditional tools while introducing additional concerns. Firstly, the large datasets used in predictive models further obscure the slippage between causation and correlation. They also produce adverse effects or 'data harms' that disproportionately affect minorities by ignoring errors, proxies for protected attributes, and the political and social meanings disguised in the inferred objectivity. Secondly, machine learning techniques deepen the 'black-box' problem: the opacity, proprietary nature, and fluid characteristics of predictive models that further undermine legal protections. Hence, although machine learning risk assessments promise more accurate and fair predictions by assuming and trying to sanitize bias in the data, this promise is not realized, and different disciplinary norms encumber it.

Moreover, a risk assessment will never be completely bias-free. The data used to inform assessment tools reflect the structural inequality of our societies; data extraction itself can reproduce unfair discrimination patterns, or even inherit unconscious biases from humans involved in data gathering and processing (Barocas & Selbst, 2016; Brayne, 2017). Machine learning frameworks continue to be constrained by models that resist the inclusion of how broader social policies (i.e. availability of health, community, welfare, and housing resources), political and criminal justice priorities (i.e. the war on drugs, stop and frisk) and growing economic inequality inform risk assessments. Machine learning and big data analytics have yet to consider how these realities interact and produce conditions for drawing people into the web of criminal justice and bolster mass incarceration.

However, the techniques offered by fair representation models can go some way to limiting bias in some contexts. Scholars will have to be more precise in separating and defining biases that produce discriminatory outcomes for individuals and groups, as opposed to differential treatment that can enhance equity. Disparate outcomes are not always problematic, and there are instances when like cases ought to be treated differently justifiably. Determining which differences matter and ought to be integrated into algorithms, and under which circumstances, is legally complicated. New developments in fair representation models enable new methods of controlling and weighting variables.

That said, a more cross-disciplinary dialogue is needed between developers, data scientists, analysts, criminologists, and others about the legal, socio-political, and discriminatory effects of algorithms. But even then, we are not guaranteed to insulate predictive recidivism models from bias. Arguably, the prediction of recidivism probabilities will always be fraught with bias given the data and variables used by predictive models. What may be possible is to design algorithms that enhance consistency of decisions by adhering to strictly defined legal criteria, which may, in and of itself, be of limited statistical value in predicting outcomes like recidivism. In such cases, concerns shift from a preoccupation with bias, equity, accuracy and fairness to a consistent application of law or policy. Jurisprudence shows, however, that this approach can also be equally fraught because it does not allow for a consideration of extenuating circumstances.

Perhaps, then, what we are left with are a host of technological innovations in the science of algorithms that cannot be neatly applied to the messy and complicated realities of law and the art of decision-making. There may be only some areas of law wherein such technologies can enable more efficient decisions by processing vast tombs of information about legal choices. If the criminal justice system continues to rely on algorithms to augment decision-making, it will be necessary to proactively engage with the rapidly evolving technological realm and to develop new safeguards and principles to preserve and protect individual rights against the arbitrary nature of risk assessments based on machine learning.

Note

1   Fair representation models do not necessarily rely on artificial intelligence and machine learning, but some data scientists do embed fairer representation models into their machine learning algorithms.

References

Alexander, M. 2010. *The new Jim Crow: Mass incarceration in the age of colorblindness.* New York: New Press.

Andrews, D. 1989. Recidivism is predictable and can be influenced: Using risk assessments to reduce recidivism. *Forum on Corrections Research*, 1: 2–4.

Andrews, D. and J. Bonta. 2010. *The psychology of criminal conduct*, 5th ed. Albany, NY: Lexis Nexis/Anderson Pub.

Angwin, J., J. Larson, S. Mattu, and L. Kirchner. 2016. Machine bias: There's software used across the country to predict future criminals. And it's biased against blacks. *ProPublica.* https://www.propublica.org/article/machine-bias-risk-assessments-in-criminal-sentencing.

Ashworth, A. and L. Zedner. 2014. *Preventive justice*, 1st ed. Oxford Monographs on Criminal Law and Justice. Oxford, United Kingdom: Oxford University Press.

Barabas, C., K. Dinakar, J. Ito, M. Virza and J. Zittrain. 2018. Interventions over predictions: Reframing the ethical debate for actuarial risk assessment. ArXiv:1712.08238 [Cs, Stat], July. http://arxiv.org/abs/1712.08238.

Barocas, S. and A.D. Selbst. 2016. Big data's disparate impact. *California Law Review*, 104 (3): 671-732.

Benjamin, R. 2019. *Race after technology: Abolitionist tools for the new Jim Code.* Medford, MA: Polity.

Berk, R., H. Heidari, S. Jabbari, M. Kearns and A. Roth. 2017. Fairness in criminal justice risk assessments: The state of the art. ArXiv:1703.09207 [Stat], March. http://arxiv.org/abs/1703.09207.

Bhui, H.S. 1999. Race, racism and risk assessment: Linking theory to practice with black mentally disordered offenders. *Probation Journal*, 46 (3): 171–181. https://doi.org/10.1177/026455059904600303.

Boldt, E.D., L.E. Hursh, S.D. Johnson and K.W. Taylor. 1983. Presentence reports and the incarceration of natives. *Canadian Journal of Criminology*, 3: 269–276.

Bonta, J. 1996. Risk-needs assessment and treatment. In *Choosing correctional options that work: Defining the demand and evaluating the supply*, edited by A.T. Harland, 18–32. Thousand Oaks, CA: Sage Publications, Inc.

Bonta, J.L. (Ed.). 2005. *Presentence reports in Canada.* User Report 2005–03. Ottawa: Public Safety and Emergency Preparedness Canada.

Brayne, S. 2017. Big data surveillance: The case of policing. *American Sociological Review*, 82 (5): 977–1008. https://doi.org/10.1177/0003122417725865.

Breiman, L. 2001. Random forests. *Machine Learning*, 45 (1): 5–32. https://doi.org/10.1023/A:1010933404324.

Brennan, T., W. Dieterich and B. Ehret. 2009. Evaluating the predictive validity of the Compas risk and needs assessment system. *Criminal Justice and Behavior*, 36 (1): 21–40. https://doi.org/10.1177/0093854808326545.

Burgess, E.W. 1928. Factors making for success or failure on parole. *Journal of Criminal Law and Criminology*, 19 (2): 239–306.

Campbell, M.A. and P. Gendreay. 2008. *Assessing the utility of risk assessment tools and personality measures in the prediction of violent recidivism for adult offenders.* Ottawa: Public Safety and Emergency Preparedness Canada [i.e. Public Safety Canada]. https://central.bac-lac.gc.ca/.item?id=PS3-1-2007-4E-r&op=pdf&app=Library.

Chouldechova, A. 2016. Fair prediction with disparate impact: A study of bias in recidivism prediction instruments. ArXiv:1610.07524 [Cs, Stat], October. http://arxiv.org/abs/1610.07524.

Cole, D.P. and G. Angus. 2002. Using pre-sentence reports to evaluate and respond to risk articles and addresses. *Criminal Law Quarterly*, 3: 302–364.

Corbett-Davies, S., E. Pierson, A. Feller, S. Goel and A. Huq. 2017. Algorithmic decision making and the cost of fairness. In *Proceedings of the 23rd ACM SIGKDD International Conference on Knowledge Discovery and Data Mining - KDD '17*, 797–806. Halifax, NS, Canada: ACM Press. https://doi.org/10.1145/3097983.3098095.

Courtland, R. 2018. Bias detectives: The researchers striving to make algorithms fair. *Nature*, 558 (7710): 357–360. https://doi.org/10.1038/d41586-018-05469-3.

Deane, H. 2000. The influence of pre-sentence reports on sentencing in a district court in New Zealand. *Australian & New Zealand Journal of Criminology*, 33 (1): 91–106. https://doi.org/10.1177/000486580003300107.

Dwork, C., M. Hardt, T. Pitassi, O. Reingold and R. Zemel. 2011. Fairness through awareness. ArXiv:1104.3913 [Cs], April. http://arxiv.org/abs/1104.3913.

Eubanks, V. 2017. *Automating inequality: How high-tech tools profile, police, and punish the poor*, 1st ed. New York: St. Martin's Press.

Fass, T.L., K. Heilbrun, D. DeMatteo and R. Fretz. 2008. The LSI-R and the Compas: Validation data on two risk-needs tools. *Criminal Justice and Behavior*, 35 (9): 1095–1108. https://doi.org/10.1177/0093854808320497.

Feeley, M. and J. Simon. 1992. The new penology: Notes on the emerging strategy of corrections and its implications. *Criminology*, 30 (4): 449–474. https://doi.org/10.1111/j.1745-9125.1992.tb01112.x.

Feeley, M. and J. Simon. 1994. Actuarial justice: The emerging new criminal law. In *The futures of criminology*, edited by D. Nelken, 173–201. New Delhi: Sage.

Ferguson, A.G. 2017. *The rise of big data policing: Surveillance, race, and the future of law enforcement*. New York: New York University Press.

Gajane, P. and M. Pechenizkiy. 2018. On formalizing fairness in prediction with machine learning. ArXiv:1710.03184 [Cs, Stat], May. http://arxiv.org/abs/1710.03184.

Garrett, B.L. and J. Monahan. 2020. Judging risk. *California Law Review*, 108: 439–493. https://doi.org/10.2139/ssrn.3190403.

Gavazzi, S. M., C.M. Yarcheck, J.M. Sullivan, S.C. Jones and A. Khurana. 2008. Global risk factors and the prediction of recidivism rates in a sample of first-time misdemeanant offenders. *International Journal of Offender Therapy and Comparative Criminology*, 52 (3): 330–345. https://doi.org/10.1177/0306624X07305481.

Greene, D., A.L. Hoffmann and L. Stark. 2019. Better, nicer, clearer, fairer: A critical assessment of the movement for ethical artificial intelligence and machine learning. In *Proceedings of the 52nd Hawaii International Conference on System Sciences*, 2122-2131.

Haines, K. and R. Morgan. 2013. Services before trial and sentence: Achievement, decline and potential. In *Handbook of probation*, edited by L. Gelsthorpe and R. Morgan, 182-209. Cullompton: Willan. https://doi.org/10.4324/9781843926184.ch7.

Hannah-Moffat, K. 2009. Gridlock or mutability: Reconsidering 'gender' and risk assessment. *Criminology & Public Policy*, 8 (1): 209–219. https://doi.org/10.1111/j.1745-9133.2009.00549.x.

Hannah-Moffat, K. 2013. Actuarial sentencing: An 'unsettled' proposition. *Justice Quarterly*, 30 (2): 270–296. https://doi.org/10.1080/07418825.2012.682603.

Hannah-Moffat, K. 2016. A conceptual kaleidoscope: Contemplating 'dynamic structural risk' and an uncoupling of risk from need. *Psychology, Crime & Law*, 22 (1–2): 33–46. https://doi.org/10.1080/1068316X.2015.1114115.

Hannah-Moffat, K. 2019. Algorithmic risk governance: Big data analytics, race and information activism in criminal justice debates. *Theoretical Criminology*, 23 (4): 453–470. https://doi.org/10.1177/1362480618763582.

Hannah-Moffat, K. and P. Maurutto. 2010. Re-contextualizing pre-sentence reports: Risk and race. *Punishment & Society*, 12 (3): 262–286. https://doi.org/10.1177/1462474510369442.

Hannah-Moffat, K., P. Maurutto and S. Turnbull. 2009. Negotiated risk: Actuarial illusions and discretion in probation. *Canadian Journal of Law and Society*, 24 (3): 391–409. https://doi.org/10.1017/S0829320100010097.

Hannah-Moffat, K. and P. O'Malley. 2007. *Gendered risks*. London: Routledge.

Hannah-Moffat, K. and K. Struthers Montford. 2019. Unpacking sentencing algorithms: Risk, racial accountability and data harms. In *Predictive sentencing: Normative and empirical perspectives*, edited by J.W. de Keijser, J.V. Roberts and J. Ryberg, 175–196. Oxford: Hart Publishing. https://doi.org/10.5040/9781509921447.

Harcourt, B.E. 2007. *Against prediction: Profiling, policing, and punishing in an actuarial age*. Chicago, IL: University of Chicago Press.

Harcourt, B.E. 2015. Risk as a proxy for race: The dangers of risk assessment. *Federal Sentencing Reporter*, 27 (4): 237–243. https://doi.org/10.1525/fsr.2015.27.4.237.

Horn, R. and M. Evans. 2000. The effect of gender on pre-sentence reports. *The Howard Journal of Criminal Justice*, 39 (2): 184–197. https://doi.org/10.1111/1468-2311.00161.

Hudson, B. and G. Bramhall. 2005. Assessing the 'other'. *The British Journal of Criminology*, 45 (5): 721–740. https://doi.org/10.1093/bjc/azi002.

Hyatt, J. and S.L. Chanenson. 2016. The use of risk assessment at sentencing: Implications for research and policy. *Villanova Law/Public Policy Research*, no. Paper No. 2017-1040. Available at SSRN: https://ssrn.com/abstract=2961288.

Johndrow, J.E. and K. Lum. 2017. An algorithm for removing sensitive information: Application to race-independent recidivism prediction. ArXiv:1703.04957 [Stat], March. http://arxiv.org/abs/1703.04957.

Kamishima, T., S. Akaho, H. Asoh and J. Sakuma. 2012. Fairness-aware classifier with prejudice remover regularizer. In *Machine learning and knowledge discovery in databases*, edited by P.A. Flach, T. De Bie and N. Cristianini, 35–50. Berlin, Heidelberg: Springer Berlin Heidelberg.

Kemshall, H. 2003. *Understanding Risk in Criminal Justice*. Maidenhead: McGraw-Hill International (UK) Ltd. https://public.ebookcentral.proquest.com/choice/publicfullrecord.aspx?p=290424.

Kleinberg, J., S. Mullainathan and M. Raghavan. 2017. *Inherent trade-offs in the fair determination of risk scores*. Schloss Dagstuhl - Leibniz-Zentrum Fuer Informatik GmbH, Wadern/Saarbruecken, Germany. https://doi.org/10.4230/lipics.itcs.2017.43.

Kohler-Hausmann, I. 2014. Managerial justice and mass misdemeanors. *Stanford Law Review*, 66 (3): 611–693.

Kusner, M.J., J.R. Loftus, C. Russell and R. Silva. 2017. Counterfactual fairness. ArXiv:1703.06856 [Cs, Stat], March. http://arxiv.org/abs/1703.06856.

Madras, D., T. Pitassi and R. Zemel. 2017. *Predict responsibly: Improving fairness and accuracy by learning to defer*. ArXiv:1711.06664 [Cs, Stat], November. http://arxiv.org/abs/1711.06664.

Marks, A., B. Bowling and C. Keenan. 2017. Automatic justice? Technology, crime, and social control. In *The Oxford handbook of law, regulation and technology*, edited by R. Brownsword, E. Scotford and K. Yeung, Vol. 1. Oxford: Oxford University Press. https://doi.org/10.1093/oxfordhb/9780199680832.013.32.

Maurutto, P. and K. Hannah-Moffat. 2006. Assembling risk and the restructuring of penal control. *The British Journal of Criminology*, 46 (3): 438–454.

Mayson, S.G. 2019. Bias in, bias out. *Yale Law Journal*, 128: 2218.

Mehrabi, N., F. Morstatter, N. Saxena, K. Lerman and A. Galstyan. 2019. A survey on bias and fairness in machine learning. ArXiv:1908.09635 [Cs], September. http://arxiv.org/abs/1908.09635.

Motiuk, L. 1997a. *Classification for correctional programming: The Offender Intake Assessment (OIA) process.* In, 9:18–22. CORRECTIONAL SERVICE OF CANADA.

Motiuk, L. 1997b. *The Community Risk/Needs Management Scale: An Effective Supervision Tool.* In, 9:8–12. CORRECTIONAL SERVICE OF CANADA.

Motiuk, L. 1998. Using dynamic factors to better predict post-release outcome. *Forum on Corrections Research,* 10 (3): 12–15.

Noble, S.U. 2018. *Algorithms of oppression: How search engines reinforce racism.* New York: New York University Press.

Norman, M.D. and R.C.Wadman. 2000. Utah presentence investigation reports: User group perceptions of quality and effectiveness. *Federal Probation,* 1: 7–12.

O'Malley, P. 2004. The uncertain promise of risk. *Australian & New Zealand Journal of Criminology,* 37 (3): 323–343. https://doi.org/10.1375/acri.37.3.323.

O'Malley, P. 2010a. *Crime and risk.* London: SAGE.

O'Malley, P. 2010b. Simulated justice: Risk, money and telemetric policing. *British Journal of Criminology,* 50 (5): 795–807. https://doi.org/10.1093/bjc/azq036.

O'Neil, C. 2016. *Weapons of math destruction: How big data increases inequality and threatens democracy.* London: Allen Lane, Penguin Books.

Pasquale, F. 2015. *The black box society: The secret algorithms that control money and information.* Cambridge: Harvard University Press.

Pridemore, W.A. 2004. Review of the literature on risk and protective factors of offending among Native Americans. *Journal of Ethnicity in Criminal Justice,* 2 (4): 45–63. https://doi.org/10.1300/J222v02n04_03.

Shaw, M. and K. Hannah-Moffat. 2000. Gender, diversity and risk assessment in Canadian corrections. *Probation Journal,* 47 (3): 163–172. https://doi.org/10.1177/026455050004700301.

State v. Loomis. 2016. Supreme Court of Wisconsin.

Tata, C., N. Burns, S. Halliday, N. Hutton and F. McNeill. 2008. Assisting and advising the sentencing decision process: The pursuit of 'quality' in pre-sentence reports. *British Journal of Criminology,* 48 (6): 835–855. https://doi.org/10.1093/bjc/azn055.

Tata, C. 2010. A sense of justice: The role of pre-sentence reports in the production (and disruption) of guilt and guilty pleas. *Punishment & Society,* 12 (3): 239–261. https://doi.org/10.1177/1462474510371734.

Taxman, F.S. and A. Dezember. 2016. The value and importance of risk and need assessment (RNA) in corrections & centencing. In *Handbook on risk and need assessment: Theory and practice,* edited by F.S.Taxman. The ASC Division on Corrections & Sentencing Handbook Series, volume 1. New York: Routledge, Taylor & Francis Group.

Thorpe, J. and K. Pease. 1976. The relationship between recommendations made to the court and sentences passed. *The British Journal of Criminology,* 16 (4): 393–394. https://doi.org/10.1093/oxfordjournals.bjc.a046771.

Tonry, M. 2019. Predictions of dangerousness in sentencing: Déjà vu all over again. *Crime and Justice,* 48: 439–482. https://doi.org/10.1086/701895.

Van Eijk, G. 2017. Socioeconomic marginality in sentencing: The built-in bias in risk assessment tools and the reproduction of social inequality. *Punishment & Society,* 19 (4): 463–481. https://doi.org/10.1177/1462474516666282.

Verma, S. and J. Rubin. 2018. Fairness definitions explained. In *Proceedings of the International Workshop on Software Fairness - FairWare '18,* 1–7. Gothenburg, Sweden: ACM Press. https://doi.org/10.1145/3194770.3194776.

Vose, B., F. Cullen and P. Smith. 2008. The empirical status of the level of service inventory. *Federal Probation,* 72: 22–29.

Wadsworth, C., F. Vera and C. Piech. 2018. Achieving fairness through adversarial learning: an application to recidivism prediction. ArXiv:1807.00199 [Cs, Stat], June. http://arxiv.org/abs/1807.00199.

Wandall, R.H. 2010. Resisting risk assessment? Pre-sentence reports and individualized sentencing in Denmark. *Punishment & Society*, 12 (3): 329–347. https://doi.org/10.1177/1462474510369446.

Western, B. and C. Wildeman. 2009. The black family and mass incarceration. *The ANNALS of the American Academy of Political and Social Science*, 621 (1): 221–242. https://doi.org/10.1177/0002716208324850.

Završnik, A. 2019. Algorithmic justice: Algorithms and big data in criminal justice settings. *European Journal of Criminology*, September. https://doi.org/10.1177/1477370819876762.

Zemel, R., Y. Wu, K. Swersky, T. Pitassi and C. Dwork. 2013. Learning fair representations. In *Proceedings of the 30th international conference on machine learning*, edited by S. Dasgupta and D. McAllester, 28: 325–333. Atlanta, Georgia, USA: PMLR.

Chapter 7

Rethinking predictive policing

Towards a holistic framework of democratic algorithmic surveillance

Rosamunde van Brakel

Introduction

Digital transformations have led to an increase of the use by police of what criminologist Clive Norris (1995) has called 'algorithmic surveillance'. The first examples of algorithmic surveillance can be found in the 1990s, when CCTV systems were coupled to computer software, which allowed the images to be converted into numerical data and analysed by complex algorithms (Norris, 1995). More specifically, it refers to 'surveillance technologies that make use of computer systems to provide more than the raw data observed. This can range from systems that classify and store simple data, through more complex systems that compare the captured data to other data and provide matches, to systems that attempt to predict events based on the captured data' (Introna & Wood, 2004: 181). In the last decade, the use of algorithmic surveillance for policing has expanded exponentially as the result of developments in big data and machine learning algorithms (Van Brakel, 2016; Bennett Moses & Chan, 2016; Ferguson, 2017; Brayne, 2017; Peeters & Schuilenburg, 2018). These technological developments have accompanied broader societal trends in policing, such as the commodification and pluralisation of policing, intelligence-led and pre-emptive policing, and platform policing (Loader, 1994, 1999; Jones & Newburn, 1998, Garland, 2001; Van Brakel & De Hert, 2011; Wilson, 2019).

These socio-technical transformations are affecting the way in which algorithmic surveillance is constructed with profound implications for democracy. Surveillance is often characterised as being undemocratic, as it opens up people to examination and control, while constraining individual autonomy, and generally relies on opacity not transparency. Further, as closed systems they resist opportunities for democratic participation in how they are designed, used, critiqued and regulated (Monahan, 2010). However, as sociologist David Lyon (2001) and others have stressed, surveillance has two faces – care and control. These ideas stem forth from a new ethics that asks 'what might happen if surveillance were guided by an ontology of peace rather than of violence, an ethic of care rather than control, an orientation to forgiveness rather than to suspicion' (Lyon, 2001: 153). It is not always clear which of the two faces is behind the actions of the surveyors, nor can the motivations between care and control always be separated. This is the reason why by only focusing on the coercive and disempowering effects of surveillance, there is a danger of ignoring the agency and reflexivity of the subjects of surveillance as well as the variable ways in which power and participation are constructed and enacted (Martin, Van Brakel & Bernhard, 2009; Couldry & Powell, 2014).

New algorithmic surveillance systems such as predictive policing are reshaping policing practices and criminal justice in general (Peeters & Schuilenburg, 2018). However, the question arises: Are they reshaping them in a democratic way? This leads to a question that this chapter attempts to answer: Can algorithmic surveillance become democratic and what would be the conditions to achieve this? Drawing on literature on democratic technology and surveillance, positive criminology and democratic policing, the main goal of this chapter is to explore if predictive policing, which is a prime example of algorithmic surveillance, can be rethought and reconfigured as democratic surveillance. This implies a shift in thinking towards concepts of participation, empowerment, care, compassion, co-creation, belonging, trust and social justice. I will explore the extent to which, and the ways in which, democracy, as a core priority for policing, potentially can reconfigure the very purpose of predictive policing.

The chapter is structured as follows. In the first part of the chapter, I begin with analysing what has already been written about democratic surveillance and the interplay between surveillance and democracy. In the second part, I will discuss predictive policing, how it is currently implemented and the social, ethical and cultural costs that accompany it. In the final part, I will explore in what way predictive policing and the discourses and rationalities that characterise it can be rethought and reconfigured in a democratic way.

Democratic algorithmic surveillance

The starting point for this analysis is the presupposition that algorithmic surveillance should be considered as a social structure, just like laws, dominant political and economic institutions, and systems of cultural belief. Social structure 'refers to the background features that help define or regulate patterns of human interaction' (Sclove, 1995: 11). Social structures are ambiguous and restrict opportunities in some respects, but enhance them in others if appropriately designed and implemented (Sclove, 1995). Algorithmic surveillance technologies have become so much embedded and normalised in society that they affect every member of society and are part of everyday life. Algorithmic surveillance as social structure can play transformative roles in influencing social, symbolic and cultural experiences in both empowering and disempowering ways. Technology is not deterministic and there is always a certain extent of flexibility in how existing technological artefacts may be used or operated and for what purpose (Sclove, 1995). Therefore, it is possible, both before and after implementation, to imagine alternative intentions, designs and applications. The process by which one set of designs rather than another comes into being is influenced by prevailing social structures and forces, including the pre-existing technological order. However, this process also reflects explicit or tacit social choices, including political negotiations or struggles. After a society has habituated itself to a technology, alternatives tend to become less accessible and thought of (Sclove, 1995). Considering algorithmic surveillance as social structure allows one to imagine what democratic algorithmic surveillance could look like.

How does surveillance relate to democracy? Often democracy is seen as the opposite of surveillance. Ball, Bellanova and Webster (2019) show how surveillance and democracy enact each other's limits in a number of ways. First, surveillance practices can compromise democratic rights: the sifting and sorting of populations inherent in surveillance practices can endanger rights, opportunities and life chances because of their distributive justice consequences. Surveillance practices can distribute access to resources throughout the population, but the decision criteria driving these distributions – particularly if they are automated – are opaque and difficult to challenge (Haggerty & Samatas, 2010). Second, surveillance practices can simultaneously underpin and undermine democratic processes. They may help target welfare at the neediest, facilitate democratic participation through voting and distribute public resources efficiently. Nevertheless, surveillance may also erode the institutional trust required for democratic governance. Fear of having one's opinions, movements or activities monitored can suppress debate within targeted groups. Third, surveillance also affects the nature of participation in different spheres of life, liberating some and constraining others. For instance, automatic number plate recognition (ANPR) delimits the mobility of those associated with a suspicious vehicle or who are recorded as being of interest to a police investigation (Ball, Bellanova & Webster, 2019).

The above analysis suggests that surveillance and democracy are not inherently opposed to each other. Considering algorithmic surveillance as a social structure and considering surveillance can be both about care and control opens up avenues to think about alternative surveillance futures. Starting from an ethics of care, could democratic surveillance be possible? Torin Monahan argues that social scientists may be doing a disservice to progressive social change when surveillance is equated with only disempowerment or oppression: 'If surveillance systems are to be designed and regulated as locally based and local accountability mechanisms, small-scale, open-ended, transparent and participatory systems they will be inherently more democratic and less prone to abuse' (Monahan, 2010: 101).

Although there are many structural issues to organise democratic surveillance, Monahan (2010) proposes some concrete possibilities. Accordingly, the most democratic and socially empowering designs are those that work to correct power asymmetries. These are designs that explicitly intend to include social groups that have been historically marginalised or discriminated against. He gives the example of Scorecard.org:

> This site serves as clearing house for information about releases of toxic chemicals and other contaminants in local neighbourhoods. It synthesizes 'toxic release inventory data' data compiled by the United States federal government, along with maps of 'superfund sites', lists of likely polluters in one's neighbourhood, comparisons with pollution in other cities, and action items for

direct public involvement. It is a surveillance system in the sense that it manipulates data for purposes of control, meaning, ideally, the policing of potential and actual industrial polluters and the clean-up of toxic materials in one's community. While this is not a completely transparent, open, or participatory form of surveillance, it is democratic in that it invites participation, fosters learning, and affords a degree of power equalization among local communities and institutions, be they industry or government.

(Monahan, 2010: 103)

A more convincing example of democratic surveillance is the radical citizen science project 'Science for Change Kosovo'. The project is an attempt to address environmental concerns in one of the most polluted regions in Europe through 'citizen science' – involving young people and ordinary citizens in the monitoring of air pollution in their local communities. The approach of this project draws on critical pedagogies like that of 1960s educator Paulo Freire, for whom learning was the co-operative activity of understanding how our lived experience is constructed, and how to make a difference in the world (McQuillan, 2014):

At the time, local young technologists, students, and community members from around Kosovo joined environmental advocates, journalists, representatives from Kosovo's local and central institutions and international experts in the citizen science movement – 'Science for Change' – to co-create and collaboratively implement an air quality monitoring project and policy advocacy campaign for three sites around Kosovo (Prishtina, Drenas and Plemetina). Using digital (Smart Citizen Kits) and non-digital technologies (diffusion tubes, ghost wipes, etc.), the youth-led action groups discovered high levels of NO2 in several parts of Prishtina.[1]

It is a surveillance system in the sense that it uses surveillance technology to monitor pollution with the purpose of influencing policy and policymakers. What is interesting about this project is that it tries to avoid the attribution of agency to data, or an assumption that participation is the same as empowerment. Many data and open data projects seem to assume that action will inevitably flow from aggregating data and visualising transparency and that participation of communities in gathering data will increase people's sense of responsibility and lead to the generation of solutions. But, as Dan McQuillan (2014) argues, the idea that collective measurement leads to collective action seems questionable.

According to Richard Sclove (1995), to envision democratic technology requires taking the concept of 'strong democracy' suggested by political theorist Benjamin Barber as starting point. This theory claims that, as a matter of justice, people should be able to influence the basic social circumstances of their lives. This implies organising society along relatively egalitarian and participatory lines and subordinating managerialism and neoliberalism to democratic prerogatives. Only then can surveillance begin to actively support, rather than coerce or constrict people's chosen ways of life (Sclove, 1995). Similar ideas can be found in philosopher John Dewey's

(1916) model of democracy. Dewey understood democracy as more than a form of government. He saw it as a way of life and as a social idea:

> [E]ach individual shall have the opportunity for release, expression, fulfilment, of his distinctive capacities, and that the outcome shall further the establishment of a fund of shared values. Like every true ideal, it signifies something to be done rather than something already given, something ready-made.
>
> (Dewey, 1916: 91)

For surveillance to be democratic it requires constant public vigilance and engagement and it needs to contribute to shared values and a faith in social justice. This approach implies intentionally harnessing the control functions of surveillance for social ends of justice and equity; involves reprogramming socio-technical codes to encourage transparency, openness, participation and accountability; and has the objective to produce new systems and new configurations of experts and users, subjects and objects, which requires a set of protocols or criteria against which to measure social value (Monahan, 2010). This is in contrast with the managerialist efficiency logic of government and markets that characterises most surveillance technologies. What becomes clear from approaching surveillance as social structure and democracy as social idea is that for algorithmic surveillance to become democratic it requires a holistic socio-technical approach.

Predictive policing

Predictive policing is an increasingly popular policing strategy and will be used here as a case study to explore if democratic algorithmic surveillance is possible. Predictive policing is a strategy that can be situated in a broader pre-emptive policing model. Pre-emptive policing is specifically geared to gather knowledge about what will happen in the future with the goal to intervene before it is too late (Van Brakel & De Hert, 2011). Pre-emptive policing can be data-driven, just like with predictive policing, but also analogue, as with pre-emptive arrests or 'Behaviour Detection Officers' at airports (Van Brakel & De Hert, 2011; Lawrence, 2016; Van Brakel, 2020). Predictive policing relies on the idea that crime is predictable and that societal phenomena are, in one way or another, statistically and algorithmically calculable (Egbert & Krasmann, 2019). In the context of this chapter, I understand predictive policing as a policing strategy that uses algorithmic surveillance to predict future crimes, criminals and victims to intervene before crimes occur. Considering algorithmic surveillance as social structure, this also implies that predictive policing cannot be seen as independent from its sociotechnical embeddedness.

A distinction can be made between two types of predictive policing: predictive mapping and predictive identification (Van Brakel, 2016). The most commonly used type is predictive mapping. This refers to advanced geospatial analyses to predict when and/or where a crime may take place at an aggregate level of analysis. Since the 1990s, theories of situational crime prevention led to the development of hot-spot analysis and later to prospective hot-spot analysis. What is new about predictive mapping is the use of big data and predictive analytics (Van Brakel, 2016). Predictions are made by an algorithm that analyses different types of aggregated, often anonymised, data. The majority of these applications are geared to predict in which neighbourhoods a burglary is more likely to take place. Illustrations of this type of predictive policing software include, but are not limited to, PredPol in the United States and the United Kingdom (Kentonline, 2013; PredPol, 2020), Criminality Awareness System (CAS) in the Netherlands (Willems & Doeleman, 2014), Precobs in Germany and Switzerland (Egbert & Krasmann, 2019), Keycrime in Milan, Italy (Mastrobuoni, 2014) and POL-INTEL in Denmark (Jansen, 2018).

The second type of predictive policing is predictive identification, where the analysis is at the individual or group level and personal data is processed; this can focus on predicting potential offenders, offenders' identities, criminal behaviour, and potential victims of crime. In practice, applications have focused on prediction of recidivism. The United Kingdom has been a forerunner of experimenting with these types of technologies. Again, these technologies build upon a long history of using risk assessments in criminal justice settings (Van Eijk, 2017). The difference is that the risk profiles are now generated from data instead of coming from scientific research (Van Brakel, 2018). Examples here are the COMPAS system in the US (Angwin et al., 2016), Metropolitan Police London & Accenture Gangmatrix used in the United Kingdom (Jansen, 2018), Durham Constabulary's Harm Assessment Risk Tool (HART) used in the United Kingdom (Oswald et al., 2018) and PROKID used in the Netherlands (Wientjes et al., 2017).

Evaluations of the effectiveness of predictive policing in preventing crime have, so far, been inconclusive (Hunt, Saunders & Hollywood, 2014; Lum & Isaac, 2016; Van Brakel, 2016; Mali, Bronkhorst-Giesen & Den Hengst, 2017; Santos, 2019; Egbert & Krasmann, 2019; Wientjes et al., 2017). For instance, an evaluation of a predictive policing application by the West Midlands Police in the United Kingdom concluded that the system was so unreliable and full of bias that it would be irresponsible to implement it (Marsch, 2019). Apart from inconclusive evaluations, several police forces have also stopped using the software. The use of PredPol by Kent Police was discontinued in 2019 and the German police forces of Karlsruhe and Stuttgart decided to stop using PRECOBS software because there was insufficient crime data to make reliable predictions (Mayer, 2019).

What is becoming increasingly clear is that the benefits of predictive policing are focused more on making bureaucratic systems more efficient than on preventing crime. These technologies are, just like analogue measurements, scores and scales, a way to standardise and enhance the objectivity of the professional claim, and to increase its capacity for transparency and oversight to increase trust and legitimacy. When something goes wrong, it is easier to establish why, how and/or by whom. By entering information into standardised forms, work becomes more transparent and predictable and classification and processing of data becomes easier (Van Brakel, 2018).

There is increasing evidence that predictive policing applications entail social and ethical costs that go beyond privacy; they are discriminatory for vulnerable groups in society (Van Brakel, 2016; Lum & Isaac, 2016; Ferguson, 2017; Williams & Kind, 2019; Richardson, Schultz & Crawford, 2019). In the United Kingdom, the country where predictive applications are the most widespread in Europe, a recent study concluded that national guidance is urgently needed to oversee the police's use of data-driven technology amid concerns it could lead to discrimination (Babuta & Oswald, 2020). Moreover, these technologies are often piloted and implemented without the necessary safeguards and without conducting any form of impact assessment, even though this is now required under the EU law enforcement directive.[2]

When considering predictive policing as a social structure it becomes clear that surveillance technologies do not just involve social and ethical costs, they also constitute policing to a certain extent and involve cultural costs. They contribute to defining policing practices and the role of police officers, what they can and cannot do. Predictive policing technologies shape policing in the sense of what sociologist Nikolas Rose (1998) has called 'governing at a distance' whereby 'professional conduct is reshaped through the imperative to undertake the interminable tasks of inscription – information systems, registers, documentation and the like that are intrinsic to these new risk-based technologies' (Rose, 1998: 190). By using measures and scales, the gaze of the police officer becomes increasingly standardised and turned into a uniform instrument of measurement. As such, algorithmic surveillance does not merely have social effects, but also plays a role in changing power relations within policing practices.

First, police officers find themselves cast in a 'subordinate role while managerial policy formation is allowed to develop into a completely autonomous force totally beyond the surveillance of the operative on the ground, who is now reduced to a mere executant' (Castel, 1991: 281). The police officer used to have a certain discretion in decision-making, but now this agency is reduced by an algorithm. Even though it is legally required to have a 'human in-the-loop',[3] there is a risk of automation bias, whereby practitioners tend to trust decisions made by automated systems over their own judgements (Skitka, Mosier & Burdick, 1999).

Second, software companies increasingly wield power over police work and culture. Managerialism and commodification already influenced the police in the 1990s (see, for instance, Loader, 1994, 1999 for the United Kingdom). However, societal developments over the last decade and the growth in power of technology companies have changed the landscape even more. In the political economy of informational capitalism (Cohen, 2019) or platform capitalism (Srinicek, 2017), platforms have become the key drivers of the datafication of society. This has also led to 'platform policing' which can be described as the techno-organisational domestic security configurations that have been emerging since 2008, whereby private enterprises enter into legal supply and maintenance agreements with police agencies; and the data capture and processing by police feeds into larger cloud infrastructures and data markets (Wilson, 2019). In other words, police forces are increasingly dependent on these enterprises through the software they provide. Predictive policing software such as PredPol has a vendor lock-in, meaning that the police cannot tweak the software themselves and that they are reliant on the companies for any adjustments (Van Brakel, 2016). Not only is there increased dependence, police are also becoming an active contributor to informational capitalism through the use of predictive policing platforms that provide data to the enterprises. This has implications for transparency, accountability and the extent to which the police themselves are an active participant in developing policing strategies. Finally, the use of the software is not only changing policing itself but, in some cases, even regulation. For instance, in Denmark the law was changed to allow the use of Palantir's POL-INTEL (EDRI, 2017).

Third, choices regarding the use of technology are also shaped by specific police cultures and the cultural and gendered identities that characterise them. For instance, as Bethan Loftus (2008) shows, resistance and resentment to the police in the United Kingdom has sustained an increasingly endangered culture within police forces. This dominant culture, which is especially over-represented in the higher ranks of the police, resists diversity in the police force and will be less favourable to using technology in a more caring and empowering way and will be less attentive to discriminatory outcomes of technology.

When police forces invest in and acquire predictive policing technologies, they are often only minimally aware of the demands that effective operation will impose as well as of the eventual financial, environmental, emotional, societal and cultural costs. The expertise to be aware of all these costs of algorithmic surveillance technologies is often not present within the police services, nor in police oversight bodies. In conclusion, the lack of evidence that predictive policing helps to prevent crime and the numerous social, ethical and cultural costs in combination with a lack of transparency, accountability, oversight and safeguards raise questions regarding the democratic nature of contemporary algorithmic surveillance.

Rethinking predictive policing as democratic algorithmic surveillance

Taking strong democracy as a starting point and considering the conclusions about the costs of predictive policing, predictive policing can be seen as undemocratic in four ways. First, predictive policing is disempowering police officers on the ground and impacts police discretion. Power and agency are shifting towards algorithms and companies who develop them. Second, the intentions and outcomes of predictive policing practices are about cost-efficiency and management and do not focus on social justice, equity, empowerment and care. Third, decisions about investing in surveillance technologies are often made top-down, being 'spur of the moment' or 'just in case' policies without public scrutiny or participation by citizens and police officers on the ground. There is little accountability for decision-making. Fourth, the design of predictive policing is often the prerogative of software companies. Police officers and the communities targeted by the technologies are generally not involved in the design process.[4]

To rethink and reconfigure predictive policing as democratic algorithmic surveillance it will be necessary to address these four problems. This requires a new way of thinking about policing and criminal justice using a holistic socio-technical framework of 'close governance' through care, empathy, empowerment, trust and equity in contrast to 'governance at a distance' (Rose, 1998) that considers the socio-technical embeddedness of algorithmic surveillance technologies. It is inspired by concepts from positive criminology such as participation, care, belonging and trust, and takes into account human connectedness and local capacity building in contrast to more punitive and disciplinary approaches to crime prevention (Schuilenburg, Van Steden & Oude Breuil, 2014; Haines & Case, 2015). In this spirit, crime prevention policies should be shaped from the bottom up and match community needs with police needs. Police should consider positive and caring alternatives to empower communities and individuals and to remove conditions that tempt people into crime. This implies a focus on long-term policies that will have a lasting effect, instead of symbolic policing (Garland, 2001; Coomber, Moyle & Mahoney, 2019).

What follows below is an attempt to rethink predictive policing from this holistic perspective. It is not meant to be exhaustive but, instead, to explore a new democratic way of thinking about predictive policing and algorithmic surveillance in general. The framework distinguishes between four socio-technical levels of analysis: police practices, intentions and outcomes, policy and oversight, and design. These levels are overlapping and interrelated and cannot be seen apart from each other. An approach to democratic algorithmic surveillance needs to address them as a whole.

Police practice

To make police practice more democratic and empowering it is necessary to take seriously the concerns and impacts of technologies on police officers' work and discretion. Moreover, it calls for a new police professionalism that expresses the values of participation, care, compassion and empathy in their work, at both management and street levels. For instance, initiatives in community policing are showing positive results such as a 'guardian policing' project in New York which has managed to overcome bias and replace the 'spiral of despair' in poor neighbourhoods with opportunity and justice. Its vision of a new approach to policing relies on community or neighbourhood policing as a fundamental building block, whereby, for instance, officers are not promoted for making arrests, but for demonstrating how they diverted a child from prison and increased trust in the community (Beck & Rice, 2016). According to Peter Neyround (2017), these findings are a key starting point for a new police professionalism. Such a new police professionalism also implies rethinking police training, how the police are managed and on which basis police officers are recruited. It implies rethinking current police cultures and police models such as pre-emptive policing.

Intentions and outcomes

Most predictive policing applications address crime prevention in a repressive manner, i.e. the focus is not on trying to do something about the causes of crime but on trying to apprehend offenders in a more efficient way. The intentions and outcomes are no longer about preventing crime but focus instead on cost-efficiency and better management strategies. Intentions and outcomes need to be democratic and set out in dialogue with the targeted communities. An example here is the CinCity project, which is focused on knife crime in London and the loss of trust in the police among young people. Using the Mental Model Approach, the project explores the underlying assumptions and perspectives that shape young people's and police officials' perceptions of knife crime, safety and trust in policing with the goal to identify gaps, misconceptions, needs and directions for tangible solutions. The ambition is to help re-establish trust in policing, while simultaneously empowering London youth.[5] This is not a project that originated with the police. However, the police could be involved in co-organising such projects in the future. In conclusion, predictive policing as democratic algorithmic surveillance should rethink its intentions to align with a more empowering and caring view on public safety.

Policy and oversight

Governance of the police use of algorithmic surveillance is generally through *ex post* oversight and judicial review, which at best ensures policing practices are lawful. However, this often does little to assure democratic accountability or sound policymaking (Friedman & Ponomarenko, 2015; Van Brakel, 2020). As John Dewey already observed in the first half of the twentieth century: 'merely legal guarantees of the civil liberties of free belief, free expression, free assembly are of little avail if in daily life freedom of communication, the give and take of ideas, facts, experiences, is choked by mutual suspicion, by abuse, by fear and hatred' (Dewey, 1939).

Officers on the ground and the affected communities need to be actively involved in the governance of police use of algorithmic surveillance. Interdisciplinary local *ex ante* oversight commissions across different sectors including elected representatives of the police, social services, industry, civil society and the public should be established in order to create accountable and democratic technologies and police cultures. These new coalitions of engagement would have to focus on making sure policy measures take a long-term perspective in contrast to the opportunist and neoliberal drivers that currently characterise policy decisions. Following Ian Loader's (1994) ideas of police accountability, local oversight commissions should be complemented with regional and/or national police commissions to avoid concentrating all power at any one level of government. The police commission shall at all times

1   Elicit and take account of the views of all individuals and social groups likely to be affected by the relevant decision;
2   Arrive at the decision that secures the broadest level of public consent without (a) prejudicing the fundamental active rights of any affected individual or social group, or (b) being disproportionately detrimental to the other interest and aspirations of such individuals and groups, in such a way as might prejudice the future operation of decision-making processes (Loader, 1994: 533).

Design

As indicated above, democratic surveillance should be designed in such a way that it corrects power asymmetries in societies by including social groups that have historically been marginalised and discriminated (Monahan, 2010). Hence, the design process of democratic predictive policing should be participatory and involve all parties, both police and the affected communities in co-creation with the company that develops the technology. This implies they should all be engaged in diagnosing the problems before the design of the technology takes place. As has been shown in relation to electronic health technologies, disregard for the interdependencies between technology, human characteristics, and the socioeconomic environment lead to technology use that has a low impact on health care practices (Van Gemert-Pijnen et al., 2011). Making the design of predictive policing democratic also implies sufficient attention for building in robust legal, ethical, technical and social justice safeguards from the beginning, with clear evaluation criteria. And it implies a robust democratic policy underpinned by accountable scientific evidence about effectiveness. Charles Manski and Daniel Nagin (2017) show how measuring police effectiveness always requires balancing the effectiveness with the costs. They advocate a scientific approach to finding the right balance between proactive policing and community trust. It is important to underscore that discussions about effectiveness and evidence-based policy are tricky as it is often unclear if the evaluations themselves are reliable and valid. As long as the methodological design behind these technologies is not critically discussed during an evaluation and no quality standards exist for these evaluations (see Farrington, 2003), their results will be of little value (Van Brakel, 2015). Similar questions need to be asked about the use of statistical methods in predictive policing models and their evaluations. A way to counter some of the problems is by involving all relevant parties in the creation of the evaluation criteria.

Conclusion

The main goal of this chapter was to explore if it is possible to rethink predictive policing as democratic algorithmic surveillance. In the first section of this chapter, it was argued that it is necessary to consider surveillance as a social structure and democracy as a social idea in order to develop a conceptualisation of democratic algorithmic. In the second part, contemporary predictive policing practices were analysed as an example of algorithmic surveillance practices. The lack of evidence regarding predictive policing's efficiency in preventing crime and the numerous social, ethical and cultural costs in combination with lack of transparency, accountability, oversight and safeguards raise questions about its democratic nature. In the third part of this chapter, I explored how predictive policing can be rethought and reconfigured as democratic surveillance using a holistic sociotechnical framework that encompasses four levels of analysis: police practices, intentions and outcomes, policy and oversight, and design.

I have argued that it is possible to rethink ways in which predictive policing can be implemented as democratic algorithmic surveillance. However, it is important to take into account how socially embedded both surveillance and democracy are. The development of democratic algorithmic surveillance must, therefore, be approached in a socio-technical and participatory way. There are a number of structural problems that hinder this pursuit. Apart from platform capitalism being dominant, the current political climate in many countries and the increased power of technology companies will make this endeavour for democratic algorithmic surveillance difficult. In addition, it is important to situate the problem of democracy within policing in a broader framework that is concerned with the structural limits of policing and police reform (Loader, 1994). Finally, there should always be caution when using surveillance and monitoring. Surveillance as social structure always has the potential to coerce and disempower. There is a risk that democratic surveillance paradoxically disempowers rather than empowers if citizens merely participate by sitting in councils and generating data, while the real policy decisions are made elsewhere. This does not mean this endeavour is in vain. It challenges us to do more research together with police, civil society and affected communities to explore best practices of empowering and democratic surveillance technologies.

Notes

1   Embassy of the Czech Republic in Pristina (2015) https://www.mzv.cz/pristina/en/bilateral_and_multilateral_relations/science_for_change_how_kosovo_s_young.html.
2   Directive (EU) 2016/680 of the European Parliament and of the Council of 27 April 2016 on the protection of natural persons with regard to the processing of personal data by competent authorities for the purposes of the prevention, investigation, detection or prosecution of criminal offences or the execution of criminal penalties, and on the free movement of such data, and repealing Council Framework Decision 2008/977/JHA.
3   Directive (EU) 2016/680
4   An exception here is the CAS system that was developed by the police of Amsterdam itself.
5   https://uclexcites.blog/2020/02/05/civic-innovation-in-community-safety-policing-and-trust-with-young-people/.

References

Angwin, J., J. Larson, S. Mattu et al. 2016. Machine bias: There's software used across the country to predict future criminals. And it's biased against blacks. *ProPublica*, 23 May, https://www.propublica.org/article/machine-bias-risk-assessments-in-criminal-sentencing.

Babuta, A. and M. Oswald. 2020. *Data analytics and algorithms in policing in England and Wales: Towards a new policy framework*, Royal United Services Institute for Defence and Security Studies, https://rusi.org/sites/default/files/rusi_pub_165_2020_01_algorithmic_policing_babuta_final_web_copy.pdf.

Ball, K., R. Bellanova and W. Webster. 2019. Surveillance and democracy: Sympathies and antagonisms. In *Surveillance and democracy in Europe*, edited by K. Ball and W. Webster. London: Routledge.

Beck, C. and C. Rice. 2016. How community policing can work. Opinion. *The New York Times*, 12 August 2016, https://www.nytimes.com/2016/08/12/opinion/how-community-policing-can-work.html.

Bennett Moses, L. and J. Chan. 2016. Algorithmic prediction in policing: Assumptions, evaluation, and accountability. *Policing & Society*, 28 (7): 806–822.

Brayne, S. 2017. Big data surveillance: The case of policing. *American Sociological Review*, 82 (5): 977–1008.

Castel, R. 1991. From dangerousness to risk. In *The Foucault effect: Studies in governmentality*, edited by G. Burchell, C. Gordon and P. Miller, 281–298. Chicago: Chicago University Press.

Coomber, R., L. Moyle and M. Knox Mahoney. 2019. Symbolic policing: situating targeted police operations/'crackdowns' on street-level drug markets. *Policing & Society*, 29 (1): 1–17.

Cohen, J. 2019. *Between truth and power: The legal constructions of informational capitalism, the legal constructions of informational capitalism*. Oxford: Oxford University Press.

Couldry, N. and A. Powell. 2014. Big data from the bottom-up. *Big Data and Society*, July–September: 1–5.

Dewey, J. 1916. *Democracy and education: An introduction to the philosophy of education*. New York: MacMillan.

Dewey, J. 1976 [1939]. Creative democracy: The task before us. In *John Dewey: The later works, 1925–1953*, Vol. 14, edited by J. Boydston, 224–230. Carbondale: Southern Illinois University Press, http://chipbruce.files.wordpress.com/2008/11/dewey_creative_dem.pdf.

EDRI. 2017. New legal framework for predictive policing in Denmark, https://edri.org/new-legal-framework-for-predictive-policing-in-denmark/.

Egbert, S. and S. Krasmann. 2019. Predictive policing: Not yet, but soon preemptive? *Policing and Society*, doi:10.1080/10439463.2019.1611821.

Farrington, D. 2003. Methodological quality standards for evaluation research. *The Annals of the American Academy of Political and Social Science*, 587 (1): 49–68.

Ferguson, A.G. 2017. *The rise of big data policing*. New York: NYU Press.

Friedman, B. and M. Ponomarenko. 2015. Democratic policing. *New York University Law Review*, 90 (6): 1827–1907.

Garland, D. 2001. *The culture of control, crime and social order in contemporary society*. Chicago: University of Chicago Press.

Haggerty, K.D. and M. Samatas. 2010. Introduction: Surveillance and democracy: An unsettled relationship. In *Surveillance and democracy*, edited by K.D. Haggerty and M. Samatas. London: Routledge.

Haines, K. and S. Case. 2015. *Positive youth justice: Children first, offenders second*. Bristol: Policy Press.

Hunt, P., J. Saunders and J.S. Hollywood. 2014. *Evaluation of the Shreveport predictive policing experiment. Rand Safety and Justice Program*. Santa Monica: Rand.

Introna, L. and D. Wood. 2004. Picturing algorithmic surveillance: the politics of facial recognition systems. *Surveillance & Society*, 2 (2/3): 177–198.

Jansen, F. 2018. *Data-driven policing in the context of Europe*. Data Justice Working Paper, https://datajusticeproject.net/wp-content/uploads/sites/30/2019/05/Report-Data-Driven-Policing-EU.pdf.

Jones, T. and T. Newburn. 1998. *Private security and public policing*. Oxford: Clarendon Press.

KentOnline. 2013. Predpol Software Which Targets Crime Down to Small Zones Has Slashed North Kent Crime by 6%, *KentOnline* 14 August 2013, https://www.kentonline.co.uk/kent/news/crime-in-north-kent-slashed-4672/.

Lawrence, P. 2016. The Vagrancy Act (1824) and the persistence of pre-emptive policing in England since 1750. *The British Journal of Criminology*, 57 (3): 513–531.

Loader, I. 1994. Democracy, justice and the limits of policing: Rethinking police accountability. *Social & Legal Studies*, 3: 521–544.

Loader, I. 1999. Consumer culture and the commodification of policing. *Sociology*, 33 (2): 373–392.

Loftus, B. 2008. Dominant culture interrupted: Recognition, resentment and the politics of change in an English police force. *The British Journal of Criminology*, 48 (6): 756–777.

Lyon, D. 2001. *Surveillance society: Monitoring everyday life*. Buckingham: Open University Press

Lum, K. and W. Isaac. 2016. To predict and serve? *Significance Magazine Royal Statistical Society*, October 2016, https://rss.onlinelibrary.wiley.com/doi/epdf/10.1111/j.1740-9713.2016.00960.x.

Mali, B., C. Bronkhorst-Giesen and M. Den Hengst. 2017. *Predictive policing: Lessen voor de toekomst*, Politieacademie, https://www.politieacademie.nl/kennisenonderzoek/kennis/mediatheek/PDF/93263.PDF.

Manski, C.F. and D.S. Nagin. 2017. Assessing benefits, costs, and disparate racial impacts of confrontational proactive policing. *PNAS*, 114 (35): 9308–9313.

Marsch, S. 2019. *Ethics committee raises alarm over 'predictive policing' tool. The Guardian*, 20 April 2019, https://www.theguardian.com/uk-news/2019/apr/20/predictive-policing-tool-could-entrench-bias-ethics-committee-warns.

Martin, A.K., R.E. van Brakel and D.J. Bernhard. 2009. Understanding resistance to digital surveillance. Towards a multidisciplinary, multi-actor framework. *Surveillance & Society*, 6 (3): 213–232.

Mastrobuoni, G. 2014. Crime is terribly revealing: Information technology and police productivity. Unpublished Paper. Available at: www.tinbergen.nl/wp-content/uploads/2015/02/Crime-is-Terribly-Revealing_-Information-Technology.pdf.

Mayer, N. 2019. Strobl entscheidet sich gegen Precobs, *Stuttgarter Nachrichten*, 3 September 2019, https://www.stuttgarter-nachrichten.de/inhalt.aus-fuer-die-einbruchvorhersage-software-strobl-entscheidet-sich-gegen-precobs.19a18735-9c8f-4f1a-bf1b-80b6a3ad0142.html.

McQuillan, D. 2014. *Smart slums: Utopian or dystopian vision of the future? The Guardian*, 6 October 2014, https://www.theguardian.com/global-development-professionals-network/2014/oct/06/smart-slums-smart-city-kenya-mapping.

Monahan, T. 2010. Surveillance as governance. Social inequality and the pursuit of democratic surveillance. In *Surveillance and democracy*, edited by K.D. Haggerty and M. Samatas, 91–110. London: Routledge.

Neyround, P.W. 2017. Balancing public safety and individual rights in street policing, commentary. *PNAS*, 114 (35): 9231–9233.

Norris, C. 1995. Video charts: Algorithmic surveillance. *Criminal Justice Matters*, 20: 7–8.

Oswald, M., J. Grace, S. Urwin and G.C. Barnes. 2018. Algorithmic risk assessment policing models: lessons from the Durham HART model and 'Experimental' proportionality. *Information & Communications Technology Law*, 27 (2): 223–250.

Peeters, R. and M. Schuilenburg. 2018. Machine justice: Governing security through the bureaucracy of algorithms. *Information Polity*, 23 (3): 267–280.

PredPol. 2020. *What. Where. When. Predict critical events and gain actionable insight with PredPol*. The Predictive Policing Company, https://www.predpol.com.

Richardson, R., J. Schultz and K. Crawford. 2019. Dirty data, bad predictions: How civil rights violations impact police data, predictive policing systems, and justice. *New York University Law Review*, 94: 192–233.

Rose, N. 1998. Governing risky individuals: The role of psychiatry in new regimes of control. *Psychiatry Psychology and Law*, 5 (2): 177–195.

Santos, R.B. 2019. Critic: Predictive policing: Where's the evidence? In *Police innovation: contrasting perspectives*, edited by D. Weisburd and A.A. Braga, 366–396. Cambridge: Cambridge University Press.

Schuilenburg, M., R. van Steden and B. Oude Breuil. 2014. *Positive criminology: Reflections on care, belonging and security.* The Hague: Eleven Publishing

Sclove, R.E. 1995. *Democracy and technology.* New York: Guilford Press.

Skitka, L.J., K.L. Mosier and M. Burdick. 1999. Does automation bias decision-making? *International Journal Human-Computer Studies*, 51: 991–1006.

Srinicek, N. 2017. *Platform capitalism.* Cambridge, UK: Polity.

Van Brakel, R. 2015. Iedereen verdacht? De effectiviteit en impact van het gebruik van preëmptieve surveillance voor publieke veiligheid, *Orde van de Dag*, 69: 35–42.

Van Brakel, R. 2016. Pre-emptive big data surveillance and its (dis)empowering consequences: the case of predictive policing. In *Exploring the boundaries of big data*, edited by B. van der Sloot, D. Broeders and E. Schrijvers, 117–141. Amsterdam: Amsterdam University Press.

Van Brakel, R. 2018. *Taming by chance? A rhizomatic analysis of pre-emptive surveillance of children*, PhD dissertation. Vrije Universiteit Brussel.

Van Brakel, R. 2020. Een reflectie over het huidig toezicht van het gebruik van surveillancetechnologie door de lokale politie in België. *Cahiers Politiestudies*, 55: 139–160.

Van Brakel R. and P. De Hert. 2011. Policing, surveillance and law in a pre-crime society: Understanding the consequences of technology-based strategies. *Cahiers Politiestudies*, 20 (3): 163–192.

Van Eijk, G. 2017. Socioeconomic marginality in sentencing: The built-in bias in risk assessment tools and the reproduction of social inequality. *Punishment & Society*, 19 (4), 463–481.

Van Gemert-Pijnen, J., N. Nijland, M. van Limburg, H. Ossebaard, S. Kelders, G. Eysenbach and E. Seydel. 2011. A holistic framework to improve the uptake and impact of eHealth technologies. *Journal of Medical Internet Research*, 13 (4): e111.

Williams, P. and E. Kind. 2019. *Data-driven policing: The hardwiring of discriminatory policing practices across Europe*, ENAR, https://www.enar-eu.org/IMG/pdf/data-driven-profiling-web-final.pdf.

Willems, D. and R. Doeleman. 2014. Predictive policing – wens of werkelijkheid? *Het Tijdschrift voor de Politie*, 76 (4/5): 39–42.

Wilson, D. 2019. Platform policing and the real-time cop. *Surveillance & Society*, 17 (1/2): 69–75.

Wientjes, J., M. Delsing, A. Cillessen, J. Janssens and R. Scholte. 2017. Identifying potential offenders on the basis of police records: Development and validation of the ProKid risk assessment tool. *Journal of Criminological Research, Policy and Practice*, 3 (4): 249–260.

Chapter 8

Algorithmic reasoning
The production of subjectivity through data

Gwen van Eijk

Introduction

In a letter to *Inside Time*, the English National Newspaper for Prisoners and Detainees, former prisoner Charles Hanson writes about the algorithmic tool OASys (Offender Assessment System), describing it as a 'dehumanising process of risk assessment'. Since 2001, OASys informs parole and probation decisions and case management (Robinson, 2017). Hanson situates his comments within a broader critique of rehabilitation programmes, but takes aim particularly with the role of OASys in how 'prisoners are seen as "things" to be measured, assessed, quantified and computerised' which 'has tended to dehumanise the offender':

> Taking groups of offender's human identities apart and categorising them into axis, tables, graphs and risk assessments by the use of computers and assuming that this is scientific is an act of intellectual dishonesty which distorts what makes up the human condition and the potential for change.
>
> (Hanson, 2009)

Hanson's letter indicates how algorithmic practices have transformed criminal justice, in this case probation and rehabilitation practices. His letter touches on various long-standing concerns about predictive justice. First, predictive justice conflicts with individual justice – the notion that each case should be assessed on its own merits (Binns, 2019). Algorithmic predictions are not individualized but rather assess the extent to which an individual shares certain characteristics with a group of individuals that is known to reoffend (Hannah-Moffat, 2013). Predictive sentencing has therefore been criticized because it 'would be legally and morally wrong to take action against a person based on membership in a specific class or other group status' (Simmons, 2018: 1076). According to Laurel Eckhouse and others (2019: 189), the decision to use data on groups to make decisions about individuals is the 'base layer' of bias that is fundamental to other layers of bias (such as biased data or biased models). This is specifically problematic when risk assessment includes information about socioeconomic status, which produces class, racial and gender bias in criminal-legal decisions (cf. Starr, 2014; Hannah-Moffat, 2016; Van Eijk; 2017).

Because of concerns about bias, various commentators, including myself, have concluded that the use of predictive algorithms cannot be legitimized in sentencing decisions but have left the door open for legitimate use in treatment decisions (Hamilton, 2015; Van Eijk, 2017; Tonry, 2019a). This is not to say that there are no concerns about algorithmic justice in the context of rehabilitation. Hanson rightfully expresses concern that OASys 'distorts what makes up the human condition and the potential for change' which touches on the question of human dignity in algorithmic justice. From a human rights perspective, Tony Ward (2011: 106) has suggested that labelling individuals as 'high-risk' could violate the moral principle of human dignity, as it could impact 'the degree to which a person is free to form his or her own intentions and is able to act in accordance with them without interference'. This raises the question whether algorithmic rehabilitation practices are compatible with the core idea of rehabilitation, that is, that desistance requires *agency*: a sense of having control to change one's course in life (McNeill, 2006; Healy, 2013). An important aspect of transformative agency is that individuals can envision an alternative future self (Paternoster & Bushway, 2009; King, 2013). The prediction of future behaviour may conflict with envisioning a positive future self, which may even be reinforced by algorithmic prediction.

In this chapter, I will argue that the problem of algorithmic justice in the context of risk-based rehabilitation is not in the first place a technological problem but a problem of human–algorithm interaction and the rationalization of algorithms. Interpretative errors seem inherent to what algorithmic predictions aim to do, namely, predict an individual's future behaviour based on group data. In this way, prediction conflicts with the principle of individual justice, which may subsequently result in violating the principle of respect for human dignity. Prediction of future behaviour and the way in which prediction are decontextualized from structural factors may discourage individuals to re-envision a positive future self, which may hamper agency and, consequently, desistance. In the conclusion, I offer several principles for improving ethical use of algorithms in the context of rehabilitation.

Human–algorithmic practices: rehabilitation, risk and marginality

The use of algorithmic predictions has proliferated and algorithms now inform decision-making processes at an increasing number of stages of the criminal justice system, from pre-trial detention to release (for an overview and discussion of different uses for different decisions, see Van Eijk, 2020). To give an idea: in the United States, 28 states and several counties use risk assessment tools for sentencing decisions (Stevenson & Doleac, 2018), while at the Federal level algorithmic risk assessment has a role in allocating treatment and resources (Monahan & Skeem, 2016; Bussert, 2019). In addition, an increasing number of states and counties is using risk assessment for pretrial decisions, which in many states is introduced as an alternative to the bail system (Desmarais & Lowder, 2019). In Canada, Hong Kong and a number of European jurisdictions, among which are the United Kingdom, the Netherlands and Finland, algorithmic tools inform pre-sentencing reports and treatment plans in the context of rehabilitation (Hannah-Moffat, 2013; Van Wingerden, Van Wilsem & Moerings, 2014; Salo, Laaksonen & Santtila, 2016; Robinson, 2017).

To worry about human decision-makers being replaced by machines is unfounded, however, as humans continue to be involved in criminal-legal decisions. Rather, algorithmic tools *inform* decisions made by judges, parole boards and probation officers about individuals (Green & Chen, 2019). Kelly Hannah-Moffat, Paula Maurutto and Sarah Turnbull (2009) have even spoken of an 'actuarial illusion' as they saw that Canadian correctional workers engaged with predictive tools on their own terms: they may overrule predictions, devalue predictive tools and prefer to rely on their own expertise (see also Van Wingerden, Van Wilsem & Moerings, 2014; Werth, 2017). Reuben Binns (2019: 19) similarly notes that 'screen-level bureaucrats' dealing with algorithmic systems exercise discretion according to their own commitments which may conflict with the goals of their organization. Based on observations, Hannah-Moffat, Maurutto and Turnbull (2009) contend that risk assessment is best understood as a negotiated process: practitioners simultaneously embrace and resist risk technologies.

However, keeping humans 'in-the-loop' of algorithmic decision-making, as Hanson as well as other critics suggest (e.g. La Diega, 2018; Simmons, 2018; Binns, 2019), is no guarantee for justice. One reason for this is that we should understand risk-based decision-making as the outcome of the *interplay* of humans and algorithms. Therefore, to understand the uses and consequences of predictive justice it is essential to investigate the human–algorithm interaction and to not reduce one aspect to the other (Winner, 1980; Binns, 2019). Indeed, we need not only ask how we can improve algorithms but also look at how to improve professional engagement with algorithmic predictions (Green & Chen, 2019).

A central question of an ethics of algorithms is 'What do algorithms do to subjects?' (Matzner, 2017: 28). This concerns not only the question of how algorithms shape decisions, but also how algorithmic reasoning shapes the production of the 'criminal subject': they shape how practitioners view justice-involved individuals as moral subjects (cf. Hannah-Moffat, 2005; Werth, 2019). Such insight is particularly important when algorithms inform rehabilitation practices that require convicted individuals to reflect on their behaviour and to transform from a 'high-risk offender' to a law-abiding individual. I started this chapter with Hanson's letter because the literature on algorithmic justice tells us surprisingly little about how justice-involved individuals who are subjected to algorithmic practices experience it. Ric Simmons (2018) has theorized that algorithmic decisions may violate the principle of procedural justice, which implies a negative experience for those who are subjected to algorithms. Indeed, in the context of loans, insurance, hiring and other day-to-day situations, Reuben Binns and others (2018) observe that algorithmic decision-making is considered unfair by people subjected to it, as it 'reduces a human being to a percentage'. Studying algorithmic and human decisions in managerial decisions that require human skills (e.g. hiring and work evaluation), Min Kyung Lee (2018) found that people perceive human decisions as fairer and more trustworthy than algorithmic decisions, and that people expressed more negative emotions in response to algorithmic decisions. Decisions in the criminal justice system pre-eminently involve human skills, which suggests that involving algorithms in these decisions is likely to be negatively experienced by those subjected to them.

To fully understand what algorithms 'do' to people, we need to study them in the context of criminal-legal policies and practices in which they are shaped and used. In this chapter, I focus on rehabilitation practices, specifically the use of predictive tools in the context of risk-based justice. The use of algorithmic tools is embedded in a currently dominant approach to rehabilitation: the Risk-Needs-Responsivity (RNR) model developed in the 1990s by Canadian psychologists Donald Andrews and James Bonta (2010a; see also Hannah-Moffat, 2013; Taxman, Caudy & Maass, 2014). The RNR model is used in Northern American and European jurisdictions and follows several principles. The risk principle prescribes *who* should be treated: direct intensive services to the higher-risk offenders and minimize services to the low-risk offenders; the needs principle prescribes *what* should be treated: criminogenic needs; while the responsivity principle addresses *how* the intervention should be delivered: characteristics of the intervention are important as well as individual 'strengths, ability, motivation, personality, and bio-demographic characteristics such as gender, ethnicity, and age' (Andrews & Bonta, 2010b: 47).

The categorization of individuals according to their risk level is based on predictive risk tools, of which the Level of Service Inventory-Revised (LSI-R), also developed by Andrews and Bonta, is the most studied and probably the most influential. The LSI-R is used by probation agencies in Canada, the United States., the United Kingdom, several European countries, Hong Kong and Australia (Hannah-Moffat, 2013; Van Wingerden, Van Wilsem & Moerings, 2014; Monahan & Skeem, 2016). The tool has inspired OASys in England and Wales (Robinson 2017), which in turn has inspired the Dutch tool RISc ('Risico Inschattings Schalen') and the Finnish tool RITA ('Riski-ja tarvearvio') (Van Wingerden, Van Wilsem & Moerings, 2014; Salo, Laaksonen & Santtila, 2016). LSI-R is a 'risk/needs assessment tool' that predicts general recidivism. Because Andrews and Bonta were not only interested in risk but also in opportunities for rehabilitation, they included 'dynamic' risk factors – also called 'criminogenic needs' – that are changeable and correlated to recidivism. Therefore, LSI-R is considered a 'third-generation' tool (for detailed overviews of the evolution of risk assessment tools, see Hannah-Moffat, 2005; Harcourt, 2008). The LSI-R aims to measure the major risk and needs factors, the 'Central Eight', for both assessing risk of recidivism and targeting criminogenic needs (Andrews & Bonta, 2010a). The 'Central Eight' consist of the 'Big Four' factors (History of Antisocial Behaviour, Antisocial Personality Pattern, Antisocial Cognition and Antisocial Associates) and the 'Moderate Four' factors (Family/Marital Circumstances, School/Work, Leisure/Recreation and Substance Abuse). According to Andrews and Bonta (2010a), the Central Eight are the best predictors to future offending and are criminogenic needs that can be altered through rehabilitation in order to decrease reoffending.

A major concern in the debate about predictive justice is bias based on social marginality, race/ethnic background, and gender (e.g. Harcourt, 2008; Starr, 2014; Hannah-Moffat, 2016; Van Eijk, 2017). As long as predictive tools exist, social marginality has played a role in predicting risk, although some risk tools have eventually excluded socioeconomic factors due to their correlation to race (Harcourt, 2008; Tonry, 2019a). In current general risk assessment tools, such as the LSI-R but also COMPAS, OASys and RISc, socioeconomic bias is 'built-in' because they measure socioeconomic items to calculate risk scores (Van Eijk, 2017). In addition to items that measure socioeconomic status directly, other items correlate with socioeconomic marginality, such as leisure activities (depend on money, time and geographical location) and attitudes (trust in police is affected by actual experiences with police, and relations with police tend to be problematic in poor neighbourhoods and communities of colour) (Harcourt, 2008; Goddard & Myers, 2017). Furthermore, qualitative evaluations of attitudes and lifestyle require human interpretation, which make standardized assessments vulnerable to subjective judgment and thus class prejudice or implicit bias (Hannah-Moffat, Maurutto & Turnbull, 2009).

While it may seem evident to many scholars, policymakers and practitioners that socioeconomic factors are criminogenic, there is reason to reconsider. Andrews and Bonta (2010a) acknowledge that school and work are among the 'Moderate Four' factors of the 'Central Eight' criminogenic factors, whereas Faye Taxman, Michael Caudy and Stephanie Maass (2014) consider school, work, housing and neighbourhood as non-criminogenic factors that indirectly impact offending behaviour. John Monahan and Jennifer Skeem (2016: 19) similarly argue that understanding criminogenic needs as causal factors is highly questionable, as we lack rigorous experimental studies to determine causality (and in many cases it would be unethical to design randomized controlled trials). Yet, including socioeconomic factors in predictive algorithms is a 'fundamental conceptual layer of bias' (Eckhouse et al., 2019) which, by and large, is accepted by many practitioners and experts. This is particularly problematic given that socially marginalized individuals are over-represented in Western criminal justice systems, even in relatively equal societies such as the Netherlands. Predictive justice thus affects marginalized groups most and it affects them most negatively, as decisions are made based on social marginality. Socioeconomic disparities, and consequently racial/ethnic and gender disparities, in criminal-legal decisions may thus be exacerbated by predictive algorithms (Van Eijk, 2017). This has not led to abandoning socioeconomic items from risk tools.

The production of the abstracted 'high-risk' subject

Rehabilitation according to the RNR model starts with predicting an individual's risk of reoffending based using an algorithmic tool. Algorithmic prediction is a process that simultaneously deindividualizes and individualizes risk. It deindividualizes risk because actuarial assessment relies on aggregate data and averages (Miller & Morris, 1988; Hannah-Moffat, 2013). While concrete decisions about individuals are 'individualized', risk assessment is not: 'the riskiness attributed to an individual is not his or her own, but the average of a group in which he or she is included for purposes of statistical analyses' (Tonry, 2019a: 446). The abstracted risk score should be distinguished from 'individual risk intrinsic to the subject herself' (ibid.). Punishing individuals based on aggregate statistics has been criticized on theoretical, methodological and ethical grounds (e.g. Hannah-Moffat, 2005, 2013; Harcourt, 2008; Simmons, 2018). It may still be useful for decision-makers to know the reoffending rate of categories of individuals that are similar to a particular individual (Monahan & Skeem, 2016), but in essence it is impossible to say anything meaningful about the future behaviour of one individual.

However, from studies on how practitioners interpret algorithmic predictions we know that professionals tend to interpret risk scores in such a way that risk becomes intrinsic to the individual. Kelly Hannah-Moffat (2013: 278) observes that despite being trained in the use and interpretation of risk tools, practitioners tended to struggle with the meaning of probability scores:

> Instead of understanding that an individual with a high risk score *shares characteristics* with an aggregate group of high-risk offenders, practitioners are likely to perceive the individual *as* a high-risk offender. In practical terms, *correlation becomes causation* and potential risk is translated into administrative certainty.
>
> (ibid., italics in original)

Thus, in interpreting algorithmic outcomes, causal explanations are inferred from correlations and because an individual is assessed as 'high risk' they are assumed to be more dangerous to society (ibid.; see also Harcourt, 2008). In his study on parole in California, Robert Werth (2019) similarly observes that the abstracted risk assessment becomes an individualized evaluation: the individual that is assessed as 'high risk' becomes an inherently dangerous subject (Werth, 2019). In line with these observations, Monahan and Skeem (2016) describe a tendency among judges to conflate risk and blame, while these judgements should play a role in different types of decisions: blame is relevant for conviction while risk is relevant only for sentencing.

These interpretative slippages are not solely the product of the use of algorithms; they are inherent to risk thinking. According to Werth (2017: 822), risk assessment is the result of a 'techno-moral assemblage': practitioners bridge and integrate different 'ways of knowing (file-based, actuarial, experiential, moral and affective)' (see also Hannah-Moffat, Maurutto & Turnbull, 2009). However, even if the actuarial way of knowing is one among other ways, the use of algorithms seems to impact other ways of knowing. Such technologies are seen as rational, scientific and value-neutral and therefore fair and just – and for these reasons fairer and more just than humans (Silver, 2000). This 'rationalization process' works to conceal the ways in which criminal justice policies and practices engage in social classification that distinguishes deserving and undeserving offender categories (ibid.; Lamont, Beljean & Clair, 2014). Rationalization also tends to push aside ethical questions about procedural and individual justice and social consequences such as the reproduction of inequality.

Eric Silver (2000) has pointed out that the social sciences contribute to rationalization in at least two ways: first, by advancing risk assessment technologies for managing populations, and second, by providing an interpretive framework that justifies population management. The RNR literature is a case in point that 'the causes of crime claimed by theory and research underpin and provide a framework for actuarial assessments or risk-based technologies' (Metcalf & Stenson, 2004: 8). Indeed, manuals for algorithmic tools present them as insightful for understanding not just correlation but causation. For example, the OASys manual published by the British National Offender Management Service states that OASys can be used to 'help assessors in understanding the "why" of offending' (NOMS, 2009: 8) and the COMPAS manual details many criminological theories, from psychological to sociological and situational theories, that 'help us understand more about why people make their behavioural choices' (Northpointe, 2012: 6). Given this contradictory information and lack of statistical expertise, it is not surprising that there is tendency among judges, parole and probation officers to understand risk factors as causal factors that explain an individual's behaviour.

The focus on risk thus has not displaced a focus on the causes of crime. Rather, risk factors are interpreted as causal to offending behaviour. Like risk scores, risk factors should be understood as 'statistical predictions', not actual predictions about an individual, let alone as causal factors. But in the context of rehabilitation it seems virtually impossible not to draw the erroneous conclusion that probabilities are certainties and that risk factors are causal to offending, as insights into risk scores and risk factors serve the purpose of informing correctional treatment (Hannah-Moffat, 2013). Even more than in the context of sentencing, for decision-makers involved in rehabilitation the individual with a high risk score is likely to become *known* as a high-risk offender based on identified criminogenic characteristics and problems.

Understanding risk factors as explanations for behaviour is particularly problematic when these factors are part of an individual's identity or lie outside an individual's scope of action. Sonja Starr (2014) problematizes including factors such as age and gender, but also employment status and residential neighbourhood, because it makes punishment dependent upon a person's identity rather than what the person has done. For Michael Tonry (2019b), this is one of the problems that leads him to conclude that predictive sentencing is morally unjustifiable, although his argument is slightly different. Tonry considers it 'per se unjust' to use variables such as age, gender and race in predictive sentencing because individuals have no control over them or are not morally responsible for them, but for socioeconomic factors, Tonry argues that:

> These are quintessentially *personal choices*; people in free societies are entitled to make those decisions for themselves and not to suffer because of the choices they make.
>
> (2019b: 14–15, italics added)

Within the RNR model, Andrew and Bonta's (2010a) argue for including 'socioeconomic achievement' in risk/needs assessment because it would be an 'achieved' status, as opposed to social class (family background) as an 'ascribed' status. It is, however, questionable that current socioeconomic circumstances are 'quintessentially personal choices' or that they are achieved rather than ascribed. Decoupling socioeconomic achievement from one's social class ignores that even in relatively equal and egalitarian societies intergenerational social mobility is more limited than the meritocratic ideal presents it (e.g. Corak, 2013). And while it is true that individuals cannot be punished for choosing unemployment, as Tonry argues, this argument ignores the structural factors that impact an individual's educational level, their socioeconomic opportunities, housing situation or residential neighbourhood: the role of parental socioeconomic status, limited social mobility, austerity, spatial segregation, employment rates, the rising costs of housing and living expenses, and unequal access to education.

Here we see the process of how risk factors are simultaneously deindividualized and individualized. Predictive justice produces an understanding of social marginality as 'decontextualized': it disregards that social marginality is shaped by socio-structural inequality (Hannah-Moffat, 2016; Goddard & Myers, 2017). Through decontextualization, the 'high-risk' subject is made individually responsible for their risk factors, which conveys the message that individuals are to blame not only for their offending but also for their socioeconomic marginality (Van Eijk, 2017). Put differently, risk assessment produces the individual as an inherently 'high-risk' subject, responsible for their own marginalized position, ignoring the context in which education, employment as well as attitudes and coping mechanisms – criminogenic or protective factors – are shaped. Andrews and Bonta (with Wormith, 2011) have responded to critics that their RNR model does consider contextual factors because it addresses employment, education and such. However, it is not sufficient to account for these circumstances as contextual to behaviour – these circumstances should be reviewed in their wider socio-political context as well, to account for the limited influence of individuals over their own circumstances.

Addressing racial inequality – but we may consider this more broadly – Hannah-Moffat (2013: 282) suggests that 'it is impossible to treat individuals fairly if they are treated as abstractions, unshaped by the particular contexts of social life'. The problem of de/individualization of risk and risk factors is inherent to what algorithms aim to do – predict future behaviour – and to how algorithms work – analysing aggregate, not individual, data. In addition, humans have trouble understanding how probabilities relate to individuals. Their understanding of risk and risk factors as inherent to an individual violates with the notion of individual justice: individuals are not really evaluated on their own merits. In the next section, I investigate how this may impact human dignity and the process of desistance.

Re-envisioning a 'low-risk' future self *against all odds*?

After an individual is assessed and labelled as a 'high-risk' subject who is inherently dangerous due to risk factors which are seen as causal to their behaviour, individuals are expected to engage with the process of rehabilitation and, ultimately, to desist from offending behaviour. While we know very little about how justice-involved individuals experience algorithmic evaluation, studies on desistance provide relevant insights into how individuals may negotiate algorithmic predictions about their future. Researchers agree that desistance follows from a combination of structural and subjective factors, although theories may emphasize one or the other as the most important catalyst for change (Farrall et al., 2011; Bersani & Doherty, 2018). In any case, it is clear that desistance requires 'agency', a sense of having some degree of control over the future direction of one's life (Farrall et al., 2011; King, 2013; Healy, 2013). Agency is future oriented, it involves reflection on the past but also hope and optimism, a readiness for change (Healy, 2013). Individuals may re-envision their past self and, more or less intentionally, construct a new self that is different, leaving behind their past self (McNeill, 2006; Bersani & Doherty, 2018; Hunter & Farrall, 2018). According to Ray Paternoster and Shawn Bushway (2009), in the process of desistance individuals imagine different possible selves and must in the long run find a balance between positive and negative possible selves. It is important to understand that re-envisioning a 'future self' requires effort and time and that there may be a tension between the current self and the future self, which can cause frustration (Harris, 2011; Hunter & Farrall, 2018).

However, while the process of desistance requires re-envisioning a future self that is different from the past (or current) self, predictive algorithms predict a future self that is at high risk to reoffend and thus to stay the same. This dilemma is illustrated by an anonymous writer to *InsideTime* who responds to Hanson's letter about the dehumanizing effects of risk assessment and proposes to put OASys to the test:

> It is time to elect a new prime minister/world leader and only your (OASys) vote counts.
> Candidate A associates with crooked politicians and consults with astrologists; has had two mistresses; he also chain-smokes and drinks 8–10 Martinis a day.
> Candidate B was kicked out of office twice; sleeps until noon; used opium in college and drinks a quart of whiskey every evening.
> Candidate C is a decorated war hero; he's a vegetarian; doesn't smoke; drinks an occasional beer and has never committed adultery.
> Which candidate would be chosen by 'OASys scoring'?
> Candidate A is Franklin Roosevelt; Candidate B is Winston Churchill; Candidate C is Adolf Hitler… Does OASys work?
>
> (Anonymous, 2010)

The writer's thought experiment could be read as a critique on the poor predictive accuracy of algorithmic tools, but it also echoes Hanson's (2009) concern that predictive justice 'distorts what makes up the human condition and the potential for change'. People can and do change, but can we re-envision radically different futures for these three candidates based on their past behaviour? If algorithmic tools predict that an individual will likely be a 'persister' in the future, how does this shape how they – and others – imagine a different future self as a 'desister'? In other words, is algorithmic justice compatible with the principle of human dignity (cf. Ward, 2011)?

The role of algorithmic prediction of risk may have a significant impact on re-envisioning potential future selves. Paternoster and Bushway (2009) argue that an individual's 'feared self' supports the initial motivation to change, as an individual does not want to become what they fear they will become. In this way, the production of the 'high-risk' subject through algorithmic reasoning could stimulate agency and desistance. However, other scholars warn of the limiting force of assessing future risk of reoffending, as 'risk' may keep individuals trapped in past behaviours. Fergus McNeill and others (2014), for example, are critical of how the RNR rehabilitation model and its focus on individual risk factors impacts desistance as it is retrospective, whereas desistance requires a prospective outlook. Risk assessment informs the imagined possible future selves as it calculates the probability of a certain future in which the individual repeats similar behaviour in the future, based on past behaviour. This may be counter-productive to desistance, McNeill (2006: 53) argues, as measures that label, exclude and segregate 'seem designed to confirm and cement "condemnation scripts" and thus to frustrate desistance'. Risk assessment may limit the imagination of a positive future self by assuming that past behaviour continues in the future, especially when risk factors – erroneously interpreted as causal to the undesired behaviour – are difficult to change.

Furthermore, the presentation of algorithmic tools as scientific, evidence-based and thus accurate – even though predictions are never fully accurate – may strengthen the sense that the 'feared future self' is unavoidable. For a 'feared future self' to motivate individuals to change, there should be space for people to imagine that they will not become their feared future self. Put differently, a negative possible self is unlikely to motivate change of it means that individuals must re-envision change *against all odds*. Desistance is difficult as is, and it can become even more difficult if it involves 'proving the computer wrong'. Whether individuals are discouraged or encouraged by future images of the self as likely reoffender depends on how risk predictions are interpreted by both the practitioner and the individual subjected to algorithmic prediction. To respect human dignity, acknowledge potential and foster change, it is essential that algorithmic predictions are taken as probabilities, not certainties. Certainties cannot be changed, while probabilities offer alternatives and thus opportunities for change. It is thus essential that rehabilitation practitioners avoid the interpretative mistakes that the studies described earlier have observed: to respect human dignity, they should resist the tendency to individualize the patterns that are found on an aggregate level.

Desistance studies furthermore show how structural factors may hinder and discourage individuals from reconstructing their identity. Desistance is, according to Stephen Farrall and others (2011: 224), 'best approached as the result of the interplay between individual choices and a range of wider social forces, institutional and societal practices which are beyond the control of the individual'. In other words, agency is enabled or constrained by structural factors and social context. Shadd Maruna (as quoted in McNeill, 2006) describes how both persisters and desisters have a sense of 'fatalism' in how they see their criminal career – as an individual overcome by criminogenic structural pressures. Desisters succeed in '"discovering" agency in order to resist and overcome' these pressures, while persisters viewed their future as a script that has been written for them long ago (ibid.: 48). The process of changing one's identity and one's behaviour may thus feel as if individuals are 'changing fate' (Healy, 2013). Desistance requires optimism about one's future, perhaps more optimism than a risk score would warrant (Cobbina & Bender, 2012). Alexes Harris (2011) observes that the motivation of individuals to change can be short-lived, as they are confronted with structural forces as barriers to change – for example, limited options for housing, work, family support and the stigma of a criminal record. As 'individuals could go only so far in creating these structural changes' (ibid.: 83), practical support is needed to keep individuals motivated.

It is possible that individuals may come to experience algorithmic predictions as structural (institutional) forces that hamper their imagination and ability to change. If in everyday situations individuals feel that algorithms reduce them to a number (Binns et al., 2018) and have negative emotional responses to algorithmic decisions (Lee, 2018), it is not difficult to imagine that individuals in the criminal justice context feel negatively about algorithmic justice as well. Prediction scores add yet another factor over which individuals have limited control – especially when decisions are black-boxed and practitioners only provide insight into the risk score and priorities co-produced by the tool (Hannah-Moffat, Maurutto & Turnbull, 2009). Defending the RNR model, Donald Andrews, James Bonta and Stephen Wormith (2011: 742) argue that in order to motivate individuals, practitioners should

> offer the client important information regarding the findings of the assessment. Open reviews of the results and implications of RNR-based assessments with moderate and higher risk individuals are a fundamental approach to the initiation of mutually agreed on service plans.

However, discussing outcomes with individuals but not the way in which prediction works, may result in viewing predictions as fixed rather than seeing them as probabilities.

Especially for marginalized offender categories, algorithm predictions may be discouraging, as their risk score depends in part on their marginalized position in society. Education, employment and housing are at least partly outside an individual's scope of action and thus difficult to change in a way that supports identity change. Yet, through algorithmic reasoning, marginalized individuals are made responsible for their criminogenic factors and expected to imagine a positive possible self that can negotiate structural inequalities (Hannah-Moffat, 2016). Reviewing the potential of criminogenic needs for treatment, Taxman, Caudy and Maass (2014) conclude that socioeconomic factors should be considered only as 'stabilizers' to an individual's life. Given structural social inequalities, it seems fairer to consider socioeconomic factors as non-criminogenic factors that are contextual and not causal to desistance. Such an approach to socioeconomic marginality as criminogenic need may prevent that algorithmic predictions become experienced as unavoidable futures that discourage individuals to re-envision a different self and future. In this context, we should also consider that in many jurisdictions individuals are subjected to multiple predictive tools during their involvement in the criminal justice system, from pre-trial detention to release (Van Eijk, 2020). Prior predictions that have informed decisions on freedom and resources may produce criminogenic circumstances that, once an individual enters treatment, may work as structural obstacles to agency and desistance (Hannah-Moffat, 2016). In short, studies on the process of desistance demonstrate that change is difficult for structural and subjective reasons, and we need to investigate the real possibility that involving algorithms makes this process even more difficult for individuals.

Principles for algorithmic justice

It is clear that algorithmic practices have transformed practices of justice, although many questions remain about how algorithms are used in practice and how they impact principles of justice and fairness. Based on what we know about risk-based justice in rehabilitation, in this chapter I have argued that what algorithmic justice aims to do – predict future behaviour – and how it does so – based on aggregate, group data – contradicts notions of individual justice (that individuals should be evaluated based on their own behaviour) and, consequently, human dignity (that individuals have agency: a sense of control over their own future). However, the most fundamental problems of algorithmic reasoning are the result of human decisions and human interpretation rather than a problem of technology. Tony Ward (2011) argues that predictive justice requires 'extreme care' in gathering data about criminogenic needs and 'that any subsequent decisions that restrict offenders' freedom, and possibly well-being, are rationally (and ethically) justified'. While in principle I agree, I would also caution against focusing on rational justifications, as they tend to push aside ethical considerations. The RNR model and measures for the accuracy and effectiveness of predictive tools offer rational justifications that invite us to treat algorithmic justice as evidence-based and data-driven and thus authoritative, value-free and apolitical evaluations of behaviour and its causes. In practice, however, algorithms are imbued with value, as decisions about how to use algorithms 'are, in the end, not a statistical or scientific matter, but a political and social judgment about what risks are unacceptable, and what responses to risks should be allowed' (Miller & Morris, 1988: 268). The question whether prediction should play a role at all in criminal-legal decisions is fundamentally an ethical question but is usually treated as a technical issue of accuracy. Categories of 'low', 'medium' and 'high' risk are constructed and for each category 'false positives' and 'false negatives' are accepted as unavoidable. Similarly, including certain risk factors or not, and which arguments are put forward by academics, experts and decision-makers, is a moral-political negotiation. For example, including racial factors in risk assessment is now seen as unacceptable, while socioeconomic factors are still seen as acceptable despite concerns of class, racial/ethnic and gender bias. Rationalization seems to neutralize concerns about constructing social marginality as risk factor and thus facilitates the alignment of technological approaches with political interests (cf. Winner, 1980), as social marginality is decontextualized and individualized through algorithmic reasoning, making individuals fully responsible for their own (deprived) situation.

It is essential to understand the human–algorithm interplay within the context of specific practices, as predictive sentencing presents different problems than predictive rehabilitation. To investigate and improve the ethics of algorithmic justice, we should thus consider algorithmic technologies not as independent from human practices but as integrated with it and view algorithms as reflections and extensions of human practices. Many fundamental problems of predictive justice arise from the problematic nature of risk-thinking and from erroneous interpretations of algorithmic prediction. It is crucial that practitioners are trained to interpret and explain algorithmic predictions, as experiences of individuals subjected to algorithms are mediated through a human expert who interprets algorithmic outcomes. Furthermore, if practitioners make interpretative mistakes, it is likely that justice-involved individuals make similar mistakes. As decision-makers in the criminal justice system are not experts on statistics, education could help to correct errors in interpreting algorithmic predictions or algorithms could be designed differently to improve interpretability (Green & Chen, 2019). From the perspective of individuals who are subjected to algorithmic justice, more effort to explain not just outcomes but the logic of algorithmic prediction helps them to evaluate the fairness of algorithmic decisions (ibid.; Binns et al., 2018). This implies that the use of black-boxed algorithms – specifically algorithms that are secret due to their proprietary nature – is unethical. In the context of rehabilitation, practitioners have an ethical duty to explain algorithmic tools correctly to justice-involved individuals in order to avoid discouraging the re-envisioning of a positive future self. Working towards an ethical use of algorithms requires addressing the inherent tensions between prediction on the one hand and individual justice and human dignity on the other. Rethinking this tension may result in a decision to not use algorithmic justice in a rehabilitation context, as to fully respect human dignity and foster agency and personal change.

While there are many reasons to be concerned about algorithmic justice – not only in the context of sentencing but also in relation to rehabilitation – it has also created opportunities for critical evaluation by a wider group of experts of decisions in criminal justice that were long hidden from the public and considered the exclusive domain of legal professionals (Peeters & Schuilenburg, 2018). The use of more advanced technology, embedded in broader concerns about digitalization and big data, has attracted new experts – statisticians, AI experts, investigative journalists, among others, in addition to social scientists and legal scholars – to scrutinize the design, use and consequences of predictive justice. This critical debate is mirrored by a growing academic and professional literature and unprecedented private sector involvement that reinforce the image of algorithmic justice as scientific and fundamentally unproblematic. The voices that are still missing from this debate are those of the individuals who are subjected to algorithmic justice. If the act of prediction itself is perceived as unfair, no algorithm is going to make prediction fair. To further the debate about ethical use of algorithmic justice we need to include the experiences of individuals who are subjected to algorithmic tools in order to ensure that they experience algorithmic justice as fair and constructive to their rehabilitation and well-being.

References

Andrews D.A. and J. Bonta. 2010a. *The psychology of criminal conduct*. London: Routledge.

Andrews, D.A. and J. Bonta. 2010b. Rehabilitating criminal justice policy and practice. *Psychology, Public Policy, and Law*, 16 (1): 39.

Andrews, D.A., J. Bonta and J.S. Wormith. 2011. The risk-need-responsivity (RNR) model: Does adding the good lives model contribute to effective crime prevention? *Criminal Justice and Behavior*, 38 (7): 735–755.

Anonymous. 2010. Standardised structured approach. *InsideTime*, 1 June, https://insidetime.org/standardised-structured-approach/

Bersani, B.E. and *E.E. Doherty*. 2018. Desistance from offending in the twenty-first century. *Annual Review of Criminology*, 1: 311–334.

Binns, R., M. Van Kleek, M. Veale, U. Lyngs, J. Zhao, and N. Shadbolt. 2018. '*It's reducing a human being to a percentage': Perceptions of justice in algorithmic decisions. Proceedings of the 2018 CHI Conference on Human Factors in Computing Systems*, 377: 1–14. doi:10.1145/3173574.3173951

Binns, R. 2019. *Human judgement in algorithmic loops: Individual justice and automated decision-making*. https://papers.ssrn.com/sol3/papers.cfm?abstract_id=3452030.

Bussert, T. 2019. What the first step act means for federal prisoners. *The Champion* (May): 28–36. Accessed 18 July 2019. https://www.frostbussert.com/files/what_the_first_step_act_means_for_federal_prisoners.pdf

Cobbina, J.E. and K.A. Bender. 2012. Predicting the future: Incarcerated women's views of reentry success. *Journal of Offender Rehabilitation*, 51 (5): 275–294.

Corak, M. 2013. Income inequality, equality of opportunity, and intergenerational mobility. *The Journal of Economic Perspectives*, 27 (3): 79–102.

Desmarais, S.L. and E.M. Lowder. 2019. *Pre-trial risk assessment tools: A primer for judges, prosecutors, and defense attorneys*. MacArthur Foundation Safety and Justice Challenge.

Eckhouse, L., K. Lum, C. Conti-Cook and J. Ciccolini. 2019. Layers of bias: A unified approach for understanding problems with risk assessment. *Criminal Justice and Behavior*, 46 (2): 185–209.

Farrall, S., G. Sharpe, B. Hunter and A. Calverley. 2011. Theorizing structural and individual-level processes in desistance and persistence: Outlining an integrated perspective. *Australian & New Zealand Journal of Criminology*, 44 (2): 218–234.

Goddard, T. and R.R. Myers. 2017. Against evidence-based oppression: Marginalized youth and the politics of risk-based assessment and intervention. *Theoretical Criminology*, 21 (2): 151–167.

Green, B. and Y. Chen. 2019. Disparate interactions: An algorithm-in-the-loop analysis of fairness in risk assessments. *Proceedings of the Conference on Fairness, Accountability, and Transparency* (January): 90–99. doi:10.1145/3287560.

Hamilton, M. 2015. Adventures in risk: predicting violent and sexual recidivism in sentencing law. *Arizona State Law Journal*, 47 (1): 1–62.

Hannah-Moffat, K. 2005. Criminogenic needs and the transformative risk subject: Hybridizations of risk/need in penality. *Punishment & Society*, 7 (1): 29–51.

Hannah-Moffat, K. 2013. Actuarial sentencing: An 'unsettled' proposition. *Justice Quarterly*, 30 (2): 270–296.

Hannah-Moffat, K. 2016. A conceptual kaleidoscope: Contemplating 'dynamic structural risk' and an uncoupling of risk from need. *Psychology, Crime & Law*, 22 (1–2): 33–46.

Hannah-Moffat, K., P. Maurutto and S. Turnbull. 2009. Negotiated risk: Actuarial illusions and discretion in probation. *Canadian Journal of Law & Society*, 24 (3): 391–409.

Hanson, C. 2009. The dehumanising process of risk assessment. *InsideTime*, 1 December, https://insidetime.org/dehumanising-process-of-risk-assessment/

Harcourt, B.E. 2008. *Against prediction*. Chicago: University of Chicago Press.

Harris, A. 2011. Constructing clean dreams: Accounts, future selves, and social and structural support as desistance work. *Symbolic Interaction*, 34 (1): 63–85.

Healy, D. 2013. Changing fate? Agency and the desistance process. *Theoretical Criminology*, 17 (4): 557–574.

Hunter, B. and S. Farrall. 2018. Emotions, future selves and the process of desistance. *The British Journal of Criminology*, 58 (2): 291–308.

King, S. 2013. Transformative agency and desistance from crime. *Criminology & Criminal Justice*, 13 (3): 317–335.

La Diega, G.N. 2018. Against the dehumanisation of decision-making. *Journal of Intellectual Property, Information Technology and Electronic Commerce Law*, 9 (1): 3–34.

Lamont M., S. Beljean and M. Clair. 2014. What is missing? Cultural processes and causal pathways to inequality. *Socio-Economic Review*, 12 (3): 573–608.

Lee, M.K. 2018. Understanding perception of algorithmic decisions: Fairness, trust, and emotion in response to algorithmic management. *Big Data & Society*, 5 (1): 1–16.

Matzner, T. 2017. Opening black boxes is not enough – Data-based surveillance in discipline and punish and today. *Foucault Studies*, 23: 27–45.

McNeill, F. 2006. A desistance paradigm for offender management. *Criminology & Criminal Justice*, 6 (1): 39–62.

McNeill F., S. Farrall, C. Lightowler and S. Maruna. 2014. Desistance and supervision. In *Encyclopedia of Criminology and Criminal Justice*, edited by G. Bruinsma and D. Weisburd, 958–967. New York: Springer.

Metcalf, C. and K. Stenson. 2004. Managing risk and the causes of crime. *Criminal Justice Matters*, 55 (1): 8–42.

Miller, M. and N. Morris. 1988. Predictions of dangerousness: An argument for limited use. *Violence and Victims*, 3 (4): 263–283.

Monahan J. and J. Skeem. 2016. Risk assessment in criminal sentencing. *Annual Review of Clinical Psychology*, 12: 489–513.

NOMS. 2009. *Public Protection Manual. Chapter 9. Risk of Harm*. National Offender Management Service/HM Prison Service. 2020. https://www.gov.uk/government/publications/public-protection-manual-chapter-9-risk-of-harm.

Northpointe. 2012. *Practitioners Guide to COMPAS*. Northpointe. http://www.northpointeinc.com/files/technical_documents/FieldGuide2_081412.pdf.

Paternoster, R. and S. Bushway. 2009. Desistance and the 'feared self': Toward an identity theory of criminal desistance. *Journal of Criminal Law and Criminology*, 99 (4): 1103–1156.

Peeters, R. and M. Schuilenburg. 2018. Machine justice: Governing security through the bureaucracy of algorithms. *Information Polity*, 23 (3): 267–280.

Robinson, G. 2017. Stand-down and deliver: Pre-sentence reports, quality and the new culture of speed. *Probation Journal*, 64 (4): 337–353.

Salo, B., T. Laaksonen and P. Santtila. 2016. Construct validity and internal reliability of the Finnish risk and needs assessment form. *Journal of Scandinavian Studies in Criminology and Crime Prevention*, 17 (1): 86–107.

Silver, E. 2000. Actuarial risk assessment: Reflections on an emerging social-scientific tool. *Critical Criminology*, 9 (1–2): 123–143.

Simmons, R. 2018. Big data, machine judges, and the legitimacy of the criminal justice system. *U.C. Davis Law Review*, 52 (2): 1067–1118.

Starr, S.B. 2014. Evidence-based sentencing and the scientific rationalization of discrimination. *Stanford Law Review*, 66: 803–872.

Stevenson, M.T. and J.L. Doleac. 2018. *The Roadblock to Reform*. American Constitution Society. https://www.acslaw.org/wp-content/uploads/2018/11/RoadblockToReform Report.pdf.

Taxman F.S., M. Caudy and S. Maass. 2014. Actualizing risk-need-responsivity. In *Encyclopedia of Criminology and Criminal Justice*, edited by G. Bruinsma and D. Weisburd, 1–11. New York: Springer.

Tonry M. 2019a. Predictions of dangerousness in sentencing: Déjà vu all over again. *Crime and Justice*, 48 (1): 439–482.

Tonry, M. 2019b. Fifty years of American sentencing reform: Nine lessons. *Crime and Justice*, 48: 1–34.

Van Eijk, G. 2017. Socioeconomic marginality in sentencing: The built-in bias in risk assessment tools and the reproduction of social inequality. *Punishment & Society*, 19 (4): 463–481.

Van Eijk, G. 2020. Inclusion and exclusion through risk-based justice: analysing combinations of risk assessment from pretrial detention to release. *British Journal of Criminology*, doi:10.1093/bjc/azaa012.

Van Wingerden, S., J. van Wilsem and M. Moerings. 2014. Pre-sentence reports and punishment: A quasi-experiment assessing the effects of risk-based pre-sentence reports on sentencing. *European Journal of Criminology*, 11 (6): 723–744.

Ward, T. 2011. Human rights and dignity in offender rehabilitation. *Journal of Forensic Psychology Practice*, 11 (2–3): 103–123.

Werth, R. 2017. Individualizing risk: Moral judgement, professional knowledge and affect in parole evaluations. *British Journal of Criminology*, 57 (4): 808–827.

Werth, R. 2019. Theorizing the performative effects of penal risk technologies: (Re)producing the subject who must be dangerous. *Social & Legal Studies*, 28 (3): 327–348.

Winner, L. 1980. Do artifacts have politics? *Daedalus*, 109 (1): 121–136.

Part III

Algorithmic cities

Chapter 9

Smart city imaginaries
Looking beyond the techno-utopian vision

Marc Schuilenburg and Brunilda Pali

Introduction

> *Maybe smart cities, these vast open-air labs,*
> *point the way to a new global civilization.*
>
> Thierry Happe, Founder CEO Netexplo

Many urban imaginaries circulate, but few are as popular as the smart city. Packaged primarily with a visual language of spectacular techno-futurism, the smart city has become an urban utopia for policymakers and urban planners promising to rationalize both the planning and governance of cities with technology that can monitor, manage and regulate various urban processes (Kitchin, 2015; Joss et al., 2019). In this techno-utopian vision, technological devices are deployed in large numbers in the public space and are integrated with mobile computing devices used by citizens, such as mobile phones, laptops and smart glasses. In order to better depict, model and predict urban processes, they are connected in a centralized network, so that large sets of collected data can be constantly analysed ('the urban dashboard') through algorithms and turned into clear predictable, intelligible and governable patterns. Central to this minute-to-minute governance is the idea that the urban environment needs to be as flexible as possible to accommodate the constantly shifting needs, demands and requirements of urban life (Zandbergen, 2018).

In less than two decades, the smart city has become a global narrative that promises to improve city-wide efficiency, decision-making, and safety (Townsend, 2013; Datta, 2015; Ersoy, 2017). Tech corporations like IBM[1] and Cisco, in particular, have been decisive in this process. Through "corporate storytelling" (Söderström, Paasche & Klauser, 2014: 307) and sheer "propaganda" (Schürer, 2020), they popularized a smart city global imaginary (Greenfield, 2013; Townsend, 2013). This imaginary is configured as a solution to all kinds of catastrophic events that cities face now and will face in the future, such as natural disasters due to climate change, high rates of criminality, and democratic fallacies, presented in scenarios (Tyszczuk, 2020). To make cities crisis- and disaster-resilient, smart technologies are used purporting to involve people, improve city services, and enhance urban systems. Singapore's smart traffic cameras, for example, restrict traffic depending on volume and ease the commute of thousands of passengers every day. In Eindhoven, one of the biggest Dutch municipalities, tension and aggression in the public space are reduced through adjusting lighting; sound analysis algorithms that can detect things like breaking glass, and release specific odours, such as the smell of oranges. In Santander, Spain, residents can turn their smartphones into the 20,000 sensors the city has installed, by downloading the 'Pulse of the City' app. City officials analyse the data in real time to adjust energy use, the number of trash pickups needed in a given week, and even how much water to sprinkle on the lawns of city parks. In each of these examples, the key belief and promise is that the advances and integration of smart technologies, data, and algorithms into urban life will bring about economic, democratic and safety benefits.

Although there is no such thing as *the* smart city, the power of the concept captures the minds of corporations, policymakers and citizens – making it an important tool through which cities are being reconfigured and reconstructed in the 21st century. An important reason why the smart city has become such a popular brand is the fact that it is presented as a value-neutral, objective, rational, and evidence-based concept. A claim of objectivity is often used by developers and policymakers in order to guarantee that societal decisions are based on what appear to be rational findings, based exclusively on data and algorithms with no human interference (Gillespie, 2014; Kitchin, 2014). This means that these decisions can be approached from a completely 'non-ideological' perspective. However, as Jathan Sadowski and Frank Pasquale (2015) argued, there is nothing more ideologized than the deployment of the term 'non-ideology', as it enables the concealing of the assumptions that drive those supposedly neutral, objective and common-sense solutions (see also Thrift & French, 2002; Kitchin & Dodge, 2011). In fact, all urban planning initiatives, including smart cities, which are motivated by political and commercial interests, are 'inherently ideological, because they constitute a dominant agent's vision for what urban changes or perceived improvements to public space should be implemented' (Scott, 2016: 7). As a consequence, the smart city demands deconstruction, critique, and social and cultural theory interpretations (Vanolo, 2014; Sadowski & Pasquale, 2015; Schuilenburg & Peeters, 2018; Sadowski & Bendor, 2019).

Fashionable and unquestioned city visions, whether they are 'smart', 'creative', or 'green', need particular scrutiny and must be interrogated in relation to the social imaginaries which they feed and on which they are fed (Campbell, 1996; Peck, 2005; Hollands, 2008; Lindner & Meissner, 2018). Without such interrogation, the arguments used by smart city proponents will remain unchallenged in their claims to a kind of universal and depoliticized approach to the economic, natural and societal crises cities are facing. In interrogating their underpinning imaginaries and visions, we must apply a "hermeneutics of suspicion", as Sadowski and Pasquale (2015) call for, referring to, as the word 'suspects' suggests, a critical analysis of 'obvious or self-evident meanings in order to draw out less visible and less flattering truths' (Ricoeur, 1970: 356). Who sets, for instance, the priorities and who drives the agendas of these urban imaginaries? What are the implications for those who will live or work there? Which people are included in these visions and which are excluded? In short, by which social imaginaries are smart cities governed?

This chapter examines and unpacks the social imaginary of the smart city. Starting by tracing the link between social imaginaries and urban imaginaries, we turn our attention in the ensuing paragraphs to the specific social imaginaries of the smart city. We argue that while smart technologies have become the dominant driver in the making of smart cities, they are essentially a way of rethinking cities' economic, democratic and social ways of working. Therefore, we propose to look 'beyond' the dominant driver of smart cities – smart technologies – in order to understand which imaginaries are nourished that generate and justify the need for smart technologies. We discern three types of social imaginaries that are embedded in the smart city: an economic, a democratic, and a security imaginary. By analysing these three types, we show how an economization of fields and practices, which were previously understood and analysed in non-economic terms, is taking place in our urban environment.

On social imaginaries

Several scholars have argued that social imaginaries are central to the construction of social institutions, subjectivities, and practices. They have used the imaginary as a heuristic tool in the study of societies that challenges the primacy given to material structures over cultural and symbolic ones (see Anderson, 1983; Castoriadis, 1987; Appadurai, 1996; Taylor, 2004). Although these scholars deal with quite different aspects of the concept of the imaginary, they all recognize the non-material and symbolic dimensions in the constitution of the material, while focusing on ways in which imaginaries shape and reshape reality (Vandevoordt, Clycq & Verschraegen, 2018). In other words, rather than adhering 'to a false dichotomy of reality and imaginary' (Armstrong, 2013: 142), there is a need to recognise the imaginary's place in the constitution of past, present and future realities. While it is outside the scope of this chapter to discuss in detail the concept of social imaginaries, following Sheila Jasanoff and Sang-Hyun Kim (2009: 120), we understand them to be 'collectively imagined forms of social life and social order which are reflected in the design and fulfilment' of scientific, technological, national, global and other social projects.

While the nation state (Anderson, 1983) is a paradigmatic case of social imaginary, other modern social imaginaries have at different times come to the foreground, such as public sphere, civil society, the globe, the market – and, as we will argue in this chapter, the smart city. As suggested by political theorist Benjamin Barber (2013), currently, it is cities, and no longer the nation state, that are becoming the playground for politics and the main referent of late modern social imaginaries. Parag Khanna (2011), writing for the McKinsey Global Institute, argues that 'in a world that increasingly appears ungovernable, cities – not states – are the islands of governance on which the future world order will be built'. Cities have been therefore gradually imagined and reclassified as crucial "engines" (Raco & Imrie, 2000) of social and economic development.

Different scholars have used the concept of the imaginary to understand cities in general and smart cities in particular (see Soja, 2000; Merricks White, 2016;

Vanolo, 2016; Wang, 2017; De Waal & Dignum, 2017; Lindner & Meissner, 2018; Sadowski & Bendor, 2019). Martijn De Waal and Marloes Dignum (2017: 264) define urban imaginaries as 'a set of visions, hopes, and fears that may directly affect government policy decisions, urban design criteria, capitalist investment, people's attitudes, etc.' Situating the urban imaginary of the smart city in time and space, Frederico Cugurullo (2018) showed how the faith in technology and innovation, professed by the proponents of the smart city, dates back to the publication of Francis Bacon's *New Atlantis* in 1627. An iteration of a modern impetus to imagine and shape the future of the city and of urban society, the smart city is presented as the most desirable model for the development of the cities of tomorrow and represents, according to Alberto Vanolo (2014), the latest phase in the "history of urban imaginaries". Other related notions that bear 'family resemblance' with the smart city are 'tech cities', 'digital cities', 'wired cities', 'cyber-cities', 'knowledge cities', 'innovation cities', 'eco-cities', 'intelligent cities', 'sim cities', 'data cities', 'City of Things', 'entrepreneurial cities', 'competitive cities', 'creative cities', and 'sustainable cities' (Kitchin, 2014). However, none has been as successful to capture and maintain the imagination as the 'smart city' has.

This all leads to the question of why 'smart' has become such a powerful imaginary. According to different scholars, the mobilisation of large amounts of data by different types of technologies is both the driving force behind smart city initiatives as well as the means by which these initiatives are implemented (Shelton, Zook & Wiig, 2015; Sadowski & Bendor, 2019). In what follows, we unpack the social imaginary of the smart city by elaborating the techno-utopian vision the smart city builds on, while focusing on the implementation of digital technologies in particular.

A techno-utopian vision

At its very core, the concept of smart city is based on a techno-utopian vision that data, digital infrastructures and technologies can enable urban governments to establish total control over, find solutions to, and govern all the complex social, cultural, political, and economic aspects of life in the city in a smarter way (Morozov, 2013; Söderström, Paasche & Klauser, 2014; Willis & Aurigi, 2017). According to Mischa Dohler and others (2013): 'It is through information and communications technologies that smart cities are truly turning "smart"'. An important element of this narrative of the smart city is that smart technologies are seen as inevitable and progressive, as a 'technocratic *pensée unique*' (Sadowski & Pasquale, 2015: 4). The driver of the integration of "techno-utopianism" (Wiig, 2015; Vanolo, 2016), "technocratic dreams" (Dunn & Cureton, 2020), or "techno-politics" (Mitchell, 2002) into urban life, is the neoliberal notion that global competitiveness among cities will automatically make them better places to live in (Harvey, 2005) and bring about 'economic, environmental and social benefits in future-focused scenarios' (Caprotti, 2019: 2467). According to Zeynep Bodur Okyay (2018), president and CEO of the Kale Group, 'it is no longer countries that are in competition, but cities. Every city will have to gain a competitive edge to differentiate itself from the rest. (…) Cities will compete and collaborate globally as interdependent entities and will drive the future.' Inside this technocratic dream, futures are imagined to be "frictionless" (Dunn & Cureton, 2020).

Smart city narratives emphasize primarily the possibility of collecting and processing digital data and the possibility of interconnecting different types of data, such as people's movement and their spatial behaviour, traffic mobility, public transportation, energy usage, water supply, and garbage collection. Matteo Pasquinelli (2015) used the concept of 'algorithmic governance' to point out that we are more than ever trying to create and manage relations and patterns between different types of data, and as a second step identify and manage deviations or abnormalities from those patterns. As Humberto Iglesia of the smart Medellin city-pilot states: 'For us a Smart City is a city that uses data and analyses this data. For us, a Smart City is a city that is totally interconnected' (cited in Cathelat, 2019: 112). Turning big data into usable information and knowledge that can be interpreted by machines for further urban governance processes is where smart data come in. Smart city policies presume that data-driven urbanisation allows for better decision-making, optimal mobilisation of resources, coordinated public service delivery, safe and better living conditions, and overall smart governance. A good example is the Intelligent Operations Center of IBM in Rio de Janeiro, which draws together data from more than 30 different types of agencies. This enables the scrutinization, control, and management of different parts of the city. As the mayor of Rio de Janeiro stated, the system 'allows us to have people looking into every corner of the city, 24 hours a day, seven days a week' (cited in Malik, 2019).

Data-driven urbanisation is in part a consequence of increased opportunities to link technological innovation with the urban environment. Rather than the construction of new cities from scratch, smart technologies are built into existing forms of urban governance and the material infrastructure of cities, such as networked sensors and actuators that both allow the monitoring of the urban environment in real time as well as act on their own intelligently with little or even no human intervention, from street lighting to automated water and electricity meters. The success of these kind of initiatives relies, to a large extent, on the invisibility of smart technologies, and also on the lack of awareness of citizens of the fact that their data are being collected. Cities, or parts of them like streets, neighbourhoods, districts, or university campuses,[2] have become literally test areas and laboratories in real-life conditions, so-called Urban Living Labs, that do not follow the ethical requirements that usual lab research requires. Similar to what Silicon Valley libertarians call "permissionless innovation" (Thierer, 2016), according to which technological progress should not be stifled by public regulations, smart cities are claiming their absolute freedom to experiment, test and innovate. As a consequence, surveillance technologies, understood as data gathering for the purpose of governing, are becoming so ubiquitous and subtle as to become totally 'subsumed into the background of everyday life' (Sadowski & Pasquale, 2015: 9). As an illustration, we can recall the famous statement made in 1991 by chief technology officer at Xerox PARC, Mark Weiser, that '[t]he most profound technologies are those that disappear… [those that] weave themselves into the fabric of everyday life until they are indistinguishable from it' (1991). The heavily disputed smart city project of Sidewalk Labs on the Toronto waterfront, for example, is one of the most highly evolved versions to date of surveillance with the prospect of collecting massive data. The information, when analysed, offers new insights to modify both the behaviour of citizens in public space and the urban space accordingly.

All that is required to understand, manage and fix the problems that a city faces, is a suitable technology, sufficient data and smart algorithms (Galič, 2019). While these features reveal a great deal about the attractiveness of the smart city, a deeper and more critical understanding of the smart city is necessary in order to understand how it serves as a principle for managing our urban environments. Against the background of the currently growing debate on smart cities, we need to ask a number of questions: Which specific values and ideas underpin the concept of the smart city? Which urban visions, policies and practices are promoted by smart cities? Which imaginaries are translated into practice and policy and what is their role in the future of our cities?

A tale of three imaginaries

With the aforementioned questions in mind, we look beyond the described techno-utopian vision to unearth specific social imaginaries that drive and shape the visions of the smart city. For this, we have collected available literature, policy papers and reports of smart cities around the world in order to investigate what we call the 'social lives' of smart technology. Drawing on several practices that purport to make cities smart, we discern three different, but interrelated social imaginaries: an (a) economic, (b) democratic, and (c) security imaginary.[3] How were these imaginaries born, how have they developed, which are the shared features and differences between them?

Economic imaginary

The central discursive trope that captures the social imaginary of the smart city is, without a doubt, an economic one: smart technologies foster growth, prosperity, knowledge, education, and more. According to this argument, 'smart' adds value and capital in cities, makes them 'hip and thriving' hubs of growth, and improves the lives of the citizens and businesses that inhabit it. Through technological ways that make cities better for the people who inhabit them, smart cities will 'force economic growth and societal progress', as Ginni Rometty, President and Chief Executive Officer of IBM, proclaimed in a speech on how organizations and people can become more competitive in the "era of smart" (Rometty, 2013). The construction of a smart city is promoted as useful to attract investments, leading sector professional workers and tourists (Brand, 2007; Hollands, 2008; Kitchin, 2014). Driven by innovation and entrepreneurship, its central goals are attracting businesses and jobs while focusing on efficiency, savings and productivity (Caragliu, Del Bo & Nijkamp, 2011). As market proponents love to point out, cities are massive economic engines and therefore we need to "unleash the entrepreneurial power of them" (Hwang, 2014).

The limitations of municipalities in working in a problem-solving way form a central feature of the economical perspective on governing public issues in smart cities. Worldwide, municipalities are seen as failing to live up to the expectations of those whom they govern. Where they are unable to govern effectively, the restructuring of public services is not merely a question of developing good policies but more a managerial question of organizing close collaboration between government and private parties (Meijer & Bolivar, 2015). Governments are no longer called upon to govern, command, and control. In smart cities, modest government relies on 'steering', as opposed to 'rowing', to achieve public objectives (cf. Osborne & Gaebler, 1992). This leads to networked forms of governance based on public–private partnerships, new public management, market governance, and privatization of municipal services, supported by the belief that smart city suppliers, such as Cisco, Siemens, Microsoft and IBM, can deliver immense savings on the provision of similar or even better type of services. A good example is the French city Nice, winner of the Smart Innovation 2016, where the municipality collaborates with major industrial groups, local SMEs and start-ups, especially those linked to the French Tech network and the world of research and education, in order to optimize the management of the city and the creation of jobs.

In the literature on the smart city, many scholars have voiced the need for caution regarding the neoliberal political economy that prioritizes market-led and technological solutions to city governance (Hollands, 2008; Kitchin, 2014; Sadowski & Pasquale, 2015; Grossi & Pianezzi, 2017; Morozov & Bria, 2018). Especially problematic is the tendency to see the use of smart technology by tech companies such as Cisco and Siemens as a kind of universal and rational way of governing in the city. Here, the concept of smart cities is presented as fundamentally 'post-political' in nature, as it disregards the political character of decision-making (Burnham, 2001; Lahiji, 2014; Wilson & Swyngedouw, 2014). This means that matters of public concern are discussed and handled in ways that foreclose questions of 'the political' (Rancière, 1995; Mouffe, 2005). Due to this process of depoliticization, governance criteria are increasingly reframed as 'objective' management criteria with an emphasis on data-driven decision protocols, measurable outputs and performance indicators to improve efficiency and effectiveness. Evgeny Morozov and Francesca Bria (2018: 10) argue that smart cities need to 'quantify the performance of their various constituent parts in order to render them more accountable, competitive, and manageable'. This is illustrated by the growing importance of rankings, competitive tables, and comparative scores of smart cities, which offer the means for cities to market their attributes and use such performance indices as a means to 'outsmart' one another (Giffinger et al., 2007).

Democratic imaginary

A second trope that captures the social imaginary of the smart city is that smart technologies enhance democratic processes. The democratic argument is rooted in the idea that smart technologies have the potential to leverage newer and richer forms of public decision-making and democratic participation. These technologies are increasingly presented as being 'citizen-based' or 'people-centred' and as having the potential to provide information to citizens in an interactive manner so that they can co-create and participate in all sorts of public policy processes that lead to smart governance (Cowley, Joss & Davot, 2017; Kumar, 2017; Cardullo & Kitchin, 2019). In Vienna, almost 600 official assistance pages facilitate or replace the physical municipal authority. Surveys among the users show: "Who 'goes online,' saves about 2 h. Very smart!" Here, the concept 'smart governance' is used to capture these new technologically mediated governance arrangements and practices. Examples of smart governance take different forms and include, amongst others, hackathons, living labs, fablabs, smart urban labs, citizen dashboards, maker spaces, smart citizens' labs, gamification concepts, and open datasets.

According to William Webster and Charles Leleux (2018: 101), the so-called participatory governance practices share four characteristics. They all have a focus on smart technology, whether it is reusing existing data or designing new applications to participate. Also, they all require the input and engagement of citizens. Next, they involve a physical as well as a virtual digital interaction. And, finally, each requires an initial stimulus from formal public agencies[4] in order to create the space and provide opportunities for engagement. Many examples of public decision-making processes emphasize the transformative potential of the use of smart technology. Key terms of these citizen-first or people-centred approaches are 'participation', 'mobilisation', 'trust', and 'inclusion'. As Mikko Rusama, Chief Digital Officer of the smart city Helsinki, puts it: 'We are working to build a culture of trust. The trust is based on openness, transparency, and the sharing of data and how decisions are made' (cited in Cathelat, 2019: 230).

The acclaimed social use of smart technology to enhance democratic processes deflects the attention away from the fact that it still remains unclear which examples of smart governance work best in which contexts. Also, and more importantly from the perspective of this chapter, it remains unclear how citizens are envisaged as democratic actors in smart cities.[5] It is not surprising that the emphasis on the role of the technologically 'empowered' smart citizen comes at a time of increased critical scrutiny of smart cities (De Waal & Dignum, 2017). In 2017, Dhaka, Bangladesh, hosted the Smart City Week to 'focus on building people-centred cities not only investing in technology and infrastructure alone but also engaging smart people who care.' A driving force behind smart projects is corporate-driven awareness that we need enough social peace and enough equity to avoid discontent among the citizens of smart cities (Cathelat, 2019). In its 2018 Trends, Cisco expresses this concern as follows: 'Ignoring the poor, the foreigners, could be a destabilising factor.' The marketing push for smart cities comes with an obligatory nod to 'bottom-up' solutions and community involvement. This means that citizens, as 'consumers' and not as 'political actors', are required to express their opinions on the quality of public services. Critics have pointed out that this 'undermines more collective imaginations of citizenship, solidarity and mutual responsibility, feeding into a neoliberal individualist ethos of consumership, where the market determines what is best for citizens' (De Waal & Dignum, 2017: 267; Cardullo & Kitchin, 2019). At the same time, critics have shown how frequently the so-called 'citizen-participation' projects are simply forms of tokenism, where citizens can have their say, but do not have any significant 'political' influence (Gordon & Mihailidis, 2016). It would be in fact utterly naïve to assume that each of the involved actors in such projects have equal or even comparable roles or power.

Security imaginary

The third trope of the social imaginary of the smart city is that smart technologies promise a safe and secure future for its citizens. When a city is considering investment in smart technologies, public safety and security are often key drivers for implementing a given initiative (Lacinák & Ristvej, 2017; Schuilenburg & Peeters, 2018; Pali & Schuilenburg, 2019). In Hangzhou, for instance, part of the corporate-driven project City Brain, a sub-project has been developed, called Community and Public Safety, where video analysis technology and video recognition algorithms are used to take preventive measures to ensure the safety and security of the public. The possibility of permanent surveillance of citizens by using smart technology that gathers and integrates big amounts of data is promoted as enhancing better protection against the dangers of criminality and disorder, but also against a varied and colourful range of natural or man-made disasters (such as floods, storms, traffic accidents, fire accidents, mass violence, terrorist attacks, water safety, network security, etc.).

The implementation of smart technologies emanates from the insight that crime levels are, and will probably remain, high in open and prosperous cities, and that local governments have only limited possibilities to deal with this situation. Tasks in this domain are increasingly being transferred to private tech companies that tackle them in their own particular way. On the one hand, commercial parties are increasingly being assigned 'police-type' duties, such as the monitoring of shopping malls, business estates, university campuses, airports, and gated communities (Shearing & Stenning, 1983; Wakefield, 2003; Schuilenburg, 2015). On the other hand, commercial parties employ the software for law enforcement agencies in order to protect citizens against crime, disorder, and other unwelcome behaviour. In this new framework, there is mention of collaboration with the local government to a greater or lesser extent. The formalization of the collaboration between municipalities and private tech companies occurs by means of contracts or similar agreements, such as protocols and covenants.

In the jumble of new smart technologies to create risk-free and safe cities, a rough distinction can be made between predictive and psycho-political technologies (Pali & Schuilenburg, 2019). Preventive technologies, such as predictive policing, facial recognition, automated license plate recognition system, biometrical control, and advanced video monitoring, have been implemented in a number of smart cities, including Amsterdam, Atlanta, Chicago, London, Stockholm, and Singapore. Singapore's government, for example, has launched the Lamppost-as-a-Platform project to install 100,000 surveillance cameras throughout the city linked to facial recognition software. Proponents of these technologies highlight the low-cost relative to more traditional crime control. According to tech company IBM, one of the first companies to employ the software for law enforcement, predictive policing, for example, is helping mayors and police departments to tackle crime on a reduced budget. It is a cost-effective way to 'do more with less' because it streamlines law enforcement operations in numerous ways, from tracking, searching and detecting suspects ('hot persons') to proactive crime prevention by identifying crime areas ('hot spots'). Several critics have emphasized the risks of these technologies for privacy, discrimination and marginalization of certain groups. John Cheney-Lippold (2011: 165), for example, highlights the problems associated with a "new algorithmic identity", an identity formation that applies mathematical algorithms to infer categories of identities based on group profiling.

Psycho-political technologies are techniques used to actively modify the behaviour of the visitors of public or semi-public spaces in smart cities. Smart sensors and devices, for instance, allow streetlights to dim or brighten automatically based on the activity on the streets, to ensure both efficiency and safety. At the same time, these sensors and devices help people to travel the most effective routes, avoiding noise and areas that have a high crime intensity. For example, GPS navigation app Waze has included an 'Avoid Dangerous Neighbourhoods' functionality and designates 'dangerous neighbourhoods' around the world (Liberatore, 2016). As a consequence, smart technologies, including apps and bots, ultra-personalize our urban experience by providing real-time information to modify our behaviour. This is made possible by wearable technology like smart watches and smart glasses, wholly centred upon individual needs. A second form of psycho-political techniques is the moulding of the atmosphere of public space through odours, light and sound manipulation by analysing large amounts of data – including amount of social interactions, police presence, waste in the street, parking density, sound level, and weather information. The aim of these techniques is to reduce tension and aggression and to establish, what the Dutch smart city Eindhoven calls, "a happy city". The colour blue, for instance, is believed to have a cooling and stringent effect. When the right shade of blue is used, it can lower heart rates and reduce people's aggression (Schuilenburg & Peeters, 2018; Pali & Schuilenburg, 2019).

Neoliberal ethos

It is important to realize that the smart city is not just a technological narrative, but rather one which involves complex political and social ordering processes, populated by images, stories, dreams and so on. We should acknowledge the ideological nature and appealing visions of these imaginaries. This means that the smart city needs to be understood as a performative term, as it allows public and private parties to reshape and transform the city according to the shared imaginaries articulated in the notion of the smart city. Following sociologist Donna Haraway (2011: 4): 'It matters what stories make worlds, what worlds make stories.' Beyond a technological narrative, we have shown that the smart city is embedded within three other social imaginaries: an economic, a democratic, and a security imaginary.

As to the shared features and differences between these social imaginaries of the smart city, it is clear that they are embedded in a neoliberal ethos of market-led and technocratic solutions to city governance and development. Neoliberalism, as scholars like Wendy Brown (2006, 2015), David Harvey (2005) and Quinn Slobodian (2018) argued, is not simply about laissez-faire, deregulation and privatization. It is also about intervention and regulation of social processes and security governance with the aim of injecting market principles of competition into these spheres of urban life. Smart infrastructure, for example, both controls and facilitates the freedom of citizens by actively regulating and managing both the atmosphere of public space and the behaviour of individuals. As a consequence, 'control comes to be so subtle that it may well present itself in the form of "choice"' (Savat, 2009: 57).

The neoliberal ethos means that economic rationality is not confined to the economic sphere of the smart city. Besides the economic sphere, both the political (democracy) and social sphere (security) of the smart city are increasingly dominated by market relations and organized according to an economic rationality. As a consequence, economic criteria are extended into urban spheres which are not economic. This means that the political and social sphere of the smart city becomes redefined as an economic domain. The model of the market is extended into the political and social arena of the smart city – even where money is not at stake – thereby collapsing the distinction between these spheres. As a consequence, the public sphere of the smart city is structured by specific forms of intervention, including new forms of decision-making processes and security provision. This is reflected in the governance criteria of democratic processes and security provision. These criteria assume that competition is the only legitimate organizing principle for the governance of both spheres. The consequence of this process of depoliticization is that governance criteria of both spheres are presented in apparently neutral terms, such as 'customers', 'consumers', 'effectiveness', 'efficiency', and 'indicators'.

The extension of entrepreneurial forms within the political and social domain of the smart city shows that criminality, for example, is no longer seen outside the market model, but is considered a market in itself. IBM has spent 'more than $14 billion on developing predictive analytics software for both commerce and law enforcement sectors' (Wang, 2018: 231). In Atlanta and Chicago, IBM provides judicial authorities with information that allows them to detect crime patterns based on big data analytics. According to the company, they are helping the police to work better because 'law enforcement's main problem is the fragmentation of information' (Willis & Aurigi, 2017: 156). Coupled with insights from the field of behavioural economics, the implications of such developments are wide-ranging, especially considering that the normative consequences can hardly be underestimated. The economization of security is 'sold' by tech companies with the message that the governance of security is measurable and controllable and therefore can be managed. As a consequence, efficient solutions are confused with good solutions, whereas the crime issue really involves difficult and long-term processes without commercial motives or a profit-and-loss mentality being involved. Does one wish to tackle urban problems by offering inhabitants more job and housing opportunities, or is one merely seeking commercial success by deploying smart security technologies to stimulate an efficient, safe and consumption-focused use of public space?

Conclusion

Nourished by a techno-utopian imaginary, which highlights decision-making algorithms based on data gathered in smart projects, the 'brave smart city' promises to solve all kinds of crises and disasters that cities will face now and, in the future, leading to smarter ways of being, living and governing. Viewed as utterly 'desirable', 'inevitable', 'rational', and 'post-political', 'smart' has colonized our urban futures. Mayors are racing to turn their cities into smart ones, and large tech corporations are selling cheap smart dreams at a high price. Against the background of the growing popularity of smart cities, it becomes important to discuss the alleged neutrality of smart technologies. While these technologies in themselves are neither good nor bad, they are also not neutral because they are hooked into a broader social imaginary of life in our cities. In other words, smart technologies are always a function of power relations – and so are their effects.

As we have shown in this chapter, taken-for-granted unquestioned smart city visions need particular scrutiny and must be interrogated in relation to the social imaginaries that govern them. Against the background of the growing debate on smart cities, we need to understand these visions, policies and practices promoted by smart cities, that are translated into practice as well as their role in the future of our cities. More specifically, we showed how smart 'storytelling' is built on a core idea that advances an integration of smart technologies into urban life that will bring about economic, democratic and security benefits. By critically interrogating the economic, democratic, and security imaginaries, we showed how a neoliberal ethos is increasingly pushing economic rationality into fields and practices which were previously understood and analysed in non-economic terms. This neoliberal ethos regulates political processes and security governance with the aim of regulating social life according to market principles and forms of competition. In other words, it favours corporate interests and is driven primarily by commercial gain, while preventing the production of alternative imaginaries of urban space.

Aiming at 'repoliticizing' the smart city debate (cf. March & Ribera-Fumaz, 2016), we claim that we need to unpack the smart city into different layers of promises, visions, and fictions that are invested in the concept and hold it together. Our core argument is that the described imaginaries are fundamental in structuring our experiences, shaping our realities, and making our futures, as much as they are crucial in disabling alternative experiences, realities, and futures. They are an intimate part of our lives as they profoundly colonize our existence. A critical understanding of the imaginaries that govern smart city projects is only the starting point. Once we understand and decode smart projects, we can find ways to disengage with them, to stop being seduced by them, and to engage ourselves with alternative imaginaries, which have nothing to do with the market and competition.

Notes

1 Debates over the meaning of smart city 'started in 2007 with an IBM marketing campaign, it culminated in 2011 with the company registering the trademark "Smarter Cities"' (Schürer, 2020: 49).
2 The University of Glasgow, for example, has been working with innovation centre Future Cities Catapult on a strategy to bring smart tech to the campus. According to Gemmy Ginty, one of the designers who worked on the strategy, universities are uniquely well placed to experiment: 'Smart cities are kind of slow-moving. Cities are so big, and there are so many players and stakeholders, it can be difficult. But universities have control over their estates. They own all the buildings, they own all the networks and they have a captive audience in terms of the students, so they can become like a living lab' (cited in Niemtus, 2019).
3 See also Hollands (2008), who presents the smart city agenda as covering four broad concerns: more efficient political and economic management through the use of networked infrastructure, business-led urban development, favorable conditions for investment in the technology and creative sectors, and social and ecological sustainability; and Rogan (2020), who deconstructs the ideology of smartness along three axioms: the economic, the political, and the spatial.
4 Barcelona is an interesting example of a pioneering smart city, which, after a technocratic turn, elected Ada Colau as a mayor on a mandate of democratizing the city and putting citizens centre stage, by opening digital platforms to greater citizen participation and oversight and promoting 'technological sovereignty'. In 2018, the Smart City Expo in Barcelona, used Henry Lefebvre's phrase 'right to the city' to demand a more inclusive and participatory city, calling for a 'right to the (smart) city'.
5 See Cowley, Joss and Davot (2017) for a typology of smart city 'public' in six different cities in the United Kingdom.

References

Anderson, B. 1983. Imagined communities. *Reflections on the origin and spread of nationalism.* London: Verso.

Appadurai, A. 1996. *Modernity at large.* Minneapolis/London: University of Minnesota Press.

Armstrong, S. 2013. Using the future to predict the past: Prison population projections and the colonisation of penal imagination. In *Crime, critique, and utopia*, edited by M. Malloch and B. Munro, 136–163. London: Palgrave Macmillan.

Barber, B.R. 2013. *If mayors ruled the world: Dysfunctional nations, rising cities.* Yale: University Press.

Brand, P. 2007. Green subjection: The politics of neoliberal urban environmental management. *International Journal of Urban and Regional Research*, 31 (3): 616–632.

Brown, W. 2006. American nightmare: Neoliberalism, neoconservatism, and de-democratization. *Political Theory*, 34 (6): 690–714.

Brown, W. 2015. *Undoing the demos. Neoliberalism's stealth revolution.* New York: Zone Books.

Burnham, P. 2001. New labour and the politics of depoliticization. *The British Journal of Politics & International Relations*, 3 (2): 127–149.

Campbell, S. 1996. Green cities, growing cities, just cities? Urban planning and the contradictions of sustainable development. *Journal of the American Planning Association*, 62 (3): 296–312.

Caragliu, A., C. Del Bo and P. Nijkamp. 2011. Smart cities in Europe. *Journal of Urban Technology*, 18 (2): 65–82.

Cardullo, P. and R. Kitchin. 2019. Being a 'citizen' in the smart city: Up and down the scaffold of smart citizen participation. *GeoJournal*, 84 (1): 11–24.

Caprotti, F. 2019. Spaces of visibility in the smart city: Flagship urban spaces and the smart urban imaginary. *Urban Studies*, 56 (12): 2465–2479.

Cathelat, B. 2019. *Smart cities: Shaping the societies of 2030*. https://unesdoc.unesco.org/ark:/48223/pf0000367762; accessed 15-01-2020.

Castoriadis, C. 1987. *The imaginary institution of society*. Cambridge: MIT University Press.

Cheney-Lippold, J. 2011. A new algorithmic identity. *Theory, Culture & Society*, 28 (6): 164–181.

Cowley, R., S. Joss and Y. Davot. 2017. The smart city and its publics: Insights from across six UK cities. *Urban Research and Practice*, 11 (1): 53–77.

Cugurullo, F. 2018. The origin of the smart city imaginary: From the dawn of modernity to the eclipse of reason. In *The Routledge companion to urban imaginaries*, edited by C. Lindner and M. Meissner. London: Routledge.

Datta, A. 2015. New urban utopias of postcolonial India: 'Entrepreneurial urbanization' in Dholera smart city, Gujarat. *Dialogues in Human Geography*, 5 (1): 3–22.

De Waal, M. and M. Dignum. 2017. The citizen in the smart city: How the smart city could transform citizenship. *Information Technology*, 59 (6), 263–273.

Dohler, M., C. Ratti, J. Paraszczak and G. Falconer. 2013. *Smart cities*. https://techblog.com-soc.org/2013/05/14/smart-cities/; accessed 15-01-2020.

Dunn, N. and P. Cureton. 2020. Frictionless futures: The vision of smartness and the occlusion of alternatives. In *Architecture and the smart city*, edited by S.M. Figueiredo, S. Krishnamuthy and T. Schroeder, 17–28. London: Routledge.

Ersoy, A. 2017. Smart cities as a mechanism towards a broader understanding of infrastructure interdependencies. *Regional Studies, Regional Science*, 4 (1): 26–31.

Galič, M. 2019. *Surveillance and privacy in smart cities and living labs. Conceptualising privacy for public space*. Rotterdam: Optima Grafische Communicatie.

Giffinger, R., C. Fertner, H. Kramar and R. Kasalek. 2007. *Smart cities – Ranking of European medium sized cities. Final report*. Vienna: The Centre of Regional Science, Vienna University of Technology.

Gillespie, T. 2014. The relevance of algorithms. In *Media technologies: Essays on communication, materiality, and society*, edited by T. Gillespie, P. Boczkowski, & K. Foot, 167–194. Cambridge, US: MIT University Press.

Gordon, E. and P. Mihailidis (Eds.). 2016. *Civic media: Technology, design, practice*. Cambridge, US: MIT University Press.

Greenfield, A. 2013. *Against the smart city*. New York: Do Projects.

Grossi, G. and D. Pianezzi. 2017. Smart cities: Utopia or neoliberal ideology? *Cities: The International Journal of Urban Policy and Planning*, 69: 79–85.

Haraway, D. 2011. *SF: Science fiction, speculative fabulation, string figures, so far. Pilgrim Award Acceptance Comments*. https://people.ucsc.edu/~haraway/Files/PilgrimAcceptance Haraway.pdf; accessed 18-03-2020.

Harvey, D. 2005. *A brief history of neoliberalism*. Oxford: Oxford University Press.

Hollands, R. 2008. Will the real smart city please stand up? Intelligent, progressive or entrepreneurial? *City*, 12 (3): 303–320.

Hwang, V.W. 2014. *Are cities our new economic engines?* https://www.forbes.com/sites/victorhwang/2014/08/14/cities-our-new-economic-engines/#7179721b1ec4; accessed 15-03-2020.

Jasanoff, S. and S.-H. Kim. 2009. Containing the atom: Sociotechnical imaginaries and nuclear power in the United States and South Korea. *Minerva*, 47: 119–146.

Joss, S., F. Sengers, D. Schraven, F. Caprotti and Y. Dayot. 2019. The smart city as global discourse: Storylines and critical junctures across 27 cities. *Journal of Urban Technology*, 26 (1): 3–34.

Khanna, P. 2011. *When cities rule the world.* https://www.mckinsey.com/featured-insights/urbanization/when-cities-rule-the-world; accessed 30-01-2020.

Kitchin, R. 2014. The real-time city? Big data and smart urbanism. *GeoJournal*, 79 (1): 1–14.

Kitchin, R. 2015. Making sense of smart cities: Addressing present shortcomings. *Cambridge Journal of Regions, Economy and Society*, 8 (1): 131–136.

Kitchin, R. and M. Dodge. 2011. *Code/space: Software and everyday life.* Cambridge, US: MIT University Press.

Kumar, V.T.M. (Ed.). 2017. *E-Democracy for smart cities.* New York: Springer.

Lacinák, M. and J. Ristvej. 2017. Smart city, safety and security. *Procedia Engineering*, 192: 522–527.

Lahiji, N. (Ed.). 2014. *Architecture against the post-political: Essays in reclaiming the critical project.* London: Routledge.

Liberatore, S. 2016. Slower but safer: Waze navigation app adds ability to avoid crime hotspots. *The Daily Mail*, June 17. https://www.dailymail.co.uk/sciencetech/article-3647262/Commuters-avoid-crime-hotspots-Waze-app-route-drivers-high-risk-areas.html; accessed 15-03-2020.

Lindner, C. and M. Meissner. 2018. *The Routledge companion to urban imaginaries.* London: Routledge.

March, H. and R. Ribera-Fumaz. 2016. Smart contradictions: The politics of making Barcelona a self-sufficient city. *European Urban and Regional Studies*, 23 (4): 816–830.

Malik, K. 2019. *As surveillance culture grows, can we even hope to escape its reach?* https://www.theguardian.com/commentisfree/2019/may/19/as-surveillance-culture-grows-can-we-even-hope-to-escape-its-reach; accessed 15-04-2020.

Meijer, A. and M.P.R. Bolivar. 2015. Governing the smart city: A review of the literature on smart urban governance. *International Review of Administrative Sciences*, 82 (2): 392–408.

Merricks White, J. 2016. Anticipatory logics of the smart city's global imaginary. *Urban Geography*, 37 (4): 572–589.

Mitchell, T. 2002. *Rule of experts: Egypt, techno-politics, modernity.* Berkeley, CA: University of California Press.

Morozov, E. 2013. *To save everything, click here: The folly of technological solutionism.* New York: Public Affairs.

Morozov, E. and F. Bria. 2018. *Rethinking the smart city: Democratizing urban technology.* New York Office: Rosa Luxembourg Stiftung.

Mouffe, C. 2005. *On the political.* London: Routledge.

Niemtus, Z. 2019. *Are university campuses turning into mini smart cities?* https://www.theguardian.com/education/2019/feb/22/are-university-campuses-turning-into-mini-smart-cities; accessed 16-01-2020.

Okyay, Z.B. 2018. *This is what a smart city should do for its people.* https://www.weforum.org/agenda/2018/10/smart-city-people-canakkale-connected-iot-urban/; accessed 19-02-2020.

Osborne, D. and T. Gaebler. 1992. *Reinventing government.* New York: Plume.

Pali, B. and M. Schuilenburg. 2019. Fear and fantasy in the smart city. *Critical Criminology: An International Journal*, doi: 10.1007/s10612-019-09447-7; accessed 28-04-2020.

Pasquinelli, M. 2015. *Anomaly detection: The mathematization of the abnormal in the metadata society.* Talk given at Transmediale. file:///C:/Users/u0058818/AppData/Local/Packages/Microsoft.MicrosoftEdge_8wekyb3d8bbwe/TempState/Downloads/Anomaly_Detection_The_Mathematization_of%20(1).pdf; accessed 22-07-2020.

Peck, J. 2005. Struggling with the creative class. *International Journal of Urban and Regional Research*, 29 (4): 740–770.

Raco, M. and R. Imrie. 2000. Governmentality and rights and responsibilities in urban policy. *Environment and Planning A: Economy and Space*, 32 (12): 2187–2204.

Rancière, J. 1995. *La mésentente: Politique et philosophie*. Paris: Galilée.

Ricoeur, P. 1970. *Freud and philosophy: An essay on interpretation*. New Haven: Yale UP.

Rogan, K. 2020. Intelligence and armament. In *Architecture and the smart city*, edited by S.M. Figueiredo, S. Krishnamuthy and T. Schroeder, 113–125. London: Routledge.

Rometty, G. 2013. *Leadership in the era of smart. Speech delivered at think forum Japan*. https://www.youtube.com/watch?v=1LfISCMahlU; accessed 26-03-2020.

Sadowski, J. and R. Bendor. 2019. Selling smartness: Corporate narratives and the smart city as a sociotechnical imaginary. *Science, Technology & Human Values*, 44 (3): 540–563.

Sadowski, J. and F. Pasquale. 2015. *The spectrum of control: A social theory of the smart city*. http://first monday.org/ojs/index.php/fm/article/view/5903/4660; accessed 15-02-2020.

Savat, D. 2009. Deleuzes objectile: From discipline to modulation. In *Deleuze and new technology*, edited by M. Poster & D. Savat, 45–62. Edinburgh: Edinburgh University Press.

Schuilenburg, M. 2015. *The securitization of society: Crime, risk, and social order*. New York: New York University Press.

Schuilenburg, M. and R. Peeters. 2018. Smart cities and the architecture of security: Pastoral power and the scripted design of public space. *City, Territory and Architecture*, 5 (13): 1–9.

Schürer, O. 2020. The answer is 'smart' – but what was the question? In *Architecture and the smart city*, edited by S.M. Figueiredo, S. Krishnamuthy and T. Schroeder, 43–55. London: Routledge.

Scott, K. 2016. *The digital city and mediated urban ecologies*. Boston, MA: Palgrave Macmillan.

Shearing, C.D. and P.C. Stenning. 1983. Private security: Implications for social control. *Social Problems*, 30 (5): 493–506.

Shelton, T, M. Zook and A. Wiig. 2015. The 'actually existing smart city'. *Cambridge Journal of Regions, Economy and Society*, 8 (1): 13–25.

Slobodian, Q. 2018. *Globalists: The end of empire and the birth of neoliberalism*. Cambridge: Harvard University Press.

Soja, E.W. 2000. *Postmetropolis: Critical studies of cities and regions*. Oxford: Wiley-Blackwell.

Söderström, O., T. Paasche and F. Klauser. 2014. Smart cities as corporate storytelling. *City*, (18): 307–320.

Taylor, C. 2004. *Modern social imaginaries*. Durham: Duke University Press.

Thierer, A. 2016. *Permissionless innovation: The continuing case for comprehensive technological freedom*. Arlington: Mercatus Center at George Mason University.

Thrift, N. and S. French. 2002. The automatic production of space. *Transactions of the Institute of British Geographers, New Series*, 27 (3): 309–325.

Townsend, A.M. 2013. *Smart cities: Big data, civic hackers, and the quest for a new utopia*. New York: W.W. Norton & Company.

Tyszczuk, R. 2020. Scenarios of interactive citizenship. In *Architecture and the smart city*, edited by S.M. Figueiredo, S. Krishnamuthy and T. Schroeder, 139–153. London: Routledge.

Vanolo, A. 2014. Smartmentality: The smart city as disciplinary strategy. *Urban Studies*, 51 (5): 883–898.

Vanolo, A. 2016. Is there anybody out there? The place and role of citizens in tomorrow's smart cities. *Futures*, 82: 26–36.

Vandevoordt, R., N. Clycq and G. Verschraegen. 2018. Studying culture through imaginaries. In *Social imaginaries in a globalizing world*, edited by H. Alma and G. Vanheeiswijk, 167–192. De Gruyter.

Wakefield, A. 2003. *Selling security: The private policing of public space*. Cullompton: Willan.

Wang, D. 2017. Foucault and the smart city. *The Design Journal*, 20 (sup1): S4378–S4386.

Wang, J. 2018. *Carceral capitalism*. South Pasadena: Semiotext(e).

Webster, C.W.R. and C. Leleux. 2018. Smart governance: Opportunities for technologically-mediated citizen co-production. *Information Polity*, 23: 95–110.

Weiser, M. 1991. The computer for the 21st century. *Scientific American*, 265 (3): 94–105.

Willis, K.S. and A. Aurigi. 2017. *Digital and smart cities*. London & New York: Routledge.

Wilson, J. and E. Swyngedouw. 2014. *The post-political and its discontents: Spaces of depoliticization, spectres of radical politics*. Edinburgh: Edinburgh University Press.

Wiig, A. 2015. IBM's smart city as techno-utopian policy mobility. *City Analysis of Urban Trends, Culture, Theory, Policy, Action*, 19 (2–3): 258–273.

Zandbergen, D. 2018. The making of a responsive city: The material (anti)politics of the Amsterdam Smart Light experiment. *CUS Working Papers Series*, 33, University of Amsterdam.

Chapter 10

Sense in the (smart) city
Where personalisation is the political

Michael McGuire

Introduction

The perception that smart cities entail 'more liveable' spaces (MGI, 2018), ones which boost economic development, enhance service levels (Rujan, 2018) and improve citizen well-being and quality of life (InfinitiLab, 2018), has become all but inseparable from the role of algorithms in underpinning such objectives (Bucher, 2018; Hildebrandt, 2018). But there is a rather narrow (computational) sense of algorithm at work here, one closely tied to an equally narrow sense of what urban life might consist in. In this chapter, I will argue that a more generous concept of algorithm – as any *procedure* or *formula* for arriving at a solution (cf. Chabert, 1999; Kahneman, 2011) – can help reorient assumptions about the ways in which cities promise the optimal human life, one found in the work of early philosophers, especially Aristotle. Aristotle would have agreed that the city (or *polis*) provides an ideal formula for engineering social well-being and happiness in that it 'exists for the sake of the good life and not for the safe of life only'.[1] This was no mere codable input–output relation, but a complex organising principle – a *politeia*, one layered in terms of the constitution of the polis and its various 'subroutines' such as laws, institutional frameworks, and the provision of tools for educating citizens of the polis as 'citizens'.

In this chapter, I will aim to revisit the sense that optimal urban life is not to be had by reducing it to the operations of ever more encompassing, ever more efficient digital algorithms, but by a more complex set of recipes (cf. Ellul, 2011). To bring this out as vividly as possible I will draw upon a dimension of urban life with a complexity which is far less amenable to digital algorithmisation than bus timetables or heating levels. This additional dimension derives from the *sensory* experience of urban space, something which sociologist Georg Simmel once argued lies beyond the 'very large and clearly visible social structures', or even the realm of micro-interaction where social scientists have usually directed their analyses (Simmel, 1997: 109). Positing the sensory aspects of cities as central to our experience of them is no mere rhetorical ploy. As I will suggest, this sensory dimension carries with it a special kind of explanatory power, one which reveals certain dynamics in urban development. And without it, what 'orients and mediates social relations' (ibid.) within the smart city will always remain incomplete.

Excess
Overload

Suppression
Control

Figure 10.1 Sensory dynamic of cities.

In what follows, I will trace the shift from the traditional to the smart city in terms of a key sensory dynamic between two (ostensibly contradictory) polarities (Figure 10.1).

I will suggest that in decoding this dynamic the new kind of *politeia* being furthered by smart cities becomes clearer. Integral to it is the phenomenon of *personalisation* – the drive towards transforming urban space into one which does not just respond to (perceived) needs, but which recognises those who have such needs. Personalisation is closely tied to the optimal living promised by smart cities, but, as a process dependent upon ravenous inputs of data to feed its outputs, it is also a paradigmatic indicator of the way algorithms (in the narrow sense) are being harnessed as vehicles of social control. I argue that this goes beyond the implications of digital connectivity and its 'variable geometry' which Gilles Deleuze proposed as the new control modularity (Deleuze, 1992: 4). By promising to simplify a new variation of sensory excess resulting from digital information, personalisation appears to offer us clarity. Worse, the illusion of autonomous preference it offers beguiles us into thinking that we 'matter' and that the smart city cares about us. By drawing upon contemporary tropes of nurturing and care, personalisation produces a corrosive *politeia* – not just to urban environments and the techno-politics of optimisation, but to the kinds of selves we are constructing within them.

Sense in the traditional city

With some notable exceptions (see, for example, Febvre, 1942; Merleau-Ponty, 1945), the influence of Simmel's insight on the impact of sensory experience upon social life was fairly limited at first. More recently, interest in developing a full-blown Simmelian-style 'sociology of the senses' (cf. Classen, 1993, Vannini, Waskul & Gottshalk, 2012; Low, 2012; Howes, 2013, 2016) has grown, though this not yet been extended to smart cities in any very developed way. But the suggestion that we *smell* and *taste* cities just as much as we see or hear them has been a persuasive one. Viewed as *sensory* environments, the 'feel' and atmosphere of a city becomes as important to its identity as other more familiar aspects like its buildings, its public spaces or its industries. The traditional city, of course, provided a veritable kaleidoscope of sensory experience. Whilst this was not always pleasant and often demanding, it was at least immediate and real (Bruce et al., 2015). And crucially, this sensory environment was as much semantic as it was physical – providing a wholly different kind of recipe for indicating where we were and what we signified as citizens. Especially significant to this recipe were our more animal, primal senses, such as smell and touch.

Take, for example, the intensities attached to the olfactory dimension. As many commentators within the developing field of sensory research have emphasised (Corbin, 1986, Classen, Howes & Synnott, 1994; Low, 2008; Jenner, 2011; Dugan 2018) pre-modern cities offered an uncompromising series of 'smell-scapes'. These comprised a vivid intermingling of many smells now stigmatised as unpleasant – such as body odour, mud, decomposing animals, rotting vegetables, decaying meat and excrement. In a single day, just one horse could typically deposit up to 24 pounds of manure and 3-4 quarts of urine onto the street (ECJ, 2013). But there were equally vivid and far more agreeable smells there to augment this olfactory intensity. The scent of meadowsweet and marjoram strewn around the floors of public buildings and manor houses was often complemented by the use of sweet rushes or herbal mixtures like lavender and thyme. And, of course, the omnipresent clouds of incense emanating from churches would have pervaded every district (Genders, 1972; Wright, 2000). Touch would also have offered a more varied and intensive range of sensory experience given the diversity of materials used – from the rough stone and smooth wood within every building to the texture of clothes, linen wall hangings and so on. Equally well, traditional cities were complex auditory spaces – with a constant din of horses' hooves, cartwheels, and light industrial noises like wood-working or the blacksmith, set against a hum of street noise and the shouts of traders. With the clatter of uneven cobblestones and the bellowing of cattle factored in to this cacophony, the volume and variety of sound experienced on a daily basis would have been significant (Garrioch, 2003; Mills, 2014).

As suggested, the point here is not just about the greater colour and intensity provided by the traditional urban sensorium. Equally significant is the recipe our senses provided for structuring the *meaning* of urban experience. Smell, as Marcel Proust famously observed, provides an untapped formula for retrieving lost memories or accessing submerged emotions (cf. Engen, 1991). In much the same way, our other senses offer visceral algorithms for situating us within urban space and making sense of its multilayered meanings. For example, differing kinds of auditory stimuli once helped structure daily life and to mark the passing of time more generally. Temporal differentiation was often conveyed to the traditional city dweller by the beating of drums at specified intervals, the ringing of the angelus bell or even the call of the cockerel (Garrioch, 2003). The local smell-scape would have assisted citizens in negotiating the geography of a city, just as the mere touch of a holy relic and the place of worship where it was situated often provided an identity and a status for a location. Taken together, it seems indisputable that our sensory faculties once provided a range of sophisticated mechanisms for 'reading' urban space.

Increasing industrialisation from the early 19th century onward did little to disrupt the intensity of urban sensory experience, or its function as a semantic tool. If anything, it merely added new ingredients into this olfactory, auditory and wider sensory mix. The burning of smoke/coal or increasingly pungent factory smells dovetailed with the new kinds of sounds produced by mechanised power, from the clatter of trains to the roar of motor vehicles, to create a new lexicon of urban meanings (Douglas, 2013; Jordan, 2018). It is only as the information age begins to exert a stronger grip upon the character of cities that a definitive sensory change in how they are experienced appears to be underway – with consequences which have only just begun to be appreciated.

Sensory suppression, urban development and rationalisation

It seems clear then that complex and 'deep' sensory landscapes have been a fundamental aspect of the urban experience until at least the mid to late 20th century. But with modernity, there also came a subtle shift in attitudes towards how best to construct an optimal formula for experiencing urban life. One trace of this shift can be seen in the increasing range of controls upon perceived 'excesses' within sensory experience, a logic which finds a natural culmination within the smart city. For example, sociologist Norbert Elias directly associated modernity with an increasing readiness to be disgusted (Eschenbaum & Correll, 2017) and suggested that the rejection of excessive sensory stimuli was a driving force within the civilising process (Elias, 2000; Miller, 2009). Sigmund Freud was arguably even more specific in making such associations. In *Civilisation and its Discontents*, he suggested that our long progress towards civil society is closely linked with the repression of our more animal senses like smell and the development of hygienic rituals to suppress them. 'Modernity', wrote sociologist Zygmunt Bauman, has 'waged a total war against smells' (cited in Jenner, 2011: 238). For Georges Bataille, a recurring aspect of modern sensibilities has been the denial of our four non-visual senses. But he refused to accept that human culture is about the progress of reason, rather the actions of a 'tube with two orifices – the anal and buccal' (1985: 88), where the excretions of the mouth (language, logic, etc.) merely mirror the excretions of the anus. For this reason, there is something more to the perceived 'abjection' of our base senses than concerns with hygiene alone. Rather, as psychoanalytic Julia Kristeva suggested, 'it is [...] not lack of cleanliness or health that causes abjection but what disturbs identity, system, order. What does not respect borders, positions, rules. The in-between, the ambiguous, the composite' (1982: 4). In other words, sensory excess becomes a cipher for social disorder – an outcome as unwelcome within the smart city as it has been elsewhere.

The minutiae of institutionalised solutions to sensory excess which emerged between the 19th and 20th centuries (see for example Laporte, 2000; Melosi, 2005) provide an instructive insight into the evolution of sensory control. The chaotic conditions within many early industrial cities which arose from rapid, unplanned expansion meant, of course, that such solutions were a priority, especially for the purposes of disease prevention. And just as within the smart city, "technological solutionism" (Morozov, 2014) was a typical response. Many such technologies were already relatively well established, given that effective disposal of human waste represents a recurring structural problem for any large human settlement. For example, modern cities often reproduced ancient water-based effluent disposal systems (Angelakis & Zheng, 2015) with Joseph Bazalgette's elegant sewer network in London (constructed as response to the 'great stink' of 1858) a prominent example of this kind (Porter, 2001). What was more novel was the introduction of approaches to hygiene with a more recognisably algorithmic component, albeit in the form of physical mechanisms, rather than digital tools.

Take, for example, the evolution of street cleaning technologies. By the first half of the 19th century, the role of the traditional road (or 'crossing') sweeper had been sufficiently well coded for it to be replaceable by machines capable of recreating their primary brushing and sweeping actions. The Patent Street Sweeping Machine of Manchester, invented by Joseph Whitworth in 1843, was the earliest example, with a fully operational sweeping machine (patented by C.S. Bishop) in action soon after (in 1849). This (mechanised) formula for street cleaning was initially very simple, requiring little more than a rotating disk with wire bristles, However, within less than 50 years such devices had acquired a far more sophisticated range of functionalities, incorporating features such as conveyor belts for carrying dirt from the broom to a designated 'dirt box'. Modern counterparts now come equipped with water tanks; sprayers designed to lessen dust by loosening up particles; the use of vacuums for sucking residues into a collection bin or a hopper; and the "regenerative air street sweeper" which uses forced air to create swirling effects that "loosens debris" (VCH, 2020).

But mechanised hygiene was only a prelude for the more complete role of algorithms in sensory management. Thus, a typical stroll through a city centre is now to enter a highly manufactured smell-scape of chemical formulae where 'natural' (ergo disorderly) odours have been replaced by artificial baking smells, scented trash bags, air fresheners and perfumed water fountains (Nassauer, 2014; Henshaw et al., 2016). A brave new world of 'synthetic aromatics' has emerged, heavily driven by commercial interests. The rise of "scent marketing" (Herz, 2010) has created a new range of sensory specialists like the 'scent consultant' to manage this regulated environment. Thus, companies such as ScentAir or Air Aroma promise to enhance customer loyalty and product recall on behalf of their 'odour clients'.[2] And, whilst scented herbs and oils have, of course, always been used therapeutically, the huge growth in popularity of contemporary techniques like 'aromatherapy'[3] underscore the idea that to manage smell is to manage human behaviour. Where smell becomes a formula, this goal becomes far more attainable. Thus, chemical processes which reproduce the fragrance of a baked potato at a bus stand can be used to sell McCains potato products (Hazell, 2012); motion-activated samples on billboards can familiarise passers-by with the Poudre range of perfumes (JCDecaux, 2019); the smell of steak, pumped out of roadside billboards, can attract passing motorists into visiting the restaurant (Frucci, 2010) just as strawberry-scented adverts at transport interchanges help advertise gin (Bellwood, 2018). All entail a transformation of smell from a thing in itself into an algorithmic simulation. The appeal of synthetic aromatics is therefore about far more than enhanced brand identity, having everything to do with the reordering of sensory space in the city.

An important indicator of this recalibrated role for the senses has been their use as a tool for more overt urban social control. One example is the way 'weaponised' sound – originally pioneered by the military as a form of torture or a strategic aid (More, 2012) – has been adapted to aid urban management. A number of local authorities and other agencies have attempted to use sound and music as way of deterring anti-social behaviour (Hirsch, 2007; Duchen, 2008; Thompson, 2018) or for mood engineering and behavioural modification. For example, Pali and Schuilenburg (2019) report how the Dutch city of Eindhoven has explored light manipulation, utilising differing intensities and colours to create more relaxed, less violent atmospheres, especially in areas of the city oriented towards the night-time economy. The Eindhoven authorities have also dabbled in olfactory control by diffusing the smell of oranges through the environment to create 'calmer' atmospheres.

Sensory control in the smart city: Singapore & the smartclean algorithm

Projects of sensory control with a more obvious (digital) algorithmic component are now unfolding across many smart cities. Asian cities provide an obvious range of case studies here with the notorious hygiene regimes being developed in Singapore amongst the most paradigmatic. Whilst these have been relatively well documented (McDonald, 2018; Clancey, 2018), their sheer scale when viewed closer up remains surprising. It is not just the variety of regulatory controls directed at deterring sensory disorder which is novel. Equally striking is the increasing trust in algorithmic solutions to this problem.

A range of legal precedents have set the scene for this enhanced role of algorithms. Under Chapter 95 of the Singapore Environmental Public Health Act, for example, anyone spitting in public place faces a maximum fine of S$1,000 for a first offence, S$2,000 for a second and up to S$5,000 for further offences (Stolarchuk, 2018) – with an additional possibility of imprisonment (Chong, 2014). The use of chewing gum is considered even more offensive in terms of hygiene – merely importing it without a licence attracts a S$100,000 fine or imprisonment of up to two years (SSO 2020). Similarly ruthless controls are enforced against littering which carries fines of up to S$2,000 (rising to S$10,000 for a third offence) and draconian 'CWO's' (corrective work orders) which require offenders to clear litter in public. These legal formulae have often gone together with more premodern solutions such as shaming rituals, where offenders are forced to wear a pink vest identifying them as 'litter louts' as they carry out their sentence. Not surprisingly, it is excremental, defecatory forms of sensory disorder which seem to be especially frowned upon. Even encouraging animal droppings by feeding a pigeon brings an immediate S$500 fine (Ng, 2018). Still more draconian are the specialist police patrols employed to perform random checks on public toilets seeking out any individual who has been careless enough to forget to flush. Fines of up to S$1,000 can result (Heong, 2019).

One variety of algorithmic power being used to enforce sensory order within Singapore can be seen in the use of specialist systems design to detect and report hygiene infractions. For example, Urine Detection Devices (UDDs) programmed to detect the scent of urine are now standardly installed in elevators throughout the city. Where an offender is identified, the UDD is programmed to set off an alarm

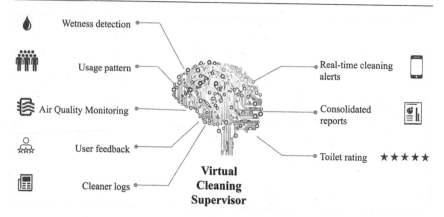

Figure 10.2 SmartClean's virtual cleaning supervisor.

and to lock the elevator doors until the police arrive (Avakian, 2015). Other examples of algorithmic control are still more comprehensive, often involving advanced AI systems with a wide range of capacities for monitoring, detecting and managing high-profile sites, such as toilets. There is an emerging range of private sector operators developing such systems – for example, the company Smartclean, a data-driven, 'intelligent' cleaning control company which offers 'smart' IoT & AI based solutions for maintaining toilet hygiene.[4] A key aim of the Smartclean mission statement is to "Standardize Cleanliness", utilising a complex algorithmic analysis of toilet usage patterns. A range of data-driven tools has been designed to manage this, including sensors for air quality monitoring, feedback modules and emergency response buttons. The resulting data are then fed into AI algorithms which schedule cleaning and suggest actionable tasks. But this is just an entrée to the level of digital ingenuity directed at producing as 'perfect' (i.e. sensorily neutral) a toilet as possible. Smartclean's premier algorithmic product is the intelligent agent they call the 'VCS' (virtual cleaning supervisor) which manages a range of tasks of the kind illustrated in Figure 10.2.

The Smartclean VCS provides a striking example of the way algorithms are being utilised to take hygiene and olfactory control into a wholly new era. But the system is really just the beginning of the way smart cities like Singapore are likely to develop digitally managed sensory environments. Already with us is the phenomenon of the self-cleaning toilet (Needham, 2019), whilst the prospect of fully intelligent hygiene robots is also now firmly on the horizon (Cogley, 2020).

From suppression to overload, sensation to the info-sensory

There is an obvious trade-off to be had in the perception of the traditional city as a site of sensory excess and the measures considered appropriate to regulate its perceived disorder. There are few who are likely to regret that human waste is no longer disposed of in the street, yet it also seems reasonable to ask whether the controls upon less offensive varieties of sensory experience have gone too far in denuding the rich atmospheres offered by urban living. In the closing part of this chapter, I want to develop these questions by considering a more recent version of the problem of sensory excess and its management, one being played out within the environment of the smart city. Though this more recent project has been less visible, its implications for our social and political order may be far more disturbing.

One way to frame this problem is to re-examine what can be taken to *constitute* sensory experience. For the assumption that this originates solely within the five modalities of smell, taste, touch, hearing and sight, is one that has been increasingly challenged. Some have argued for example, that it might be just as plausible to think of *eight* senses (see Classen, 1993). Or that, in addition to the five traditional 'exteroceptive' senses (sight, hearing, taste, smell, and touch) which provide information about the external world, we need also to consider *internal* sensory experience such as thermal perception (Fulkerson, 2014), temporal perception, our sense of balance or our sense of movement (kinesthesia) (Vannini, Waskul & Gottshalk, 2012). It is also plausible to attribute distinctive sensory experience to the way our senses *combine* or overlap – as in the phenomenon of synaesthesia, where individuals report that they 'see' smells as colours or experience visual stimuli as sound (Suslick, 2012).

Technology has always had a role in reordering our senses, whether by enhancing certain senses over others, or by increasing the range and intensity of sensory experience in general. Its role in enhancing the significance of the visual senses from the late 19th century onwards provides a useful case study of this kind of dynamic. During this period, a series of technological shifts appeared to have decisively shifted our sensory balance towards what Michel De Certeau called a 'cancerous growth of vision [...] measuring everything by its ability to show, or be shown' (De Certeau, 2002: xxi). Georg Simmel made a similar point, arguing 'modern social life increases in ever growing degree the rôle of mere visual impression' (Simmel, 2009: 356), a suggestion developed by Walter Benjamin, who highlighted the way that new visual media like the photograph shifted artistic creativity away from the hand so that it is now 'devolved only upon the eye, looking into a lens' (1969: 2). As other visual technologies like cinema – and later television – further augmented the volume of imagery in circulation, profound effects upon our perceptions and conceptions of the world resulted. Gilles Deleuze paralleled cinema with a form of *thought* – a "psychomechanics", one that 'consists of movements and thought-processes (pre-linguistic images), and of points of view on these movements and processes (pre-signifying signs)' (Deleuze, 1989: 262). With the increased importance of the visual sensorium has come an increase in the variety of visual signifiers cluttering our urban environments – from billboards and adverts to street signs, shop fronts and so on.

The role of technology in shifting and augmenting the balance of our sensory capacities has arguably now taken on a still greater power with the advent of digital information. Information is, of course, unique in sensory terms in that it is *polymorphic*, that is it can be reproduced across the visual, aural, olfactory or other sensory spectra. Perhaps more significantly, it can also *code and recode* sensory data into differing forms and so 're-present' them to us in wholly new ways. In this sense, digital information provides an entry point to wholly new kinds of sensory experience, initially centred on the cognitive but capable of being expanded across the whole spectrum. In material terms, this shift has presented itself in at least two ways. The first relates to the floods of connected data originating from the multiple interfaces we now engage with. The act of assembling, combining and synthesising this into something meaningful and manageable generates a new variety of experience requiring sensory as well as cognitive understanding. A second, still more far-reaching level is where the new information manifold offers access, via virtual technologies, into wholly alternative realities, realities with increasingly rich sensory possibilities. This goes beyond mere simulation into physical experiences of seeing and hearing and – where the interface is sophisticated enough – even touching, tasting and smelling (Soo, 2016; Kerruish, 2019). Some psychologists have already argued that the cognitive has its own sensory aspects (see, for example, Maslen, 2015), but our suggestion is that matters have now evolved much further than this. For the result, arguably, of our elevated encounters with a data-rich world is the emergence of a new, *second-order* sensory dimension. For convenience, we can call this the 'info-sensory', a new modality of sensory experience deriving from information and information-based environments.

But with this augmented info-sensory capacity there comes an inevitable complication. And it is here where certain continuities between the pursuit of an optimal algorithm for urban life in both the traditional polis and the contemporary smart city emerge. For, just as the amplification of our traditional sensorium by urban space produced a perceived excess requiring control so, in turn, have our emerging 'info-sensory' capacities begun to generate analogous problems within the smart city. New varieties of sensory excess and info-pollution are already discernible in the sheer volume of data which we now need to process on a daily basis. One outcome of this is the increasing difficulties we experience in attempting to distinguish between genuine information and mere 'noise'. The phenomenon of 'fake news' is only one variety of this – superfluous, irrelevant or 'uninformative' information is another (Stahl, 2006; Zhang & Ghorbani, 2020). Together, this information noise clogs our cognitive faculties creating degradations in knowledge, and blockages or disruptions to critical thinking (Bawden & Robinson, 2009). A second outcome is the phenomenon of "information overload" where it is the volume of data itself which creates stress, or "digital anxiety" as this is sometimes called (Bawden & Robinson, 2009; Harrison & Lucassen, 2019).

Such outcomes were not, of course, entirely unpredictable. Back in the 1970s, social psychologist Stanley Milgram's work on contemporary urban life had already highlighted the effects of its excessive stimuli upon decision-making and the stress which results (Blass, 2005). This finding has, in turn, been replicated in various research reported within the psychological literature (see Roetzal, 2019 for a comprehensive guide to this in the context of the business world). And even in the 1960s, long before the information revolution had taken hold, commentators like

Marshall McLuhan were predicting an "age of anxiety" produced by the tendency of communications technologies to heighten nervous tensions (McLuhan, 1964). However, even McLuhan may have been surprised at the scale of what has subsequently unfolded and the many ancillary effects of information overload, not least the pernicious influence of 'fake' news.

Nonetheless, social life – especially within an urban setting – now seems too attached to the addictions of information and the heady buzz of its "odours, sounds and sights and feel" to turn away from the info-sensorium. And the economic and commercial benefits of mass information to smart cities means that there is little possibility of any sustained attempt to ameliorate the impacts of information overload there either. However, the growth of interest in personal solutions to the excesses of the info-sensorium (such as going 'off-grid' or engaging in 'digital hygiene') mean that there is an increasing pressure upon data merchants or data-rich environments like the smart city to provide an impression of simplicity, whilst preserving the political and commercial advantages of mass information. I suggest that one key 'solution' of this kind lies in the phenomenon of *personalisation* and the algorithms which make this possible. On this view, personalisation has begun to transcend its roots within the marketing world, to become a kind of all-purpose 'vaccine' against the cognitive overload of the new info-sensorium. For in a personalised smart city with algorithms designed to recognise us, the excesses of the info-sensory appear to dissipate. No longer need there be any fear of drowning in data, losing control of our identity, or – worse – being insignificant. Because, in the end, the smart city is 'all about us'.

Personalisation in the smart city and beyond

In retrospect, the so-called 'me decade' of the 1970s (Wolfe, 1976) appears to have been a mere prelude to the age of social media, selfies, influencers, and status updates. The self-obsessed, narcissistic aspects of contemporary culture (Lasch, 1979; Twenge & Campbell, 2009) are manifested in any number of indicators – from the fixation upon celebrity, populist politicians who gain success by playing to our sense of self-importance, individuals who are 'famous for being famous', status updates on social media, and so on. Evidence for the shift towards a 'culture of the self' can be found across a variety of data sources. For example, one recent study found that, in the 1950s, only around 12% of 14-16-year-olds agreed with the statement "I am an important person". However, by 1989 this figure had grown to 77% of boys and more than 80% of girls (Twenge & Campbell, 2009: 34). Similarly, the number of American college students who responded to questions based on the NPI (Narcissistic Personality Inventory) test in a 'narcissistic direction' doubled between 1982 and 2009 (Twenge & Foster, 2010).

In a culture so driven by the quest for self-worth, exploiting the sense that we are 'special' or 'recognised' is proving to be a powerful strategy. One result is a world of 'personalisation', underpinned by algorithms focused upon identifying our preferences. It is a world where we appear to matter because our every need can, in principle, be acknowledged. Personalisation draws upon long-established ways of asserting self-identity – whether this involves erecting statues in public places or just carving one's name on a tree. Contemporary personalisation incorporates traditional assertions of identity like these and assimilates them within a broader control agenda. Key to this is sensory management – now reinvented as a tool for managing inflated info-sensory environments like the smart city. Personalisation algorithms help simplify the cognitive resources required to navigate complex information spaces by highlighting only what 'we want' or what we (ostensibly) need. And herein lies a further, more pernicious aspect of personalisation, one that reveals it as a fundamentally *political* process. Lulled into the easy satisfactions of a world 'made for us' any need to challenge or to question this world becomes increasingly superfluous.

The extent to which this world-made-for-us is slowly but surely becoming a new norm is widely evidenced. Access to almost any kind of online service is now, almost invariably, to be confronted by a variety of algorithms which help the service to 'know' or to 'remember' you (Manola, 2019). Many examples appear relatively innocuous. There are the reminders which quickly arrive when products are added to a basket during an online shopping session, without actually being purchased. There are the messages offering targeted encouragements for users to stay on a site when their click-through behaviour suggests they are about to leave it. There are the customised promotions and offers which appear 'foolish' to resist – offers which have been shown to increase the likelihood of purchase by over a third (Sahni, Zou & Chintagunta, 2014). And there are the semblances of autonomous choice fostered by techniques like 'back in stock' or 'price drop' notifications, where users are sent an alert (email, push, SMS, etc.) when a desirable product comes back into stock or when it drops in price. More coercive forms of personalisation algorithms are seen in marketing techniques like urgency messaging (Hassan, 2018; Taylor, 2019). Here, targeted notifications such as 'five other people are looking at this hotel room offer right now' place subtle pressures upon users to make purchases more quickly. Marketing-based forms of personalisation like these are further augmented by content personalisation in browsing, viewing or purchasing. Info-sensory simplification is an important bait here – it is far 'easier' for us if Amazon remembers what kind of soup we prefer, or Netflix selects which kind of drama we are likely to prefer (Thorp, 2015).

This wealth of customised service provision expands as we move into the environment of the smart city. As a space where functionality is dependent upon massive data processing, the smart city provides an ideal environment for the delivery of targeted 'hyperpersonalised' goods and services (Nelson-Field, 2020). Whether it is traffic updates, reminders of doctors' appointments or timetabled shopping deliveries, the smart city already offers the opportunity for a daily routine wholly centred upon individual need. Such opportunities are only likely to increase. For example, smart city dwellers will have easy access to personalised therapy services such as the Woebot app, an automated agent which uses CBT-based approaches to provide support to its users (Molteni, 2017). Or personal trainers like the Vi system which offers real-time feedback during workouts and customised guidance on specific goals like weight loss. Vi not only 'learns' from the personal data it obtains from apps like Google Fit and Apple HealthKit, it can also connect to smartphone music libraries like Spotify Premium, to provide a tailored musical backdrop to exercise programmes (Rose, 2017). Even the sports drink used during sessions can be personalised. For example, the Gx/Gatorade drink offers an app which 'connects' the Gatorade bottle to secondary support facilities like a weigh station, or hydration pods whose formulas can be personalised by flavour, sodium and carbohydrate levels. Sweat profiles are monitored and sodium levels measured to ensure the user always operates at an 'ideal hydration level' (SSO, 2017).

In its most developed form, the entire smart city will eventually become an environment which is alive to our presence. As we move through its streets and spaces, adverts, billboards and even digital signage will acquire the potential to react to cues like our gender, age and so on. The rise of drive hailing apps like Uber or Lyft already enable us to experience tailored transportation through urban spaces on the basis of our predetermined profiles. The advent of automated vehicles is likely to take this into a wholly new dimension with customised luggage storage, personalised content to entertain users along the way, driving styles tailored to preferences, and even facilities for taking a nap along the journey where needed (Hasenjaegar & Wersing, 2017). Traditional automobile companies have seen the writing on the wall here with brands like Mini, and its MINI Vision Next 100 project welcoming drivers with personalised greetings as they approach the car or allowing them to customise their driving preferences (Hope, 2016).

Two kinds of technological innovation are likely to further strengthen the personalisation regimes of the smart city. The first of these is wearable technologies like glasses, wrist-devices and even the clothes we wear (Ortiz, 2018). On one level, these will increasingly permit users to access the ultra-personalised services on offer as they navigate their environment, engaging in work and leisure activity (Bowman, 2014). The whole gamut of services essential to urban life, from health care to entertainment, will be instantly available and tailored to the real-time needs of the wearable tech user (see, for example, Dunn, Runge & Snyder, 2018). Even where a user has arrived in an unfamiliar city, 'itinerary personalisation' will be there to ensure that no forms of cognitive stress or dissonance disrupt their (guided) exploration of retail and other sponsored facilities (D'Amico, Ercoli & Del Bimbo, 2013). Something, of course, will be demanded in return. As citizens move around the city they will increasingly be required to function as human data-hubs, active sensors engaged in interactive, participatory data exchanges to support applications like real-time traffic updates, pollution monitoring and so on.

The second kind of technological innovation likely to be central here will involve the role of ever more sophisticated AI and robotic systems. We are, of course, already familiar with more limited examples of this in the form of personal assistants like Siri or Alexa activated by voice commands to provide instant solutions to our requests. Over 100 million Alexa devices had been sold by 2019 (Smith, 2019), but these represent merely a first wave of what will be a far wider, more accomplished range of personalised agents serving the domestic and public spaces of smart city environments (Williams, 2018). One example of the potentials here has been explored in the EU SciRoc programme (SciRoc, 2020) which is looking specifically at the capacity of smart city robots to provide a constant available range of supports to citizens-in-need. For example, assisting customers in shops or other commercial sites, providing professional services like legal or financial advice, or offering support capacities during emergency situations.

Tapping into this world made 'just for us' provided by smart cities and their personalisation algorithms, it may well seem that we have reached a point of historic perfection. With every citizen acknowledged as special and with every point of view connected by digital communication, the 'highest form of community' represented by the polis has surely begun to be realised. But the contrast between a society of digitally customised engines for need satisfaction and the Aristotelian formula for the ultimate 'end' or *telos* for human life – *eudaimonia* or happiness – could hardly be more stark. Though, as we saw earlier, Aristotle agreed that the city/polis offers an ideal vehicle for its realisation, he also insisted that this cannot be attained without an adequate *politeia* – a formula for realising a form of community which is complex, not simplified, and active, not passive.

Thus, just as the management of sensory excess within the traditional city turned out to be a lodestone for recognising the politics of rationalisation which typified modernity, so too do the techniques of managing sensory excess in the smart city tell their own story. For as one part of our sensory net is flattened, further irregularities are emerging elsewhere – in the form of our exposure to the new dimensions of 'info-sensory' experience. And as our anxieties about the potential overload of info-sensory stimuli increase, so too do the reassurances that we are special. In order to manage the new anxieties that come with this reconfiguring of the sensory, the self is re-presented as the centre of all things we always imagined it might be.

Personalisation thereby provides one kind of window into the new politics of absorption, distraction and somatic harvesting which our contemporary polis – the smart city – is helping to advance. But the Faustian pact attached to this new arrangement remains to be properly acknowledged. For in this representation of the self as a focus of attention, its substance is simultaneously eroded. Personalised simulacra emerge, data-fied sums of connections which lack any effective connection to the sensory landscape. Within the comfortingly secure womb of nurture, where algorithms are ever more finely tuned to our needs a new, a far more powerful form of control is being conceived, one that is more about an absorption we happily yield to than a coercion we might resist. In this way, in place of a transparent *formula* for achieving human happiness, we are given *formulae* that persuade us we already have it. And it is here where personalisation becomes the political, a form of digital flattery which diverts us, whilst simultaneously absorbing us into a greater whole which can we no longer recognise, let alone criticise.

Notes

1   *Politics* 3.9.1280a 31-4
2   See https://scentair.com/ & https://www.air-aroma.com/

3 In 2018, the global aromatherapy market was valued at around $1.8 billion, with a projected growth to over $2.7 over 10% by 2025. The market for essential oils appears to be even greater, with anticipated worldwide growth from around $ 17 billion in 2017 to $ 27 billion by 2022 (Brandessence, 2019).

4 https://www.smartclean.sg/

References

Angelakis, A. and X.Y. Zheng. 2015. Evolution of water supply, sanitation, wastewater, and stormwater technologies globally. *Water*, 7: 455–463.

Avakian, T. 2015. 16 odd things that are illegal in Singapore: Urinating in a public elevator. *Business Insider*, 4 August 2015.

Bataille, G. 1985. *Visions of excess: Selected writings, 1927–1939*, Minneapolis: University of Minnesota Press.

Bawden, D. and L. Robinson. 2009. The dark side of information: Overload, anxiety and other paradoxes and pathologies. *Journal of Information Science*, 35 (2): 180–191.

Bellwood, O. 2018. Beefeater unveils strawberry-scented campaign. *The Spirits Business*, 16 May 2018.

Benjamin, W. 1969. The work of art in the age of mechanical reproduction. In *Illuminations*. edited by H. Arendt, translated by Harry Zohn from the 1935 essay, 1–26. New York: Schocken Books.

Blass, T. 2005. The urban psychology of Stanley Milgram. *Journal of Social Distress and Homelessness*, 14 (1–2): 12–22.

Bowman, J. 2014. *Wearable technology: Implications for personalisation and privacy, WARC Event Reports, I-COM Global Summit*, April 2014.

Brandessence. 2019. Aromatherapy market – Global industry analysis, size, share, trends, segmentation and forecast 2019–2025. https://brandessenceresearch.biz/Request/Sample? ResearchPostId=97516&RequestType=Methodology; accessed 15-04-2020.

Bruce, N., J. Condie, V. Henshaw and A. Payne. 2015. Analysing olfactory and auditory sensescapes in English cities: Sensory expectation and urban environmental perception. *Ambiences: International Journal of Sensory Environment, Architecture and Urban Space*. https://journals.openedition.org/ambiances/560; accessed 15-04-2020.

Bucher, T. 2018. *If…then: Algorithmic power and politics*. Oxford: Oxford University Press.

Clancey, G. 2018. Hygiene in a landlord state: Health, cleanliness and chewing gum in late twentieth century Singapore. *Science Technology & Society*, 23 (2): 214–233.

Classen, C. 1993. *Worlds of sense: Exploring the senses in history and across cultures*. London and New York: Routledge.

Classen, C., D. Howes and A. Synnott. 1994. *Aroma: The cultural history of smell*. London and New York: Routledge.

Chabert, J. (Ed.) 1999. *A history of algorithms: From the pebble to the microchip*. Berlin: Springer-Verlag.

Chong, E. 2014. Man in spitting case jailed 5 weeks. *Straits Times*, 24 March 2014.

Cogley, M. 2020. From cleaning toilets to cooking your dinner – five ways robots will transform housework. *Telegraph*, 10 January 2020.

Corbin, A. 1986. *The foul and the fragrant: Odor and the French social imagination*. Harvard: Harvard University Press.

D'Amico, G., S. Ercoli and A. Del Bimbo. 2013. A framework for itinerary personalization in cultural tourism of smart cities. *AI*HCI@AI*IA* 2013.

De Certeau, M. 2002. *The practice of everyday life*. Berkeley and Los Angeles: University of California Press.

Deleuze, G. 1989. *Cinema 2: The time image*. Minneapolis: University of Minnesota Press.

Deleuze, G. 1992. *Postscript on the societies of control*, October, 59: 3–7.

Douglas, I. 2013. *Cities: An environmental history*. London and New York: I.B. Tauris.

Duchen, J. 2008. Mind the Bach: Classical music on the underground. *Independent*, 26 March 2008.

Dugan, H. 2018. London smellwalk around 1450: Smelling medieval cities. In *The Oxford handbook of later medieval archaeology in Britain*, edited by C. Gerrard and A. Gutiérrez, 728–741. Oxford: Oxford University Press.

Dunn, J., R. Runge and M. Snyder. 2018. Wearables and the medical revolution. *Personalized Medicine*, 15, 5.

ECJ. 2013. Cleaning towns and streets – A history. *European Cleaning Journal*, 15 May 2013.

Elias, N. 2000. *The civilising process* (2nd edition). London: Wiley-Blackwell.

Ellul, J. 2011. *The meaning of the city*. Wipf and Stock; Reprint edition.

Engen, T. 1991. *Odour, sensation and memory*. New York: Praeger.

Eschenbaum, N. and B. Correll. 2017. *Disgust in early modern English literature*. London: Routledge.

Febvre, L. [1942] 1982. *The problem of unbelief in the sixteenth-century: The religion of Rabelais*. trans. B. Gottlieb, Cambridge MA: Harvard University Press.

Frucci, A. 2010. The steak-scented billboard: Advertising's stinking future. *Gizmodo*, 6 February 2010.

Fulkerson, M. 2014. Rethinking the senses and their interactions: The case for sensory pluralism. *Frontiers in Psychology*, 5, 1426. doi:10.3389/fpsyg.2014.01426.

Garrioch, D. 2003. Sounds of the city: The soundscape of early modern European towns. *Urban History*, 30, 1.

Genders, R. 1972. *A history of scent*. London: Hamish Hamilton Ltd.

Harrison, G. and M. Lucassen. 2019. Stress and anxiety in the digital age: The dark side of technology. *OpenLearn*, 1 March 2019.

Hasenjaegar, M. and H. Wersing. 2017. Personalization in advanced driver assistance systems and autonomous vehicles: A review. Conference paper, *IEEE 20th International Conference on Intelligent Transportation Systems (ITSC)*, Yokohama, Japan, 16–19 October 2017.

Hassan, O. 2018. *Why & how to use urgency in your marketing*. Optimise Press, 17 January 2018.

Hazell, K. 2012. McCain adverts that smell like freshly cooked jacket potatoes. *Huffington Post*, 7 February 2012.

Heong, S.K. 2019. Singapore the fine city: 10 offences you might not realise you're committing. *Dollars and Sense*, 6 November 2019.

Henshaw, V., D. Medway, G. Warnaby and C. Perkins. 2016. Marketing the 'city of smells'. *Marketing Theory* 16 (2): 152–170.

Herz, R.S. 2010. The emotional, cognitive, and biological basics of olfaction: Implications and considerations for scent marketing. In *Sensory marketing: Research on the sensuality of products*, edited by A. Krishna, 87–107. London and New York: Routledge/Taylor & Francis Group.

Hildebrandt, M. 2018. Algorithmic regulation and the rule of law. *Philosophical Transaction of the Royal Society A*, 376, 2128.

Hirsch, L. 2007. Weaponizing classical music: Crime prevention and symbolic power in the age of repetition. *Journal of Popular Music Studies* 19 (4): 342–358.

Hope, G. 2016. MINI vision next 100 previews MINI's future. *AutoExpress*, 6 September 2016.

Howes, D. 2013. The social life of the senses. *Ars Vivendi Journal*, 3: 4–23.

Howes, D. (Ed.) 2016. *A cultural history of the senses in the modern age*. London: Bloomsbury Academic.

InfinitiLab. 2018. *59 Per cent of millennials believe a smart city would improve their quality of life*. https://www.globenewswire.com/news-release/2018/06/04/1515979/0/en/Report-INFINITI-LAB-Finds-59-Per-Cent-of-Millennials-Believe-a-Smart-City-Would-Improve-Their-Quality-of-Life.html; accessed 16-05-2020.

JCDecaux. 2019. *Smells like ooh: The power of scent in advertising*. https://www.jcdecaux.com/blog/smells-ooh-power-scent-advertising; accessed 16-05-2020.

Jenner, M. 2011. Follow your nose? Smell, smelling, and their histories. *The American Historical Review*, 116 (2): 335–351.

Jordan, M. 2018. You cannot win the war on noise. *CityLab*, 23 April 2018.

Kahneman, D. 2011. *Thinking fast and slow*. New York: MacMillan.

Kerruish, E. 2019. Arranging sensations: Smell and taste in augmented and virtual reality. *The Senses & Society*, 14 (1): 31–45.

Kristeva, J. 1982. *Powers of horror: An essay on abjection*. New York: Columbia University Press.

Laporte, D. 2000. *A history of shit*. Boston: MIT Press.

Lasch, C. 1979. *The culture of narcissism: American life in an age of diminishing expectations*. New York and London: W. W. Norton & Company, Inc.

Low, K. 2008. *Scent and scent-sibilities: Smell and everyday life experiences*. Cambridge: Cambridge Scholars Publishing.

Low, K. 2012. The social life of the senses: Charting directions. *Sociology Compass*, 6 (3): 271–282.

Manola, S. 2019. What is personalization in digital marketing? *ABTasty*, 27 May 2019.

Maslen, S. 2015. Researching the senses as knowledge. *The Senses and Society*, 10 (1): 52–70.

Melosi, M. 2005. *Garbage in the cities: Refuse reform and the environment*. Pittsburgh: University of Pittsburgh Press.

McDonald, T. 2018. The cost of keeping Singapore squeaky clean. *BBC*, 29 October 2018.

McLuhan, M. 1964. *Understanding media: The extensions of man*. New York: McGraw-Hill.

Merleau-Ponty, M. [1945] 1962. *Phenomenology of perception*. London: Routledge and Kegan Paul.

MGI. 2018. Smart cities: Digital solutions for a more livable future. *McKinsey Global Institute*, Report June 2018.

Miller, W. 2009. *The anatomy of disgust*. Cambridge: Harvard University Press.

Mills, S. 2014. *Auditory archaeology: Understanding sound and hearing in the past*. London: Routledge.

Molteni, M. 2017. The chatbot therapist will see you now. *Wired*, 6 July 2017.

More, A. 2012. Contours of control | weaponising classical music: Waging class-warfare beneath our cities' streets. *Ceasefire*, 29 September 2012.

Morozov, E. 2014. *To save everything, click here: The folly of technological solutionism*. New York: PublicAffairs.

Nassauer, S. 2014. Using scent as a marketing tool, stores hope it – and shoppers – will linger. *Wall Street Journal*, 20 May 2014.

Needham, J. 2019. Japan's singing, self-cleaning toilets are conquering the West. *Wired*, 2 September 2019.

Nelson-Field, K. 2020. *The attention economy and how media works: Simple truths for marketers*. Singapore: Springer Nature.

Ng, C. 2018. Two men fined $1,500 and $450 for feeding pigeons in two separate cases. *Straits Times*, 3 July 2018.

Ortiz, J. 2018. *Wearable technologies*. Rijeka: Intech Open.

Pali, B. and M. Schuilenburg. 2019. Fear and fantasy in the smart city. *Critical Criminology: An International Journal*, doi: 10.1007/s10612-019-09447-7; accessed 03-01-2020.

Porter, D. 2001. The great stink of London: Sir Joseph Bazalgette and the cleansing of the Victorian metropolis. *Victorian Studies*, 43 (3): 530–531.

Roetzal, P. 2019. Information overload in the information age: A review of the literature from business administration, business psychology, and related disciplines. *Journal of Business Research*, 12: 479–522.

Rose, B. 2017. Vi is a personal assistant for your workouts, but it needs some help. *The Verge*, 31 August 2018.

Rujan, A. 2018. Thinking about becoming a smart city? 10 benefits of smart cities. *Plante Moran*.

Sahni, N., D. Zou and P. Chintagunta. 2014. Effects of targeted promotions: Evidence from field experiments. *SSRN Electronic Journal*. doi:10.2139/ssrn.2530290; accessed 30-02-2020.

SciRoc. 2020. *Smart city robotic challenge*. EU H2020 Project, https://sciroc.eu/; accessed 30-04-2020.

Simmel, G. 1997. Sociology of the senses. In *Simmel on culture*, edited by D. Frisby and M. Featherstone, 109–119. London: Sage.

Simmel, G. 2009. Sociology of the senses: Visual interaction. In *Introduction to the science of sociology*, edited by R.E. Park and E. Burgess, 356ff. Project Gutenberg version, https://www.gutenberg.org/files/28496/28496-h/28496-h.htm#Page_356; accessed 23-06-2020.

Smith, C. 2019. *Amazon alexa statistics. DMR Business Statistics*.

Soo, d. 2016. Wake up and smell the roses: Virtually. *Asian Scientist*, 1 August 2016.

SSO 2017. How Gatorade is using technology to measure sweat content and help athletes stay hydrated. *Geekwire*, 10 May 2017.

SSO 2020. Regulation of imports and exports (chewing gum) regulations. https://sso.agc.gov.sg/SL/272A-RG4; accessed 26-07-2020.

Stahl, B. 2006. On the difference or equality of information, misinformation, and disinformation: A critical research perspective. *Informing Science Journal*, 9: 83–96.

Stolarchuk, J. 2018. NEA slaps Singapore resident with hefty $300 fine for spitting in public. *Independent News (Singapore)*, 3 February 2018.

Suslick, K.S. 2012. Synesthesia in science and technology: More than making the unseen visible. *Current Opinion in Chemical Biology*, 16 (5–6): 557–563.

Taylor, M. 2019. How creating a sense of urgency helped me increase sales by 332%. *CXL Institute*, 6 May 2019.

Thompson, M. 2018. To soothe or remove? Affect, revanchism and the weaponized use of classical music. *Communication and the Public*, 2 (4): 272–283.

Thorp, J. 2015. 11 examples of website personalization. *Add This (Blog)*, 20/01/2015.

Twenge, J.M. and W.K. Campbell. 2009. *The narcissism epidemic: Living in the age of entitlement*. New York: Simon & Schuster.

Twenge, J.M. and J.D. Foster. 2010. Birth cohort increases in narcissistic personality traits among American college students, 1982–2009. *Social Psychological and Personality Science*, 1: 99–106.

Vannini, P., D. Waskul and S. Gottshalk. 2012. *The senses in self, society and culture: A sociology of the senses*. London: Routledge.

VCH. 2020. *Invention and history of street sweeper. Vacuum cleaner history*. http://www.vacuum-cleanerhistory.com/vacuum-cleaner-development/history-of-street-sweeper/; accessed 23-09-2020.

Williams, A. 2018. Smart cities are getting smarter, but challenges remain. *Robotics Business Review*, 23 October 2018.

Wolfe, T. 1976. The 'me' decade and the third great awakening. *New York Magazine*, 23 August 1976.

Wright, L. 2000. *Clean and decent: The fascinating history of the bathroom and wc*. London: Penguin Classics.

Zhang, X. and A. Ghorbani 2020. An overview of online fake news: Characterization, detection, and discussion. *Information Processing & Management*, 57, 2.

Chapter 11

Five smart city futures

A criminological analysis of urban intelligence

Keith Hayward

Introduction

We live in the age of the smart city. Evident the world over from Stockholm to Songdo, Singapore to Saudi Arabia, the Smart City Paradigm (SCP) is hegemonic in discussions of 21st-century city planning and governance such that it is now the preeminent urban ideal of our time. Much of this success stems from the fact that the SCP is actually a blended concept that combines ideas and insights from an array of different fields, including computer science, cybernetics, consumerism and 'choice-based' citizenship models, Artificial Intelligence (AI), business science and urban entrepreneurialism, big data and networked informatics, environmental resilience and the 'green technology' movement, and even virtual reality and computer gaming. This broad, constitutive heritage allows smart city models to be deployed in any number of contexts to serve any number of masters; something which, in turn, has resulted in the concept being engulfed by triumphalist claims about its ability to transform and enhance everything from urban sustainability to the life possibilities and aesthetic experiences of the contemporary city dweller.

But if the history of urban studies tells us anything it is that idealized city concepts frequently fall short of their utopian promise (Eaton, 2001).[1] Perhaps it is unsurprising, then, that alongside all the techno-optimism and corporate hyperbole surrounding urban smartness, there also exists a loud and sustained chorus of scholarly criticism. Distilled, this criticism takes three forms. First, that smart cities are little more than vessels for global corporatism and other forms of unconstrained private influence (e.g. Söderström, Paasche & Klauser, 2014; Hollands, 2015; Kitchen, 2016). This particular criticism is especially pronounced among urban studies scholars. The reason for this is clear: historically, it has been disciplines such as architecture, town planning, and urban geography that have been the wellspring of new city models/paradigms. In this case, however, the etymology and advancement of the term 'smart city' was instead a product of the corporate world. More specifically, it was developed in the executive offices of two of the world's biggest computer companies, IBM and Cisco, as a catch-all concept to explain how new Information and Communication Technology (ICT) chains could be used to reinvent the urban landscape by making it more 'intelligent', networked, automated, and, importantly, competitive (Rosati & Conti, 2016).[2] Second, at the conceptual level, there is much confusion and concern about what actually constitutes a 'smart city', with numerous commentators characterizing the term as 'fuzzy' or 'nebulous' and thus lacking a consistent ontology (e.g. Hollands, 2008; Albino, Berardi & Dangelico, 2015; Sadowski & Pasquale, 2015). Finally, because it prioritizes technology and computational prediction over and above the more serendipitous or informal aspects of urban life, some have claimed that the SCP runs the risk of transforming the city into what has been termed a neutral, "technological place" (Keymolen & Voorwinden, 2019); a one-dimensional zone of control (Krivý, 2018) and coercion (Sennett, 2012; Greenfield, 2013), where the public is managed and 'responsibilized' to such an extent that individuals are reduced to unsympathetic objects of visibility and datafication.

In this chapter, I offer a brief criminological introduction to these debates and some of the other competing claims surrounding urban smartness by outlining five putative smart city futures. Importantly, and as I have stated elsewhere when writing about emerging trends in spatial criminology (Hayward, 2012), the collection of themes offered here are not in any way intended as definitive or exhaustive, but rather a series of theoretical reflections on the direction of travel urban smartness is already taking and what these pathways might mean for theoretical criminologists interested in the crime-city dynamic.

The smart city as sociotechnical imaginary

> The city is a computer, the streetscape is the interface, you are the cursor, and your smartphone is the input device.
>
> Paul McFedries (cited in Mattern, 2017)

From the outset, the SCP has been celebrated with a confetti of tech industry puff articles – a tendency that shows no sign of abating. In a recent edition of securityinfowatch.com, for example, we are told that, 'Smart cities are safe cities' (Weagle, 2019), and that they offer 'greater energy efficiency and more convenience than ever before', whilst simultaneously enabling 'police departments and law enforcement the world over to leverage technology to enhance their commitment to protecting lives and property' (Carter, 2019). Written by corporate managers with plenty of skin in the game, such articles exemplify the type of permanent computational upside that undergirds the smart city tech sector. Yet they also illustrate a related, more general tendency (that also exists in both academia and municipal government) that views urban smartness as a panacea for all sorts of urban ills. Whether it is reducing urban crime or solving traffic congestion, enhancing civic responsibility or facilitating community-driven eco-sustainability,[3] no problem it seems is so big or small it cannot be solved by urban smart systems. To a certain extent, this is to be expected. Faced with ever more pervasive managerialism on the one hand, and shrinking financial budgets on the other, today's politicians and public officials are unsurprisingly receptive to tech-industry marketing about enhanced public safety or better cost-effectiveness, a point made by Jathan Sadowski (2019) in an article that neatly sums up the contemporary appeal of the SCP:

> You can't blame their intended targets for going along with this narrative, whether it's the planners who need help managing complex systems more effectively, the politicians who are under pressure to keep performance high, or the public who want to live in a city that serves their needs. The smart city is, after all, designed to sound awesome.

Indeed, it is. Promoted as a glittering vision of the future that is at once grandiose and practical, radical yet tantalizingly achievable, the SCP represents nothing less than a new urban imaginary in which technology is harnessed and rationalized for the betterment of all city dwellers no matter the geographic location. Casting the smart city in such open, imaginative terms has certainly been good for business. It allows vendors to market tech solutions based on positive, yet vague concepts such as 'urban development' or 'enhanced civic creativity', and customers to conceive a future in which intelligent, interconnected, and instrumentalized ICT systems help create the putative socio-political urbanscape of their choosing. It is for this reason that certain critical commentators have started to evoke the term "sociotechnical imaginary" (Jasanoff & Kim, 2015) to highlight the combination of unrelenting positivity at the heart of the SCP (March, 2016; Sadowski & Bendor, 2019).

Sociotechnical imaginaries are intellectual expressions, usually in the form of envisioned societal scenarios that breathe (normative) life into (abstract) scientific knowledge and technological expertise. Put another way, the sociotechnical imaginary is a conceptual vehicle that allows two historically compartmentalized domains – the techno-scientific and the socio-political – to reconcile their contrasting positions regarding mental and material phenomena. It is a process that, as Maureen McNeil and others (2017: 457) have pointed out, involves a deft but strategic shift away from the hard sciences' fundamental concern with "domains of facts and artefacts", and towards the more unfamiliar, subjective world of "storytelling, imaging, and imagining". According to Jathan Sadowski (2019) – the academic most closely associated with the application of this term to the SCP – the smart city should be understood as an exemplary expression of the sociotechnical imagination: 'that is, as a vision and performance of a desirable future based on marshalling technology to change society that insists on a particular model of municipal development and governance'. As Sadowski and his co-author Roy Bendor explain in an earlier paper based on their analysis of over a decade's worth of primary source material on smart urbanism produced by Cisco and IBM, this drift towards the imaginary in global smart city policymaking is overwhelmingly invoked by corporate actors:

> Although policy-making plays an important role in streamlining and applying smart city technologies [...] corporations shape and extend the sociotechnical imaginary. Large vendors set the tone, enroll other actors, and weave the narratives that make possible the smart city's actualization [...]. We should think of these corporate discourses as tools for directing and delimiting what we can

imagine as possible [...]. Their aim is to establish *their* version of smartness as *the* future – the only one available or possible

(Sadowski & Bendor, 2019: 543–544).

To ensure the scientific facts and technological logics of powerful computer companies are transposed from one context (hardware manufacture, data storage) to another (the dynamic contemporary cityscape), corporate imagineers frame and promote certain aspects of the smart city future while downplaying others. Several narratives are discernible, but here I will mention just two – the mutually-reinforcing logics of 'anticipation' and 'crisis'.

In a subtle variation of Ulrich Beck's risk society thesis, in which the German social theorist stressed the incalculability of *future* existential threats, the "anticipatory action thesis" (Anderson, 2010) stresses instead how threats to urban infrastructure are made the basis for action in the *present*. It is a common mind-set when promoting the merits of urban smartness, as James Merricks White (2016: 584) explains:

Anticipation offers a useful way to take seriously the future orientation of the smart city's global imaginary. It reveals that visions of technology-driven urban change are interwoven with the perceived challenges of a crisis-ridden world [...] Rather than rely on affirmative action toward some normative goal, the smart city's global imaginary resorts to the threat of inaction spiraling into panic and insecurity. This post-modernist turn in urban planning and policy relies not so much on a politics of optimism, as one of realistic-seeming fear, tempered by the possibility of hope – but only if action is taken now.

Fairly obviously, this emphasis on 'action now' – a ubiquitous trope among smart city boosters – dovetails nicely with the more general *crisis culture* that surrounds the SCP. In a subtle rebranding of the sort of end-of-times narratives that have been the stock-in-trade of zombie movies, horror literature, and video games for decades, the smart city sociotechnical imaginary is today driven forward by its very own set of management-approved dystopian scenarios. For example, in his insightful work on "the anticipatory logics of the smart city", White (ibid.) outlines three crises consistently mobilized by corporations and tech service providers when promoting urban smartness: 'mass urbanization', 'global climate change', and 'fiscal austerity'. It is a list that one could easily extend by including a range of other related/subsidiary crises – terrorism, urban protest/incivility, pandemic outbreak, and the imminent degradation and collapse of urban infrastructure and existing (always outdated) technology – that are oft-deployed in a bid to promote the smart city cause.

Embedding a culture of crisis within the sociotechnical imaginary of the SCP is, of course, a well-considered strategy. Dystopian futures demand solutions, and thus whatever the anticipated insecurity, the smart city is always waiting in the wings with a compelling fix that is reassuringly both innovative and immediate. This chapter is not the place to review the specific computational or material means by which smart systems aim to tackle the various emergencies outlined above. Instead, in the space available here I will simply outline three common but problematic tropes that, although rarely acknowledged, in reality constitute the ontological basis of the smart city edifice.

First, and of most significance, is *the fetishization of computational technology*: the disconcerting tendency evident across all spheres of contemporary life, from education to warfare, to cede power and problem-prioritization to reified technologies and networked systems connected to vast repositories of data in the mistaken belief that any social challenge can be solved solely by the application of computation and technological acceleration. Here, the obvious danger is that society falls victim to Morozovian "solutionism" (2013), or what James Bridle (2018) more recently termed "the chasm of computational thinking" – the belief that all of the world's problems (including some developments that, as yet, are not even considered actual problems) can be identified and overcome by the application of techno-solutions.

Second, *the over-valorization of the city (and ergo city governance) as the unit of solution* for many of the crises that smartness boosters allude to in their promotional material; or, in White's terms,

> there is a disconnect between the scale of perceived threats and the site at which they ought to be addressed […]. While the urban is framed as a substrate on which systemic crises will potentially unfold, it is rare that the consultancy companies under analysis refer to specific cities. Rather, global trends and statistics are called upon as a justification for action in particular instances
> (2016: 585).

Third, and clearly related to the previous points, is *the tech industry's failure to look beyond the smart prescription to the actual causes of the (urban) malaise*. This lack of a deeper, more rounded sociological and philosophical understanding of modern society and its inherent problems ensures that, all too often, the type of sociotechnical imagination that constitutes the creative mulch for smart city prototypes is limited and derivative in form, a point I will now develop in the next smart city future.

The smart city as corporate 'play' space

> On the surface, the dominant smart cities' storyline is about efficient and sustainable cities, but underneath it is primarily a strategic tool for gaining a dominant position in a huge market.
> (Söderström, Paasche & Klauser, 2014: 316)

As mentioned above, the smart city is often perceived as an ambiguously defined, imprecise concept. More recently, however, many commentators have sought to reject this characterization and instead view the SCP in more straightforward, critical terms as a vehicle for multinational corporations to further intensify private influence within the city (Greenfield 2013, 2017; Kitchin, 2014; Hollands, 2015). It is a view summed up by the criminologists Marc Schuilenburg and Brunilda Pali (2019) when they assert that, if 'we gaze beneath the clichés and rhetoric, the smart city appears as a "naked king" – a commercial construct designed to sell a corporate vision of capital accumulation'. While such a view may be unpalatable to those working on the technological, infrastructural, or communicative dimensions of urban smartness, it is not one easily dismissed given the short, but well-documented history of the smart city (Townsend, 2013). According to Ola Söderström, Till Paasche and Francisco Klauser (2014: 310), the term 'smart city' first appeared in the mid-1990s, when it was attached to planned autonomous garden cities in Australia and Malaysia. In these early examples, terms like 'competitiveness', 'economic efficiency' and 'business compatibility' all featured in the rhetoric, but no more so than other intrinsic elements of smartness such as sustainability, e-governance, or ICT functionality. However, that weighting equivalence quickly tilted in favour of corporate interest.

In 2008, after a decade of major financial losses, IBM was facing the economic slowdown caused by the global financial crisis. The company urgently needed something to revive its flagging revenue streams, and it found it in CEO Sam Palmisano's much-publicized talk "A Smarter Planet: The Next Leadership Agenda". Essentially, what emerged from Palmisano's intervention was IBM's 21st-century 'market creation strategy'. Registering the term 'smart cities' as a Trademark in 2009, IBM set about defining and promoting urban smartness through a series of publications, promotional tradeshows, and high-profile conference events. It was an extremely successful campaign. By solidifying their position as the key stakeholder in the field, IBM were perfectly placed to first develop and then aggressively exploit the global smart city market. In particular, they discursively constructed the smart city as a place of possibility, an *open* space for playful corporate experimentation that would simultaneously enhance urban 'creativity' and encourage inward financial investment.

On the surface, the vision of the smart city presented by IBM and its main competitor Cisco was one premised on an array of different meanings – creative, digital, intelligent, interconnected, virtual etc. – all of which supposedly operated in a neutral, non-ideological fashion. The reality, of course, was/is entirely different. Behind the sheen of openness and creative innovation was (unsurprisingly) a deep commitment to profiteering and global neoliberalism, something identified by sociologist Robert Hollands (2008) in an early critical article that portrayed the then embryonic smart city as just another form of urban entrepreneurialism. But although he was right to see the SCP as a variation/extension of the marketable 'creative city' rubric, at this point he could only sense how smartness providers would come to dominate the market and the surrounding discourse. A decade or so after the Hollands' article, IBM, Cisco, and other key players in the field, such as Siemens and Sidewalk Labs, have not just grabbed a slice of the smart city pie, they now produce the pie's ingredients, control the recipe, and operate as the preeminent pie shop retailers. By continuing to establish and promote a corporate version of the SCP (often via examples of developments taking place in cities like Singapore or Dubai, where the interests of profit and/or the perpetuation of an established hierarchical order is prioritized over democratic or civic accountability), these companies have ensured that, today, no meaningful alternative (non-neoliberal) smart city model exists. In short, a small group of tech companies have succeeded in actualizing the title of a 2015 report by the Silicon Valley Growth Partnership Company, Frost and Sullivan, and effectively constructed the *Smart City as a Service* (Cotton, 2015).

It is a situation that resonates perfectly with philosopher Slavoj Žižek's (2011) analysis of the current state of global capitalism more generally. For Žižek, the only solution we are offered for capitalism's (urban) failings is more capitalism – the only horizon, the capitalist horizon. And so we hurtle forward into a corporate urban future slathered in the familiar terminology of open border global capitalists – 'emerging markets', 'urban competitiveness', 'increased accountability and transparency', etc. This 'market realism', masquerading as a sociotechnical imaginary, has numerous criminological implications. To start with, it ensures that city governments continue to divert money towards ICT spending and away from other more traditional forms of public investment. This shift is perhaps most apparent within contemporary policing practice (Joh, 2017; Danaher, 2018; Interpol, UNICRI, 2019), but, as we shall now see, it is also manifesting itself spatially through new security and crime prevention/reduction strategies that are dramatically reconfiguring how our cities look and feel, and how we as citizens are surveyed and controlled.

The smart city as militarized tech zone

> Technologies that go to war inevitably come back home.
>
> Arthur Holland Michel, author of *Eyes in the Sky*,
> speaking at DIIS, Copenhagen, 3 March 2020

In *Surveillance Valley: The Secret Military History of the Internet,* Yasha Levine (2018) excavates a fascinating alternative account of how the Internet came into being. Initially designed and built in the late 1960s by the Pentagon's Defense Advanced Research Projects Agency (DARPA) as a network for data gathering and intelligence sharing about overseas counterinsurgency groups, the Internet (or ARPANET, as it was then known) quickly morphed into a much more pervasive and sophisticated surveillance tool. In Levine's account, this transformation from niche military network to totalizing surveillance system came about as a result of a series of often clandestine contracts and technological collaborations between US federal defence agencies and private telecommunication companies. Half a century later, and this same relational dynamic is even stronger, resulting in the hybrid private–public system of surveillance and control that is the Internet today. This backstory is important because if the smart city is anything, it is the manifestation of the Internet in material form – the Internet of Things as an urban concept. It is for this reason that many commentators view the SCP simply as an extension of the high-tech militarization of society that the Internet initiated.

The ultimate goal of all smart city designers is to create urban zones where every action, interaction, incident, and exchange, is surveilled, recorded, data-fied, and networked. In and of themselves, such practices can be entirely neutral. However, if the last two decades have taught us anything about smart cities, it is that, when it comes to matters relating to surveillance and security, it is important to situate all new technological developments along a control continuum. At the benign end of the scale, it is possible to view smart platforms like data sensors or the Internet of Things as no more than an extension of the social, as convenient feedback tools or interactive communication nodes. This is the position adopted by Alberto Vanolo (2014) who, writing from a Foucauldian perspective, calls this new world of scanners, sensors, and interconnected data architecture, *smartmentality*. For Vanolo, these new urban management/monitoring techniques are an inevitable twist along the disciplinary axis, only this time (through technology) 'citizens are very subtly asked to participate in the construction of smart cities' (2014: 893). Others are less sanguine. Sadowski and Pasquale (2015: 10), for example, view so-called "soft power biometric surveillance" as nothing less than somatic "strip mining"; a process in which the new data brokers of the tech industry dividualize individuals by monetizing the material body in the new 'face', 'iris' and 'gait economies'.[4] By such means, we travel along the smartness continuum towards its more militarized, security-oriented pole.

As smart systems start to be used more on the general public than by it, we begin to see the SCP framed in more ideological terms as a top-down site of control. Perhaps the central motif for the smart city as a quasi-militaristic domain is the Domain Awareness System (DAS) or Domain Awareness Center (DAC). Essentially a city-wide security assemblage, DACs aggregate video feeds from thousands of surveillance cameras, car number plate readers, and physical and radiological sensors, and channel them into a centralized command hub. From here, 'police are able to punch in a location and watch in real time or wind back the clock. They could turn on face-recognition and vehicle-tracking systems, plug in social media feeds, and enhance their view with data coming in from other law enforcement agencies' (Levine, 2018: 1–2). For Jathan Sadowski (2019), systems like the New York City DAS – a joint venture between the NYPD and Microsoft – have an underlying goal: to transform the city into a platform and thus create a governance model predicated on coercion and control and overseen by a combination of security agents and tech company liaisons:

> The idea of the captured city requires an adversarial view of a city's inhabitants: When the enemy can be anywhere, the battlespace is everywhere; all places and people must be accounted for at all times. With enough ubiquitous surveillance and processing power, the goal is to render the whole city – every place, every moment – knowable and controllable: They will be able to press rewind on the city, pause it at any point, and watch it unfold over time, or hit fast-forward and devise predictive models that inform anticipatory policing and planning [...]. Instead of police (and their private partners) needing to navigate a chaotic and multifarious city, 'smart' systems promise to impose machine-like order, as though the city could be made to function as predictably and programmatically as the computers that analyse it.
>
> (Sadowski, 2019)

Historian Melvin Kranzberg's first law of technology states: 'Technology is neither good nor bad; nor is it neutral'. From what we know about it so far, the DAS
is doing little to undermine this axiom. With its emphasis on 'anticipatory policing'
and 'predictive modelling', DACs and DASs represent a major shift in urban policing practices, from those aimed at detecting violations in order to enforce the law,
to those that seek to predict criminal acts in order to prevent them entirely. If this
only involved new modes of policing that relied upon the development of (algorithmic) tools to 'hypernudge' citizens into adopting certain prosocial behaviours,
this might be acceptable. However, it is already clear that what is materializing is
something far more socially corrosive (Hayward & Maas, 2020). Instead of 'objective', 'neutral' modes of policing (not that 'neutral policing' has ever been a reality),
many of these smart police systems will rely upon databases and analytic platforms
that are irrevocably skewed by baked-in biases, whether they use AI or existing
criminal statistics (Angwin et al., 2016). The inevitable result being, 'runaway feedback loops' of self-confirming predictive patterns (Ensign et al., 2017). Some criminologists have already expressed their concerns about such developments in terms
of stand-alone 'predictive policing' practices (Edwards, 2017; Kaufmann, Egbert &
Leese, 2018). Yet so far very little has been written about how such developments
will scale up when tethered to other fast-developing military technologies currently being redesigned for deployment in civilian contexts – and thus ultimately
for integration within smart city surveillance platforms.

Over a decade ago, DARPA introduced ARGUS-IS, a 1.8 gigapixel video surveillance platform attached to unmanned drones capable of observing an area of
25 square kilometres with a resolution of 15 cm, at any time (Hambling, 2009). In
2014, this program was integrated with the US Air Force as part of the 'Gorgon
Stare' system, which deploys Wide Angle Motion Imagery (WAMI) to enable
drones to track multiple targets within a large area. Developed initially to detect
the planting of IEDs by insurgents in Baghdad during the Second Gulf War, it was
not long before the system was operational as an investigative law enforcement
tool in the skies above Baltimore (Michel, 2019). The subsequent civil liberty concerns raised by Baltimoreans after it emerged that Gorgon Stare had been deployed
without authorization or local consultation did nothing, of course, to stop the
rollout of this technology in other US cities. The US military is already conducting further WAMI tests across six Midwest sates using experimental high-tech
altitude balloons placed in the stratosphere at altitudes of up to 65,000ft. Equipped
with high-tech tracking radars, the balloons are intended 'to provide a persistent
surveillance system to locate and deter narcotic trafficking and homeland security
threats' (Harris, 2019). Other developments, while also largely hidden from view,
are even more intrusive and worrying from a privacy perspective. Author Arthur
Holland Michel (2019), for example, warns that, soon, WAMI platforms will be
augmented by infrared imaging that can detect individuals inside homes and
buildings. Meanwhile the Pentagon have already tested their new 'Jetson' laser, a
device capable of identifying unique cardiac (heartbeat) signatures through clothes
at a range of 200 m. Today, it seems one can scan anyone with everything
(Hayward & Maas, 2020).

Impressive as these technologies are, for them to be harnessed effectively for use in the smart city, what is required is what counterinsurgency experts refer to as synergy across battlefield logistics (Singer, 2019). For obvious reasons, smart city imagineers tend to use alternative terminology, such as 'end-to-end solutions', but essentially it amounts to the same thing: data flow and real-time information updates between surveillance systems, command hubs, and end-user operatives. In the case of high-tech balloons, advanced 'mesh networking technologies' are used to link up WAMI platforms and share data immediately with receivers. In police DASs, the same goal is achieved through the use of smart tools and on-the-ground digital feedback loops (see, for example, Kilgannon (2020) on the NYPD's recent decision to replace officer's personnel handwritten logbooks with smartphone apps in an effort to better achieve what they call 'clean data'). In these and other developments, we see the further erosion of policing as a community resource, replaced instead with something that looks ever more like a combination of a private security patrol and a military deployment.

On undertaking this chapter, I vowed to avoid any mention of George Orwell's classic novel *1984*, but such technology leaves you no choice. There is no other standard of comparison. The difference, of course, is that what is available in the smart city today is Big Brother for the cybernetic generation (Big Brother's Big Brother?). Born out of computing and network theory, cybernetics views human beings not as individuals in charge of their own destiny, but as components in complex systems. In the urban war machine that is the contemporary DAS, humans have been relegated to just another piece in a universal machine, a series of nodes in a network linked together by circuits of information. In the next section, we explore the logical consequence of this type of thinking.

The smart city as cyborg central

> So I am not Vitruvian man, enclosed within a single perfect circle, looking out at the world from my personal perspective coordinates and, simultaneously, providing the measure of all things. Nor am I, as architectural phenomenologists would have it, an autonomous, self-sufficient, biologically embodied subject encountering, objectifying, and responding to my immediate environment. I construct, and I am constructed, in a mutually recursive process that continually engages my fluid, permeable boundaries and my endlessly ramifying networks. I am a spatially extended cyborg.
>
> (William Mitchell, 2003: 39)

Ever since Norbert Weiner, the godfather of the field, published *Cybernetics: Control and Communication in the Animal and the Machine* in 1948, theorists from numerous disciplines have predicted that, eventually, the division between humans and the larger 'cybernetic machine' in which we all live will break down. A central motif in this erosion of the line between cyber space and "meat space", as author William Gibson evocatively put it, is of course the cyborg (Gray, 1995).[5] In popular culture, the cyborg is typically presented as a social (humanoid) actor. Sentient, yet emotionally distant, liberating, but potentially destructive (Haraway, 1991). Think The Borg in *Star Trek*, or the T-800 robot in the *Terminator* movie series. However, as Matthew Gandy (2005: 28) has pointed out, among futurologists, cyberneticists, and social theorists, an equally important reading of the cyborg is as a *corporeal extension of the spatial*. Here, as a result of connected infrastructure and digital network flows, the cyborg exemplifies the growth and development of the cyber city – the replicant as a prosthetic augmentation of sociologist Manuel Castells (1996) 'space of flows'. Fast-forward to the era of the smart city and both these interpretations are evident, although not necessarily always in the way that quixotic cyberneticists or science fiction writers envisaged.

At an obvious level, fast-emerging trends in military robotics, virtual reality, and cloud-based battlefield communications, provide an excellent illustration of the cyborg as both a physical-territorial being, and a further symbol of the more general militarization of late-modern society. In the Second Gulf War, for example, we saw the deployment of what Elvin Wyly (2013: 389) calls "IBM machines-with legs" – hundreds of thousands of data-gathering soldiers and defence contractor employees functioning as networked nodes in the military-postindustrial complex. Add to this, developments in armoured exoskeletons (Scharre et al., 2018), "robot grunts", and "wetware" ("human performance modification" via genome editing and other forms of synthetic biology) and it is clear that, although we are still some way from the cybernetic police officer in Paul Verhoeven's 1987 film *Robocop* – a favourite metaphor of criminologists and police scholars – the future cyborg will eventually make good on Gandy and Mitchell's claims and function as a corporeal extension of the city, albeit in its DAC/urban battle zone variant.[6]

Less obvious, but potentially even more worrying, is another aspect of the 'cyborg city' that relates not to spatiality *per se*, but to the shifting nature of consciousness and cognition among the future smart city inhabitant. Put simply, what I am suggesting here is that the neo-'cyborg'-urbanite might be less a human-like replicant (although, of course, these are coming), and more *a replicant-like human*. A starting position here is Jennifer Gabrys' (2014) observation that, while the smart city is fundamentally an environmental phenomenon, it also has an active social function in the way it transforms urban citizens into 'citizen sensors'. For Maroš Krivý (2018: 16), this development is a central feature of what he calls 'the progressive cybernetisation of everyday life', a process by which 'the citizen is simultaneously dissolved into an automated behavioural sensor and transgressed as an environmental vector'. However, this is only the start. Within the new network individual, the blurring of data flows between humans and non-humans is growing ever greater, further eroding the dividing line between mind and machine.

This desubjectification process, or what Jerry Mander (2012) calls "the privatization of consciousness", is in turn intensified by the intrusion of market forces through evolutionary neuromarketing techniques and other forms of neural network colonization coded into the algorithm. To some, such concerns might seem far-fetched, too futuristic. But in reality aspects of these developments are already with us. In certain spheres of life, humans are already losing out to data in the networks of neural networks that now constitute the machine–human dyad.

For example, in the world of financial trading, human agency has been first tra-duced and now essentially replaced by automated trading positions set by algo-rithms, often resulting in random 'flash crashes' and other unforeseen market inflammations (Bridle, 2018: 121). In science and technology studies they call this new social physics "the neoliberal noösphere" – 'a partially autonomous realm in which informational algorithms interact with one another in ways that often defy human understanding, prediction or control' (Wyly, 2013: 390).

But what will result from this submission to the network, this acquiescence to the algorithm? How will citizens behave and negotiate the new 'smart cities of cognitive-cultural capitalism' (ibid)? In a thoughtful paper entitled "Beyond flat-land: when smart cities make stupid citizens", Michael McGuire sets out to answer such questions by predicting how existing psycho-behavioural and transactional relations might intensify within the fully-developed, hyper-connected SCP. McGuire's central point is that smart cities "risk damaging the most crucial com-ponent of any city – the citizens who constitute it". Developing sociologist Richard Sennett's (2012) notion of the "stupefying smart city", McGuire (2018: 2) asserts that 'the smarter our cities become the more "stupid" *we* all become', and so, rather than stupefaction, what is actually happening is a process of *stultification*:

> Sennett concurs with the idea that there is no "magic" behind what a smart city can offer [...]. The result is that exploration, uncertainty and the inherent irregularities of more organic urban spaces become stifled. We cease to have to "work out" how to use and interact with the city and it is at this point where what he calls "stupefaction" begins. But rather than stupefaction – which implies mere bewilderment or a (temporary) loss of sense, I argue that there may be deeper and longer lasting impacts. The smart city may *stultify* far more than it stupefies – that is, it may so actively denude and erode out traditional capacities to use urban space that its citizens (literally) become stupid.
>
> (McGuire, 2018: 4)

As we become increasingly adept 'at 'deleting' those parts of the urban senso-rium which we wish to ignore', we edge closer to the replicant-like human men-tioned above. Through processes such as 'inattentional blindness' and the 'atrophying of our critical faculties' human agency is 'filleted out', to use McGuire's terminology. As a result, smart citizens lose not only the ability to govern them-selves but, more importantly, *the will*, as they rely ever-more on the network to maintain them in 'a state of perpetual safety and total security' (ibid.: 8); a relational dynamic that itself diminishes social resilience and exacerbates passive infantiliza-tion (Hayward, 2013).

The tech utopians and "Californian ideology" (Barbrook & Cameron, 1996) merchants believed their new sophisticated creations would bring about "the end of politics" and facilitate a harmonious society built on transparent circuits of information and effortless environmental-behavioural management. Instead, they have inadvertently put in place the technological foundations of a totalizing system of control, surveillance, and exploitation.[7] In terms of human subjectivity and interpersonal dynamics, the cybernetic dream has been even more damaging. The cyberneticists' vision was of a new "citizen-sensor" who would be so enlightened by networked flows of processed data that all the petty grievances and micro competitions of the analogue world would somehow melt away as we embrace hyperconnectivity. In reality, they and their corporate adherents have created a world so reliant on digital technology that we have lost sight of what it means to be human. The inevitable question that now confronts us is this: will the rise of urban smartness and its worker-drone corollary, the replicant-like human, continue unabated? Or will individual actors, subcultural groups, or indeed the public at large decide it's now time to take the city back?

The smart city as adversarial surface

> The only good DAC is a dead DAC!
>
> Anti-surveillance protestor in Oakland (cited in Levine, 2018: 2)

As we have seen, the zones of futurity surrounding the smart city are in the main presented as overwhelmingly positive. Given the multinational companies involved and the colossal investment that has been ploughed into the technological development and marketing of urban smartness, how could it be any other way? However, peel back the thick veneer of corporate puffery and booster superficiality, and it is clear that, as a model of future urban living, the smart city is not quite the shining Jerusalem its supporters assume it to be. Explore the research produced on the margins of the field by critical journalists, academics, and radical urbanists, and it is apparent there also exists a much bleaker view of the smart city's future – a future that includes protest and urban resistance aimed at halting the advance of techno-imperialism, and adversarial/criminal practices that use smart systems as attack surfaces. Let us look briefly at each in turn. When considering future protest within/against the SCP a good place to start is with some of the ideas currently cohering around the term "tech-lash". Glossing because of space constraints, the so-called "tech-lash" is predicated on generalized concerns about the ethics of data-driven urbanism and whether forms of governance based on cybernetics and techno-solutions are ultimately compatible with a plural, open democratic society (Kitchen, 2016; Greenfield, 2017).[8] This presupposition is then compounded by secondary fears about *the technology itself* (Bridle, 2018). Specifically, the view that, by privileging and promoting only technological solutions to the problems of urbanization, we have failed to consider how these same technologies might also be used against us. Albeit nascent, the tech-lash has already taken a number of forms, including popular boycotts of certain social network platforms and the 2018 European-wide data-protection ruling. Inevitably, given its status as an emblem of AI and networked technology, the smart city is also emerging as a site of resistance and dissent. So far, pushback has been limited to certain specific aspects of urban smartness such as local campaigns against DACs and municipal face-recognition camera bans. However, if current trends are anything to go by, the anti-smartness movement will likely crystallize into something more tangible, which could potentially pose a serious challenge to the smart city's technological, and ergo operational, viability.

From what we have seen so far, two discernible "cultures of resistance" are emerging. The first functions largely within the tech community and is less interested in resistance *per se* than in stress-testing new technological initiatives in a bid to promote better risk management (see Belfield, 2020). Of central importance here is the field of AI and how its malicious use can expose vulnerabilities in smart critical infrastructure – and, of course, create new ones. Because AI is susceptible to "adversarial input" – data designed to exploit the way a system processes stimuli – it is possible to make an AI platform 'hallucinate' objects (or sounds) that are not there. In one famous example, a picture of a panda that looks normal to the human eye was imperceptibly 'altered' so the AI perceived it as a gibbon (Goodfellow, Shlens & Szegedy, 2014). Likewise, it is now possible to 3D-print a model of a turtle in such a way that it is perceived by AI as a rifle from nearly every angle (Athalye et al., 2018). Such practices have immense implications for AI-security sensors and other scanning equipment embedded in smart architecture. For example, Kevin Eykholt and others (2017) have developed "adversarial patch" stickers that, when placed on traffic signs, cause image-recognition networks (such as those in self-driving cars) to misinterpret 'Stop' signs as 'speed limit 45km/h' signs. In a similar experiment, Tencent's Keen Security Lab (2019) showed that placing three stickers on the road can spoof a Tesla Model-S car into switching lanes – sending it directly into oncoming traffic. Although such initiatives are not always welcomed by the tech community, in and of themselves they do not amount to meaningful *political* resistance.[9] Rather, the goal is to stimulate a more informed discussion about vulnerability vectors and preventative security. For something more stridently political, one must turn to a second emerging culture of resistance.

One of the defining features of the recent spate of political uprisings has been the way protestors have mobilized technology in their resistance practices.[10] For example, encrypted messaging platforms like Telegram are now a staple of any political protest. Meanwhile, decentralized apps that use QR codes to allow organizer-nodes (called 'water drops') to amalgamate small flash protests into coordinated demonstrations (or 'tsunamis') are also becoming common. However, what is of greater interest here is the way protesters around the globe now actively undertake specific 'anti-technology actions'; whether in the form of localized participatory resistance against depersonalizing forms of "digital justice" (Smith & O'Malley, 2017), or wider anti-government demonstrations in places like Catalonia and Hong Kong, where smart lampposts and face-recognition systems were torn down and ID cards were wrapped in tinfoil to avoid triggering RFID sensors. These tendencies will doubtless grow in sophistication as protestors also become adept at developing adversarial AI techniques that can confuse facial-recognition programs. Already, artists and researchers have combined to develop cosmetic "dazzle camouflage" that protects individuals against AI surveillance, while in Belgium an adversarial image has been designed which, if printed and carried around, renders a whole person invisible to specific AI computer-vision systems.[11] Adam Edwards and Marco Calaresu (2018) recently observed that in the current environment 'it would be unwise to overestimate the power of machines or to underestimate the capacity of humans for resistance and improvisation in "democratic cities"'. Both sentiments are unequivocally true. However, so far at least, critics of the SCP have been more concerned with the former than the latter issue. Going forward, it is my contention that the social sciences can do much to help redress this imbalance.

Criminologically speaking, it is at this point that the idea of the smart city as an *adversarial surface/space* gathers traction. Much has been written by criminologists and digital sociologists about cybercrime and online victimization, but very little about *the smart city as a specific vector of digital insecurity*. However, we are now on the cusp of an entirely new era of "cyber-physical threats" (Joo & Tan, 2018) and "AI crimes" (King et al., 2020) against hyper-connected critical-infrastructure systems (Kaloudi & Jungyeu, 2020) and thus the need to pivot in this direction is clear. For example, already emerging are 'AI hacks' that can exploit vulnerabilities in voice-recognition systems such as Alexa, Siri and Google Assistant. These techniques can be easily adapted to attack 'smart homes' – unlocking doors, wiring money, or triggering buy-orders for incriminating or embarrassing products – merely by, say, playing slightly 'perturbed' music over the radio. Such 'adversarial attacks' illustrate how bad actors can sprinkle a physical environment with what Paul Scharre and Michael Horowitz (2018: 15) call "cognitive landmines" – raising critical security vulnerabilities in Internet of Things systems and posing further problems for advocates of the SCP.

By developing advanced systems of surveillance and pre-emption in an attempt to make 'traditional' crime forms impossible, we have simply exposed society to a different, largely unanticipated series of catastrophic risks and threats – including a complex interplay of system failures brought about by resistance and criminal sabotage – that previously would have been considered impossible. This being the case, it is perhaps an apposite moment to remind criminologists of the words of the French 'philosopher of everyday life', Michel de Certeau:

> If it is true that the grid of "discipline" is everywhere becoming clearer and more extensive, it is all the more urgent to discover how an entire society resists being reduced to it, what popular procedures (also "miniscule" and quotidian) manipulate the mechanisms of discipline and conform to them only in order to evade them.
>
> (1984: xiv)

Conclusion

In 2022, on a 175-acre site in the foothills of Mount Fuji, the Japanese manufacturer Toyota will break ground on 'Woven City'. Described in contradictory terms by Toyota Motor Corp President, Akio Toyoda, as both a "field of dreams" and a "fully controlled site", Woven City is (unimaginatively) being promoted as the prototype for the future of urban living (Korosec, 2020). Despite the bold claims, much of the technology that will underpin Woven City is not actually new. Instead, it represents a conflation of established inventions (smart home-connected technology, sensor-based AI, and embedded health-assessment scanners), with Toyota's autonomous 'e-Palette transport and delivery shuttles' and branded in-home service and maintenance robotics. It is this latter element that is most important. Woven City will no doubt test many interesting things, but essentially what it represents is the further insinuation of corporate robots into the private and public spheres of 'Smart city 2.0'. For a world leader in robotic technology like Toyota, the shiny designer homes and spotless leisure spaces of Woven City are little more than a life-size testing ground for the new robot–human interface – a benign version of Alex Garland's *Ex Machina,* or, to reprise a term from earlier, the first fully-operational *robotic sociotechnical imaginary.* The problem for Toyota is that, even before the story of Woven City begins, we know how it ends. We know, because we have heard this story before.

Situated 25 miles South West of Seoul, the South Korean smart city of Songdo was launched in 2015 amidst the standard fanfare of publicity and crypto-futurology. The plan for Songdo was typically ambitious. It would function as both the world's first purpose-built 'smart business district', and provide a home for 300,000 new residents. Spacious, leafy, traffic-free, and of course 'ecologically sustainable', Songdo was marketed as a tranquil techno-suburban paradise; the very antithesis of the polluted, overpopulated neighbourhoods of the typical South Korean city. However, less than a decade later, things have deviated from the blueprint. Only a quarter full, bereft of businesses and major retailers, and lacking in cultural facilities, Songdo exhibits what one observer recently described as "a Chernobyl-like emptiness" (White, 2018). Big on tech innovation and hyper-connectivity it may be, but with its empty high-rises and shuttered retail spaces, Songdo today is less a smart city and more a hyper-connected ghost town.

The many problems to have beset Songdo provide an abject illustration of what happens when urban developers prioritize technological innovation over and above the lived realities of city dwellers. Why, then, if 'the World's first Smart City' offers a vivid and still unfolding example of a broken sociotechnical imaginary are Toyota so keen to break ground on yet another techno-fantasy citadel? The answer can be found in the nature of techno-computational culture itself. In the same way computer scientists attempt to correct prediction errors by adding more data to their models, many proponents of the SCP believe erroneously that the only way to tackle the real-world failings of smart technology is with *more* smart technology. However, embedding ever-more technology within urban space is a far more consequential (and irreversible) act than enlarging a dataset. As more tasks and decisions are acquiesced to machines and their associated systems, the "urban experience" (Hayward, 2004) is inevitably reconstituted. Urban space becomes more contrived and calculating, while a walk through the city starts to feel like time spent in the "code/space" (Kitchen & Dodge, 2011) of an airport; safe and sterile, but homogeneous and delimiting. But maybe this is the point. If the underlying premise of smart city proponents is, "what is not smart must be dumb", then it automatically follows that the city of digital technology is superior to its analogue (human) predecessor. It is this false binary that leads inexorably to Woven City and its doubling down on corporate robotics. Stated simply, for Toyota and other smartness service providers, the only possible smart city future is the one premised on the robotic sociotechnical imaginary. After all, the methodological and epistemological pastiche of life that will emerge out of the new robot–human interface will no doubt be much easier to manage and scale than the real thing, blighted as it is by the idiosyncrasies and existential anxieties of the 'unsmart' analogue citizen.

The opening line of this chapter declared boldly that we now live in the age of the smart city. The question we must therefore pose by way of conclusion is a stark one: whether it is Woven City, Songdo or the plug-and-play DAC soon be installed in a city near you, what will 'living' actually mean when urban life is ultimately defined and enforced by a computational system? If we fail to provide a clear answer to this question, we will only have ourselves to blame as the smart city effortlessly transitions from sociotechnical imaginary to technologically-determined reality.

Notes

1   There's nothing new about adding a prefix to the word 'city' in an attempt to herald a new urban paradigm. From Ebenezer Howard's 'Garden City' project at the end of the nineteenth century, to end-of-the-twentieth-century conceptual models such as the 'postmodern city' (Soja, 1989), the 'edge city' (Garreau, 1991), the 'fantasy city' (Hannigan, 1998), the 'dual city' (Castells, 1996), and the 'enterprise city' (Hall, 1989) (to name but a few), urban scholars, architects, and city planners have produced a dizzying array of prefixes in an attempt to predict, and in some cases influence, the future form and function of urban space. However, while these models have contributed much to our understanding of the changing nature of cities and city life in late modernity, none of them has achieved anywhere near the real-world impact of the prefix du jour – 'smart'.

2   The term [urban] 'smartness' was also the brainchild of corporate executives. ICT imagineers appropriated the term from debates taking place in the field of urban planning in the early 1990s about 'smart growth' and how this concept could be used to combat the urban sprawl underway in many US cities at that time.

3   See Viitanen and Kingston (2014) for a critique of the "conceptual adolescence" that characterizes much of the smart city hype about 'sustainability' and 'environmental resilience'.

4   Interestingly, with the onset of 5G network it will soon be possible (by a combination of geotagging and new mobile router triangulation) to create digital avatars of smart phone users, a process that will allow surveillance operatives and other interested parties to plot/track individuals not only on the Cartesian X and Y plains, but also on the Z (height) axis.

5   The term 'cyborg' is shorthand for what cybernetic organism.

6   It is interesting that Norbert Weiner, the MIT professor who did more than anybody to kick-start the cybernetic revolution in military thinking, soon came to regret his involvement. As Levine (2018: 45) notes: 'He saw scientists and military men taking the narrowest possible interpretation of cybernetics to create better killing machines and more efficient systems of surveillance and control and exploitation.'

7   Under normal conditions, the wide scale take up of these granular and predictive surveillance systems might have taken a decade or so. However, as a result of the Covid-19 crisis, the deployment of such technology will be much more rapid, as surveillance proponents utilize public health concerns to justify immediate and (permanent) deployment á la China.

8 This concern is itself a product of two interconnected anxieties. First, concerns about the smart city's ontology as a 'neo-liberal political place' and fears that, in the long run, it will diminish social trust and potentially even the rule of law (Keymolen & Voorwinden, 2019); second, a more specifically neo-Marxist argument that the new super-rich elites will utilize a combination of hyper-surveillance and special juridical zones to bring about what Doctorow (2015) has called 'a long age of [ICT] powered feudalism'.

9 On resistance in contemporary criminology, see Hayward & Schuilenburg, 2014.

10 The idea of a tech-lash, or of 'opting out' of mainstream digital culture, is also growing outside of organized resistance movements. See, for example, the massive uptick in the use of the darkweb's 'Tor' browser, or the rise of so-called "obfuscation" techniques like the browser plug-ins AdNauseam or TrackMeNot (Brunton & Nissenbaum, 2016).

11 See also Adam Harvey's 'HyperFace' project which uses textile patterns that can trick facial recognition systems.

References

Albino, V., U. Berardi and R.M. Dangelico. 2015. Smart cities: Definitions, dimensions, performance, and initiatives. *Journal of Urban Technology*, 22 (1): 3–21.

Angwin, J. et al. 2016. Machine bias: There's software used across the country to predict future criminals. And it's biased against blacks. *ProPublica*.

Anderson, B. 2010. Preemption, precaution, preparedness: Anticipatory action and future geographies. *Progress in Human Geography*, 34 (6): 777–798.

Athalye, A., L. Engstrom, A. Ilyas and K. Kwok. 2018. *Synthesizing robust adversarial examples. Proceedings of the 35th International Conference on Machine Learning*, PMLR 80: 284–293.

Barbrook, R. and A. Cameron. 1996. The Californian ideology. *Science as Culture*, 6 (1): 44–72.

Belfield, H. 2020. *Activism by the AI community. AIES '20: Proceedings of the AAAI/ACM Conference on AI, Ethics, and Society*, February, 15–21.

Bridle, J. 2018. *New dark age*. London: Verso Books.

Brunton, F. and H. Nissenbaum. 2016. *Obfuscation*. Boston: MIT Press.

Carter, B. 2019. Public safety is at the heart of the smart city movement. Securityinfowatch. com, August.

Castells, M. 1996. *The rise of the network society*. Oxford: Blackwell.

Cotton, B. 2015. *Smart city as a service: Using analytics to equip communities for data-driven decisions*. https://www.mayorsinnovation.org/images/uploads/pdf/15_-_Smart_City_as_a_ Service.pdf; accessed 23-08-2020.

Danaher, J. 2018. The automation of policing: Challenges and opportunities. https://philosophicaldisquisitions.blogspot.com/2018/10/the-automation-of-policing-challenges. html; accessed 23-08-2020.

De Certeau, M. 1984. *The practice of everyday life*. Berkeley: University of California Press.

Doctorow, C. 2015. Technology should be used to create social mobility – Not to spy on citizens, http://www.theguardian.com/technology/2015/mar/10/nsa-gchq-technology-create-social-mobility-spy-on-citizens; accessed 03-09-2020.

Eaton, R. 2001. *Ideal cities*. London: Thames and Hudson.

Edwards, A. 2017. Big data, predictive machines and security: The minority report. In *The Routledge handbook of technology, crime and justice*, edited by M. Maguire and T. Holt. London: Routledge.

Edwards, A. and M. Calaresu. 2018. Smart cities and security: Editorial preface. *City, Territory and Architecture*, 5: 19. https://doi.org/10.1186/s40410-018-0089-1.

Ensign, D. et al. 2017. Runaway feedback loops in predictive policing. *Proceedings of Machine Learning Research*, 81:1–12.

Eykholt, K., I. Evtimov, E. Fernandes, T. Kohno, B. Li, A. Prakash, A. Rahmati and D. Song. 2017. Robust physical-world attacks on deep learning models. https://arxiv.org/abs/1707.08945; accessed 03-09-2020.

Gabrys, J. 2014. Programming environments: Environmentality and citizen sensing in the smart city. *Environment and Planning D: Society and Space*, 32 (1): 30–48.

Gandy, M. 2005. Cyborg urbanization: Complexity and monstrosity in the contemporary city. *International Journal of Urban and Regional Research*, 29 (1): 26–49.

Garreau, J. 1991. *Edge city*. New York: Doubleday.

Goodfellow, I.J., J. Shlens and C. Szegedy. 2014. Explaining and harnessing adversarial examples. arXiv:14126572 [cs, stat].

Gray, C.H. 1995. *The cyborg handbook*. New York: Routledge.

Greenfield, A. 2013. *Against the smart city*. New York: Do Projects.

Greenfield, A. 2017. *Radical technologies*. London: Verso Books.

Hall, P. 1989. *Cities of tomorrow*. London: Blackwell.

Hambling, D. 2009. Special forces: Gigapixel flying spy sees all. *Wired*.

Hannigan, J. 1998. *Fantasy city*. London: Routledge.

Haraway, D.J. 1991. *Simians, cyborgs, and women*. London: Free Association Books.

Harris, M. 2019. Pentagon testing mass surveillance balloons across the US. *The Guardian*, 2 August.

Hayward, K.J. 2004. *City limits*. London: GlassHouse.

Hayward, K.J. 2012. Five spaces of cultural criminology. *British Journal of Criminology*, 53 (4): 441–462.

Hayward, K.J. 2013. 'Life stage dissolution' in Anglo-American advertising and popular culture. *The Sociological Review*, 61 (3): 525–548.

Hayward, K.J. and M. Maas. 2020. Artificial intelligence and crime: A primer for criminologists. *Crime, Media, Culture*, doi: 10.1177/1741659020917434; accessed 23-08-2020.

Hayward, K.J. and M. Schuilenburg. 2014. To resist = to create?: Some thoughts on the concept of resistance in cultural criminology. *Tijdschrift over Cultuur and Criminaliteit*, 4 (1): 22–36.

Hollands, R. 2008. Will the real smart city please stand up? Intelligent, progressive or entrepreneurial? *City*, 12 (3): 303–320.

Hollands, R. 2015. Critical interventions into the corporate smart city. *Cambridge Journal of Regions, Economy and Society*, 8 (1): 61–77.

Interpol, UNICRI. 2019. *Artificial intelligence and robotics for law enforcement*.

Jasanoff, S. and S.-H. Kim. 2015. *Dreamscapes of modernity: Sociotechnical imaginaries and the fabrication of power*. Chicago: University of Chicago Press.

Joh, E.E. 2017. The undue influence of surveillance technology companies on policing. *NYU Legal Review Online*, 101.

Joo, Y.-M. and T.-B. Tan. 2018. Smart cities: A new age of digital insecurity. *Survival*, 60 (2): 91–106.

Kaloudi, N. and L. Jungyeu. 2020. The AI-based cyber threat landscape: A survey. *ACM Computing Surveys*, 53 (1): 1–34.

Kaufmann, M., S. Egbert and M. Leese. 2018. Predictive policing and the politics of patterns. *British Journal of Criminology*, 59: 674–692.

Keymolen, E. and A. Voorwinden. 2019. Can we negotiate?: Trust and the rule of law in the smart city. *International Review of Law, Computers, and Technology*, forthcoming.

Kilgannon, C. 2020. Why the NYPD dropped one of its oldest crime-fighting tools. *New York Times*, 5 February.

King, T.C., N. Aggarwal, M. Taddeo et al. 2020. Artificial intelligence crime: An interdisciplinary analysis of foreseeable threats and solutions. *Science and Engineering Ethics*, 26, 89–120.

Kitchin, R. 2014. The real-time city? Big data and smart urbanism. *GeoJournal*, 79 (1): 1–14.

Kitchen, R. 2016. The ethics of smart cities and urban science. *Philosophical Transactions of the Royal Society A*, 374: 20160115.

Kitchen, R. and M. Dodge. 2011. *Code/Space*. Cambridge: MIT Press.

Korosec, K. 2020. Toyota is building a tiny utopian prototype city filled with people, robots and AI. https://www.yahoo.com/finance; accessed 20-01-2020.

Krivý, M. 2018. Towards a critique of cybernetic urbanism: The smart city and the society of control. *Planning Theory*, 17 (1): 8–30.

Levine, Y. 2018. *Surveillance valley*. New York: Public Affairs.

Mander, J. 2012. Privatization of consciousness. *Monthly Review*, 64 (5).

McGuire, M. 2018. Beyond flatland: When smart cities make stupid citizens. *City, Territory and Architecture*, 5.

McNeil, M., M. Arribas-Ayllon, J. Haran, A. Mackenzie and R. Tutton. 2017. Conceptualizing imaginaries of science, technology, and society. In *The Routledge handbook of science and technology studies*, edited by U. Felt et al. Cambridge: MIT Press.

March, H. 2016. The smart city and other ICT-led techno-imaginaries. *Journal of Cleaner Production*, 199: 1694–1703.

Mattern, S. 2017. *A city is not a computer*. https://placesjournal.org/article/a-city-is-not-acomputer/?gclid=EAIaIQobChMI7bDUjf6K6AIVlpQYCh0acAIbEAAYASAAEgKGGPD_BwE#ref_10; accessed 20-05-2020.

Michel, A.H. 2019. *Eyes in the sky*. HMH Books.

Mitchell, W.J. 2003. *Me++: The cyborg self and the networked city*. Cambridge: MIT Press.

Morozov, E. 2013. *To save everything, click here*. New York: Public Affairs Books.

Pali, B. and M. Schuilenburg. 2019. Fear and fantasy in the smart city. *Critical Criminology: An International Journal*, doi:10.1007/s10612-019-09447-7; accessed 02-01-2020.

Rosati, U. and S. Conti. 2016. What is a smart city project?: An urban model or a corporate business plan? *Procedia: Social and Behavioral Sciences*, 223: 968–973.

Sadowski, J. 2019. *The captured city: The 'smart city' makes infrastructure and surveillance indistinguishable*. realifemag.com.

Sadowski, J. and R. Bendor. 2019. Selling smartness: Corporate narratives and the smart city as a technological imaginary. *Science, Technology, and Human Values*, 44 (3): 540–563.

Sadowski, J. and F. Pasquale 2015. The spectrum of control: A social theory of theory of the smart city. *First Monday*, 20 (7), 6 July.

Scharre, P. and M.C. Horowitz. 2018. *Artificial intelligence*. Center for a new American security. https://www.cnas.org/.

Scharre, P., L. Fish, K. Kidder and A. Schafer. 2018. *Emerging technology*. Center for a New American Security, https://www.cnas.org/.

Sennett, R. 2012. The stupefying smart city. Available at in *LSECities* Open Transcripts: Urban Age, Electric City.

Singer, P.W. 2019. *Insurgency in 2030*. newamerica.org.

Smith, G. and P. O'Malley. 2017. Driving politics: Data-driven governance and resistance. *British Journal of Criminology*, 57 (2): 275–298.

Söderström, O., T. Paasche and F. Klauser. 2014. Smart cities as corporate storytelling. *City*, 18 (3): 307–320.

Soja, E. 1989. *Postmodern geographies*. London: Verso.

Tencent Keen Security Lab. 2019. Experimental security research of Tesla autopilot. Tencent.

Townsend, A.M. 2013. *Smarter cities*. New York: Norton.

Vanolo, A. 2014. Smartmentality: The smart city as disciplinary strategy. *Urban Studies*, 51 (5): 883–898.

Viitanen J. and R. Kingston. 2014. Smart cities and green growth: Outsourcing democratic and environmental resilience to the global technology sector. *Environment and Planning A: Economy and Space*, 46 (4): 803-819.

Weagle, S. 2019. *Smart cities are safe cities*. Securityinfowatch.com, 16 August.

White, J.M. 2016. Anticipatory logics of the smart city's global imaginary. *Urban Geography*, 37 (4): 572–598.

White, C. 2018. *South Korea's 'smart city' Songdo: not quite smart enough?* https://www.scmp.com/week-asia/business/article/2137838/south-koreas-smart-city-songdo-not-quite-smart-enough; accessed 20-05-2020.

Wyly, E. 2013. The city of cognitive-cultural capitalism. *City*, 17 (3): 387–394.

Žižek, S. 2011. *Living in the end of times*. London: Verso.

Chapter 12

Understanding the algorithmic society

Concluding thoughts

Marc Schuilenburg and Rik Peeters

The classification of societies

In the history of humankind, there have been various ways to classify a society. One classification is based on the evolution of types of pre-industrial societies, including hunting and gathering, horticultural, pastoral, and agricultural societies. Although not all hunting and gathering societies are exactly alike, anthropologists and sociologists agree that they all share the basic feature of economic relationships based on cooperation. There is no conception of private property or ownership in these societies and members simply give things to one another. Another well-known example to categorize societies is the distinction between cremating and burying societies. Scholars such as archaeologist Gordon Childe (1945) have pointed out that this distinction has several analytical implications for our understanding of past and present human societies. In the case of burial societies, their proliferation derived partially from the desire to lend order and dignity to the hour of death and burial. Subsequently, there is the assumption that burial treatment is a reflection of the hierarchical nature of society, with defined classes and elites controlling social groups. A third example of classification is the difference between the hegemonic power structures ('power over') in a disciplinary society and a communicational society in which power becomes more immanent in its processes ('power from within'). According to sociologist Scott Lash, these mutations occur in conjunction with the advent of a society of ubiquitous media 'in which power is increasingly in the algorithm' (2007: 71).

The point here is that these classifications, as anthropologists such as Morton Fried (1960) and Marshall Sahlins (1961) have stated, can be placed in broader categories and stages of social complexity. However, many ethnographic studies show that to define societies as hierarchical for example is to oversimplify and generalize the complex social order of many western and non-western societies. Other scholars have objected that these categorizations do not explain how different types of societies are related to one another, blend into one another, and ultimately partially replace one another. What causes, for example, the transition between a disciplinary society and a communicational society at a certain moment? As Gilles Deleuze remarked in his book *Foucault*: 'When a new formation appears, with new rules and series, it never comes all at once, in a single phrase or act of creation, but emerges like a series of "building blocks", with gaps, traces and reactivations of former elements that survive under the new rules' (1986: 30). This poses the question about the 'basis' of our society in terms of technology, power, and knowledge, without having to fall back on a fixed and unchangeable form or a deeply rooted essence.

Technology, power, and knowledge

It seems almost a cliché to say that algorithms are so deeply embedded in our society that they are affecting decisions everywhere. But what is not trite is analysing *how* they are affecting the key pillars of our society, such as administration, health, education, work, criminal justice and cities. Although algorithms are not confined to mathematics, there is a tendency to see algorithms, amidst the expanding capacities of Artificial Intelligence and machine learning, as a recent technological innovation that applies abstract mathematical principles to massive quantities of data. According to philosopher Matteo Pasquinelli, the first machine-learning algorithm was the Perceptron from 1957. The Perceptron was invented by the cognitive scientist Frank Rosenblatt at the Cornell Aeronautical Laboratory in Buffalo, New York. Pasquinelli writes in "Three thousand years of algorithmic rituals" (2019) that 'the Perceptron was a sort of photo camera that could be taught to recognize a specific shape, i.e. to make a decision with a margin of error (making it an 'intelligent' machine)'.

The depth of this technological change, in which the repetition of similar patterns 'teach' the machine and cause the pattern to emerge as a statistical distribution, has triggered all manner of sociocultural visions of society. One of these is the way algorithms and analytics give rise to a new power dynamic. Scholars from a range of backgrounds are increasingly investigating how new modalities of power are enfolding in our algorithmically-mediated society. Philosopher Colin Koopman, for example, speaks of "infopower", which works upon us through the formats of data. Koopman defines infopower as a 'political assembly of information [...] which is political because it disposes us as subjects of data prior to any communicative exchange' (2019b: 1334). A key element of infopower is the way it binds us in the sense that it 'both ties us down and speeds us up' (2019a: 12). Another new form of power is, what lawyer and critical theorist Bernard Harcourt (2007) calls, "expository power", revealing how unfree we are becoming because our subjectivity is moulded by algorithms. Algorithms define us as particular kinds of persons whose possibilities for action are conditioned in particular ways.

Such plural forms of power show that our present society does not bring the world together in a single harmonious entity, but regularly produces social syntheses between different forms of technology, power, and knowledge. Accordingly, the discerned forms of power and knowledge described in this volume are not mutually exclusive nor do they displace 'old' forms of power and knowledge. The example of smart cities makes this clear. Although the concept 'smart city' suggests that only smart technology is used to transform and improve life within a city, this provides a limited perspective on what smart surveillance currently entails. Smart cities still use 'dumb' tools and techniques to improve public safety – by, for instance, placing large concrete planters, heavy trucks and cement barriers along busy pedestrian streets and squares to restrict access and improve security (Pali & Schuilenburg, 2019). Another example is the digital form of predictive policing, where predictive analytics are used to assess likely future behaviours or events and to direct appropriate action by the police. In relation to the question of power, it can be argued that predictive policing is an expression of classic state surveillance ("sovereign power"), which operates, however, through data-driven technologies developed by private companies to track and monitor the behaviour and movements of people (Schuilenburg, 2021).

The main theme of this book revolves around a critical concern with how algorithms are shaping society now and how they might shape it in the future. To approach these concerns, we define *the algorithmic society* as 'a set of practices and discourses, implicating hybrid connections between governmental and private parties, that is underpinned by a repertoire of relatively new data-driven technologies, which adds new layers to the governance of society through own modes of knowledge, and particular ways of forming new subjects'. In many respects, the research conducted in the preceding chapters advances our understanding of *how* the algorithmic society functions. Based on the contributions by different scholars, we can draw five observations on the mechanisms and dilemmas regarding the impact of algorithms in our society.

Five observations

Techno-utopia

A first observation is the seemingly contradictory *techno-utopian vision* that the widespread use of algorithms implies (see, for instance, the contribution by Schuilenburg and Pali). Algorithms have been identified as an advanced technological form of solving humanity's problems that insists on a particular model of development and governance. Its sequencing and black boxing of procedural steps creates a machine-like logic, befitting of a Weberian analysis of late-modern bureaucracy. The alienation that marked the classic bureaucracy is brought to a new provisional conclusion in the automation of decision-making processes in the provision of public services, the administration of criminal justice, and the surveillance of urban spaces. Even though human agency is rarely fully eliminated and many automated decisions require a follow-up decision by human agents (civil servants, judges, police officers, etc.), the analyses presented in this volume converge around the idea that algorithms pursue a further rationalization of governance, which is closely related to our data-driven economy.

At the same time, however, the use of algorithms is also infused with a utopian vision of control, prediction and efficiency. As several contributions have outlined (see, for instance, the chapters by McGuire and by Hayward), at least three core beliefs of algorithmic governance can be identified to make governance 'smarter'. First, algorithms promote efficiency, not only in private life and the economy but also in government processes. They are both capable of processing and analysing enormous of data and finding patterns where human reason falls short. Second, the use of algorithms is believed to be positively related to equity. They reduce human bias and subjectivity, are citizen-centred, and enable participation. And third, algorithms can be applied to improve safety and security. They allow prediction of crime as well as soft forms of behavioural control (rather than strict discipline) in urban areas. However, these promises are, at least partly, utopian. Efficiency is instrumental to an economic rationale of competition and consumption. Human bias might be reduced in street-level decisions, but continues to play a major role in the design and data input of algorithms. And reliable prediction remains fundamentally unattainable while it also legitimizes new forms of control.

Inequality

A second observation that can be drawn from the contributions in this volume is that the social consequences of algorithmic governance are *distributive* (see the chapters by Van Brakel and by Ávila, Hannah-Moffat and Maurutto). The effects of, among other things, the automation of administrative decisions, risk prediction in criminal justice, and behavioural interventions in the public domain are not evenly distributed among the population. The algorithmic society has winners and losers. The winners are those that benefit from competition and consumption, that are not subjected to biased data, and that are in the 'happy flow' of standardized administration decisions. Conversely, the losers can be found where people become superfluous or unproductive in the name of efficiency, in already overpoliced urban areas and profiled high-risk groups, and where administrative errors or other bureaucratic complications occur.

At least two factors of algorithmic governance complicate the mitigation of these distributive tendencies. The first complication is that algorithms are not evenly applied nor implemented according to a grand design, but instead resemble more of a *patchwork*. There is, however, a 'logic' in this patchwork. For instance, algorithms tend to be applied in specific urban areas, such as in business improvement districts or commercial centres where 'smart city' incentives are rolled out, and in high crime areas where instruments such as hot-spot policing are commonly applied. Furthermore, algorithms are often used in exactly those administrative decisions where citizens are most vulnerable for abuse or exclusion, namely decisions regarding the access to welfare services or benefits and decisions in criminal justice sentencing and probation.

The second complication concerns safeguarding the *fairness* of decisions for individuals. Algorithmic decision-making implies a large level of standardization: processes are designed with abstractions of individual identities in mind. As a consequence, people may be profiled because of certain characteristics of a larger population group (as in the case of predictive policing). Furthermore, algorithmic decision-making is often highly opaque for citizens. They may be subjected to administrative decisions based on data they have no access to, based on obscure algorithmic processes and data sharing, and based on designed-in outcome options without individual human case assessment. As several contributions have demonstrated, a challenge remains in safeguarding fairness of algorithmic decisions for every citizen and organizing practical accountability of public organizations. The people most likely to be negatively affected by algorithms are also the most likely to be left without a clear path to appeal algorithmic decisions.

Technological usurpation

A third observation is that algorithms push towards a *technological contamination of justice* by overriding existing legal processes and safeguards (see the chapters by Meijer and Grimmelikhuijsen and by Widlak, Van Eck and Peeters). Three inter-related problems in the design of algorithmic governance can be identified in this respect. A first problem is the lack of algorithmic transparency. It is often unclear for both human decision-makers and affected citizens what kinds of data are used and how algorithms are designed, thereby complicating the possibility to assess the fairness of an algorithm. A second issue is the lack of algorithmic accountability. If a decision is automatically generated, who is to be held accountable for it? How can we tell if all relevant elements in an individual case have been weighed? And how can citizens appeal against a decision if they do not know on what data or criteria it was based? Finally, a third issue is the lack of street-level discretion. In 'analogue' decision-making, discretion by street-level bureaucrats or frontline workers serves as a key mechanism to balance general rules with the need to apply them in a fair way in highly diverse situations. The ability for organizations to weigh individual circumstances has been limited by the introduction of automated decision-making. Rather than factual assessment, algorithms now provide the default for the decisions by human agents.

A challenge remains in making algorithmic decision-making compatible with the *rule of law* (see Coglianese's contribution). As mentioned above, transparency and fairness are being redefined under the sway of emerging technologies. More in general, there has already been a strong backlash against algorithmic decision-making from privacy and human rights advocates. The issues of transparency and fairness are complicated ones for automated projects. Algorithms are designed by IT professionals rather than decision-makers and often remain secretive due to their proprietary nature. Moreover, as in the case of automated network decisions, there can be a schism between the owners of the decision and the owners of the data upon which decisions are based. Often neither the decision-making organization nor the affected citizen have insight into the source and correctness of the data.

Algorithmic agency

A fourth observation is that we can only understand the impact algorithms on the governing of society by taking into account *human–algorithm interactions* (see the chapter by Van Eijk). However, keeping 'humans in-the-loop' of data-driven regulation is in itself not enough to make a meaningful impact. Various contributions in this volume have demonstrated the behavioural elements at play in day-to-day algorithmic governance. Crucially, even if humans have to follow-up on an algorithmically-generated outcome, algorithms tend to be produce a default that decision-makers do not deviate from. Algorithms do not argue. They present an outcome without an argument or reasoning. They present a truth without revealing sources or assumptions. 'Merely' organizing discretionary space and algorithmic transparency may not suffice to overcome behavioural and organizational barriers for the actual use of human discretion. The agency of algorithms extends beyond their immediate calculations and computer codes.

Various mechanisms can make it likely that human agents stick to the algorithmic outcomes. It is a well-known fact from behavioural psychology that people in general tend to follow the default option rather than question it. In addition, algorithms are especially attractive defaults since they are usually presented as 'non-ideological' – with an aura of scientific objectivity and rationality. Moreover, research in probation and policing studies has shown that human decision-makers may fail to properly understand algorithms and, for instance, conflate correlation and causation and, consequently, attach too much weight to predictive algorithms. Various classic insights on satisficing behaviour from organizational studies are at play in algorithmic governance as well. For instance, it takes a lot of capacity – both analytically and in terms of time – to pick out the problematic cases from a large bulk of algorithmic administrative decisions or to make a factual assessment of a case rather than trust the data provided by the computer system. Furthermore, organising meaningful transparency, accountability and fairness can also be complicated by epistemological issues. The problem here is not that algorithms lack transparency, but that certain algorithms are so complicated that they become incomprehensible for human reasoning.

Big tech companies

A fifth and final observation is that a fundamental shift in *sovereignty* takes place from governments to big technology companies in the algorithmic society (see, for instance, Henman's contribution). We understand sovereignty here as the authority to make decisions within a given sphere that impact how people live, the places where they live, and the things that regulate their lives. Several contributors demonstrate that private companies have a decisive influence on which digital products and services are developed, how they will increasingly affect the governance of public affairs, and how our behaviour is influenced by their decisions. If this development continues, the most important story we will tell about algorithms is how the private sector dictates the terms of innovation and development, including what 'good governance' entails. This leads to the final question: How can we *re-politicize* the use of algorithms and data in democratic ways?

The path forward

Our goal is not to outline an argument that is simply 'against algorithms'; after all, algorithms are already deeply woven into the fabric of the social world, they will undoubtedly continue to spread, and the positive effects of algorithms can outweigh the downsides for individuals and society in specific applications. However, there are also expected and unexpected pitfalls, as the contributions in the book have convincingly shown. Therefore, it can be productive to develop local practices that offer an alternative regime for dealing with the anxieties of the algorithmic society.

In this context, critical theorists Evgeny Morozov and Francesca Bria (2018) speak of "technological sovereignty" as a way to preserve a degree of autonomy and establish a buffer between citizens and technology providers. They argue that technological sovereignty may promise a more meaningful social license to govern our lives as it denotes the capacity of citizens to have a say and participate in how the technological infrastructure around us operates and what ends it serves. In the end: humans still design algorithms, determine their objectives, and decide in which areas they should be applied. The most ambitious program to reclaim technological sovereignty to date has sprung up in Barcelona, where the government and its citizens determine their own priorities in terms of the direction and use of technological innovations, with clear social benefits and public returns. Here, there is a commitment to using open source technologies and the city council has appointed a commissioner of Technology and Digital Innovation.

The relevant problem, therefore, is what human agency should look like in an algorithmic society. In terms of initial suggestions, the following guidelines can be formulated:

- Citizen control should be central in algorithmic design – not just organizational effectiveness. How are citizens affected in their daily lives? How can they defend themselves against unfair algorithmic decisions?
- An organizational context for meaningful human discretion should be organized. To overcome the convenient default of algorithmic outcomes, human agents must have the freedom and incentives to deviate if they deem it necessary from their professional perspective.
- Independent watchdog institutions must have a crucial role in organizing voice and counter-narratives. It is unlikely that governmental agencies or private tech companies alone will organize sufficient checks and balances for algorithmic decision-making in accordance with principles of social justice and the rule of law. These independent institutions should also test in advance whether the algorithms used by governmental agencies actually work.
- The introduction of algorithmic applications should keep in step with public legitimacy and acceptance. Forcing algorithmic tools upon citizens for instrumental reasons can backfire if it undermines citizens' trust in governmental agencies.

This is an ambition we aspire to: to seek practical and political interventions that launch a new collective vision for the improvement of our algorithmically mediated society. This is by no means an easy task; it implies a tension with traditional measures of success and performance. Yet the increasing integration of algorithms in our social infrastructure requires us to widen our understanding of the functioning of technologies beyond a narrow instrumental focus.

References

Childe, G. 1945. Directional changes in funerary practices during 50,000 years. *Man*, 45: 13–19.

Deleuze, G. 1986. *Foucault*. Paris: Minuit.

Fried, M. 1960. *On the evolution of social stratification and the state*. Indianapolis: Bobbs-Merrill.

Harcourt, B.E. 2007. *Against prediction: Profiling, policing, and punishing in an actuarial age*. Chicago: Chicago University Press.

Koopman, C. 2019a. *How we became our data: A genealogy of the informational person*. Chicago: The University of Chicago Press.

Koopman, C. Koopman, C. 2019b. Information before information theory: The politics of data beyond the perspective of communication. *New Media and Society*, 21 (6): 1326–1343.

Lash, S. 2007. Power after hegemony: Cultural studies in mutation? *Theory, Culture & Society*, 24 (3): 55–78.

Morozov, E. and F. Bria. 2018. *Rethinking the smart city: Democratizing urban technology*. New York Office: Rosa Luxembourg Stiftung.

Pali, B. and M. Schuilenburg. 2019. Fear and fantasy in the smart city. *Critical Criminology: An International Journal*, doi:10.1007/s10612-019-09447-7; accessed 28-04-2020.

Pasquinelli, M. 2019. *Three thousand years of algorithmic rituals: The emergence of AI from the computation of space. E-flux*, #101.

Sahlins, M. 1961. The segmentary lineage: An organization of predatory expansion. *American Anthropologist*, 63: 322–345.

Schuilenburg, M. 2021. The security society: On power, surveillance, and punishments. In: *The Pre-crime society: Crime, culture, and control in the ultramodern age*, edited by B.A. Arrigo and B.G. Sellers. Bristol, UK: Bristol University Press and Policy Press.

Index